XProc 3.0

Programmer Reference

Erik Siegel

XProc 3.0

Programmer Reference

Disclaimer

The information in this book is provided on an "as is" basis, without warranty. While every effort has been taken by the author and XML Press in the preparation of this book, the author and XML Press shall have neither liability nor responsibility to any person or entity with respect to any loss or damages arising from the information contained herein.

This book contains links to third-party web sites that are not under the control of the author or XML Press. The author and XML Press are not responsible for the content of any linked site. Inclusion of a link in this book does not imply that the author or XML Press endorses or accepts any responsibility for the content of that third-party site.

Credits

XProc logo:	Bethan Tovey-Walsh
Author photo:	Maaike Siegel
Figure 6.1:	isado (Flickr, CC BY-ND 2.0)
XProc 3.0 specification	This book contains material, including code examples, copied from or derived from the XProc 3.0 Draft Community Group Report. Appendix D contains the copyright notices for this material.

Trademarks

XML Press and the XML Press logo are trademarks of XML Press.

All terms mentioned in this book that are known to be trademarks or service marks have been capitalized as appropriate. Use of a term in this book should not be regarded as affecting the validity of any trademark or service mark.

XML Press
Laguna Hills, CA
http://xmlpress.net

First Edition
ISBN: 978-1-937434-70-0 (print)
ISBN: 978-1-937434-71-7 (ebook)

Table of Contents

Preface

Welcome to this book about XProc 3.0, a programming language for processing XML (and other) documents in *pipelines*. XProc chains conversions and other steps together to achieve potentially complex results.

XProc is currently not a well-known or a widely used programming language. Most systems that process XML are relatively simple. A single XSLT or even some DOM manipulation in some programming language often suffices. There is no need to bother with yet another processor and programming language.

However, there are areas where XML processing gets complicated. One example is publishing, where XML is widely used to mark up content. Most publishers struggle with consolidating input from various sources (Word, InDesign, PDF, XML, HTML, etc.) into a central XML format such as DITA or DocBook. From this XML they create their output: books, magazines, newspapers, websites, etc. Both sides of this process—to and from the central XML format—involve heavy XML processing, and this is where XProc can play a starring role and sometimes even make *the* difference between impracticable and feasible.

But people love what they know, and unknown means unloved. The syntax of XProc version 1.0 also didn't help: it put off a lot of people, even seasoned XML programmers who were used to other pipeline tools such as Cocoon. In addition, introductory material for learning the language was hard to find.

XProc 3.0 was designed with these shortcomings in mind. The syntax was simplified and new features added. These language advancements, backed up by this programmer's manual, will hopefully make it a lot easier for people to learn and use XProc.

Heavy XML processing is a niche in the programming world, so the XProc language will probably never become really mainstream. However, I hope that our efforts on the specification, together with the availability of this book, will make it more likely that people will use XProc.

Who is this book for?

XProc is a programming language originating from the XML world. So, no surprise, this book is aimed at programmers and others who do XML processing and use, or are considering using, XProc. It explains the language in detail, provides examples, and contains a selected set of example use cases (Chapter 10).

Readers should have some background knowledge of XML and XML processing. Knowing, even superficially, languages like XSLT, XQuery, or XPath will certainly help you understand XProc better. This book does not set out to teach these other languages; it concentrates on XProc only. Consult the section titled "Additional resources" (p. xvii) if you want to know more about the underlying technologies, tools, and standards.

How to use this book

There are several ways you can use this book, including the following:

- If you want to learn it all, read it all. Skim the appendices and use them for reference.
- If you want an introduction, a basic understanding of what XProc is, what it can be used for, and how it does its magic, read Chapter 1 and Chapter 3.
- Use it as a reference guide as you use XProc.
- Find inspiration in the use cases in Chapter 10.

From my own experience in learning a new programming language, I know it helps to read, or at least glance at, the entire book. Simply find out what's there so you know what the capabilities are, even if you don't initially dig into all of the details.

> A personal sorry tale: I did some foolish and heavy programming to get loop counters in `<p:for-each>` loops before finding out that XProc has extension functions (Chapter 9). These would have done the job in a few keystrokes. Even just having known in the back of my head that these kinds of functions were there would have made me look them up. Functions for iterations are likely candidates for inclusion in a language, aren't they? And yes, there it is: `p:iteration-position()`...

Here is an overview of the structure of the book:

- Chapter 1 introduces XProc and provides a little (non-technical) background information.
- Chapter 2 helps you get started using XProc. It tells you how to install and run the appropriate software. Examples range from the proverbial "Hello world!" to a 101 crash course.
- Chapter 3 provides background information about XProc and how it sees the world without delving into the syntax just yet: what is a pipeline and a document, what are their main properties, how do you connect steps, etc.
- Chapter 4 explains the various programming concepts in XProc: the use of XPath, maps, Attribute and Text Value Templates (AVT/TVT), etc.
- Chapters 5–7 are key in creating XProc pipelines. They explain the full language:
  - Chapter 5 explains how to *declare* a step: what does a pipeline document look like and how do you declare input ports, output ports, and options. It's about the *prolog* of a pipeline.
  - Chapter 6 tells you how populate your pipelines with functionality: chaining steps, using variables, etc. It's about the *body* of a pipeline.
  - Chapter 7 handles the *core steps* in XProc, including looping, branching, etc.
- Chapter 8 lists the *built-in steps* that populate pipelines. There are many built-in steps. This chapter doesn't handle them in detail, it mainly provides an overview.
- Chapter 9 lists the XProc *extension functions* that are available for use in the XPath expressions in your pipeline. Among many others it contains functions for iteration information.
- Chapter 10 provides some examples of XProc pipelines for specific use cases.
- There are several appendices with reference information and a Step Index.

The XProc logo

To make absolutely sure XProc will be taken serious in the XML standards world, it has a logo (designed by Bethan Tovey-Walsh):

Figure 1 – The Kanava XProc logo

We even gave it a name: *Kanava*. This not only sounds funny and is easy to pronounce, but also appears to be Finnish for pipeline!

Conventions used

File extension

This book and its code examples use the preferred file extension for XProc documents: `.xpl`.

Explaining XML structures

This book uses a specific notation to explain XML structures. Although this notation looks like XML, it is *not* well-formed! So don't copy/paste any of these examples directly into your code and expect them to work.

Figure 2 shows an XML structure for the fictitious `<some-element>` element.

```
<some-element attribute-1-optional? = (type)
              attribute-2-required = (type)
              attribute-3-fixed-values? = "value-1" | "value-2" | "value-3" ...
              attribute-4-avt? = { (type) } >
  <elm-1-optional>?
  <elm-2-mandatory>
  <elm-3-multiple-optional>*
  <elm-4-multiple-mandatory>+
  ( <elm-in-group-1> |
    <elm-in-group-2> )*
</some-element>
```

Figure 2 – Sample XML structure for a fictitious element

Each example is followed by a table that describes the attributes and child elements in the example.

Here are some details about the syntax used in Figure 2:

- Occurrences are given in DTD fashion:

Nothing (or sometimes 1)	Exactly once (required, single)
?	Zero or once (optional, single)
*	Zero or more (optional, multiple)
+	One or more (required, multiple)

- Attributes are followed by a data type (for instance `xs:string` or `xs:boolean`) or by the list of values it can have (like the `attribute-3-fixed-values` attribute in Figure 2).

  The `xs` namespace prefix for data types must be bound to the namespace `http://www.w3.org/2001/XMLSchema` (`xmlns:xs="http://www.w3.org/2001/XMLSchema"`).

- There are some special, XProc specific, data types, for example `SelPattern` or `XPathType`. These are explained in the section titled "Special data types" (p. xvi).

- When the type of an attribute is in curly braces {…} (like the `attribute-4-avt` attribute in the example), its value is an *Attribute Value Template* (AVT, see the section titled "Attribute and Text Value Templates" (p. 68)). It can contain XPath expressions between curly braces, {…}, which will be evaluated and expanded.

- Child elements can be grouped, like the `<elm-in-group-1>` and `<elm-in-group-2>` elements in Figure 2. The elements in a group are separated with the pipe character (|) and surrounded by parentheses. This means you have a choice of elements, and you can repeat this choice as often as the occurrences indicator on the group allows.

  In Figure 2, the occurrence indicator on this group is `*` (zero-or-more), so any combination of both elements would be valid, as would an empty value.

Special data types

Some attributes have a special data type. Table 1 shows the data-type indicators used in XProc.

Table 1 – Special data type indicators

Data type indicator	Description	Examples
`ContentTypes`	A list of one or more (whitespace separated) MIME type patterns. See the section titled "Specifying content types" (p. 99).	`text/plain` `text/* */*+xml`
`ExcludePrefixes`	A list of one or more (whitespace separated) namespace prefixes to exclude. Special values are `#all` and `#default`. See the section titled "Excluding namespace prefixes" (p. 145).	`xsl myns` `#all`

`SelPattern`	An XSLT selection pattern (the pattern/expression you can use in an XSLT `match` attribute).	`/*/div[1]`
		`p | para | paragraph`
		`title[contains(.,'XProc')]`

`XPathExpr`	An XPath expression	`concat('XP', 'roc')`
		`/*/@status`
		`1 + 1`

`XPathType`	An XPath sequence type indicator	`xs:string`
		`element(div)+`
		`map(xs:string, item()*)`

Using and finding code examples

The code examples presented in this book, especially the ones in Chapters 2 and 10, can be found on GitHub at https://github.com/eriksiegel/XProc-3.0-book-sources.git. These examples are offered under the MIT License (see Appendix D). Feel free to download and use them.

Because I don't know where you'll install these source files, every reference to them is prefixed with `$SOURCES`, for example `$SOURCES/hello-world/hello-world.xpl`.

Additional resources

This section contains additional information resources. It's compiled based on my personal preferences combined with suggestions from others. Although incomplete and biased, it is nevertheless a good place to start exploring.

XProc and underlying standards

The XProc 3.0 specification (http://spec.xproc.org/)

> The XProc specification is written in the style of a W3C recommendation, using the terse prose necessary to reach the level of exactness a standard needs. This book was written based on the specification.
>
> If during your XProc adventures you're ever in doubt who is right, this book or the specification, stop asking. The specification is *always* right.

XPath 3.1 standard (https://www.w3.org/TR/xpath-31)
XPath and XQuery Functions and Operators 3.1 (https://www.w3.org/TR/xpath-functions-31)

> XProc uses XPath 3.1 as an underlying standard. These links bring you to the official standard documents.
>
> If you're new to XPath, I suggest you read Michael Kay's book *XSLT 2.0 and XPath 2.0*. Although written for a previous version, it still stands. Its core concepts are explained well, and since 3.1 is backwards compatible with 2.0, anything you read is still true.
>
> Another well-written and informative resource for learning XPath is Priscilla Walmsley's book *XQuery: Search Across a Variety of XML Data*. This book is very complete, covering

difficult subjects such as higher-order functions, maps, and arrays. However, it doesn't make the distinction between what's XPath and what's XQuery as clear as it could. So you might end up trying XQuery constructs (like FLWOR expressions) as XPath expressions. That won't work inside an XProc pipeline. The book also includes a full list of available XPath functions.

Other information

The World Wide Web Consortium (W3C) (http://www.w3c.org)

The W3C is the body that manages, among other things, the XProc specification and related XML standards. Their website is easy to use and informative.

W3 schools (http://w3schools.com)

W3Schools is a developer site with tutorials and references on web development languages, including XSLT, XQuery and XPath.[1]

XSLT 2.0 and XPath 2.0: Programmer's Reference by Michael Kay (Wiley, 2008)

Although this book is a bit outdated (XSLT is on version 3.0 and XPath is on version 3.1), it is still an excellent resource and a good place to start with XPath.

XSLT, 2nd Edition by Doug Tidwell (O'Reilly, 2008)

A good book to learn and explore XSLT. It's a bit outdated but still useful for the basics.

XSLT Cookbook, 2nd Edition by Sal Mangano (O'Reilly, 2006)

XSLT examples in cookbook style. Useful when you have an XSLT problem to crack, and you need an example to start from.

XSL-List (https://www.mulberrytech.com/xsl/xsl-list/)

The XSL-List is a place to ask XSLT questions and receive help. The list is usually very responsive. It also has an archive.

---

[1] Be aware, W3Schools is a controversial website. Just mentioning it here caused a surprising amount of criticism from reviewers. It apparently has a history of errors and is infamous for heavy advertising. Nonetheless, I personally consult it regularly and find the information well-presented. Judge it for yourself.

XQuery: Search Across a Variety of XML Data by Priscilla Walmsley (O'Reilly, 2016)

> Considered the authoritative resource for programming XQuery. Also a very good place to start when you need information about the underlying XPath standard.

Contact information

This book was written by Erik Siegel (Xatapult, http://www.xatapult.com). You can reach me at erik@xatapult.nl.

I would definitely like to hear from you. Whatever you have to say about this book, suggestions, omissions, errors, praise, likes, dislikes, disgust, please send me an e-mail. Knowing that there are people out there actually using what I've written will help me stay motivated.

Acknowledgements

I would like to thank the other members of the XProc 3.0 editorial team for their support, discussions and encouragements: Achim Berndzen, Gerrit Imsieke, and Norman Tovey-Walsh. Extra kudos for Achim and Norman because they somehow managed to work on an XProc processor in addition to their day-time jobs and working on the specification.

Beside the XProc editors, a lot of people participated in the discussions and meetings around XProc 3.0. This community group, chaired by Ari Nordström, varied in attendance and so I'm not going to mention other names, because I will undoubtedly forget someone. But if you were there you know it: thanks!

And there were, unbelievably, people that took the time and the effort to actually read all this and helped me with detailed feedback and criticism: my fellow XProc editorial crew-mates Achim, Gerrit, and Norman as well as Pieter Masereeuw, who looked at it from an outsider's viewpoint. Thanks for all your time and effort!

CHAPTER 1

Introduction

What is XProc?

Let's try to answer this question with an overview of XProc's main high-level characteristics:

- XProc is a *programming language*, expressed in XML, in which you can write *pipelines*.
- An XProc *pipeline* takes data as its input (often XML) and passes it through specialized *steps* to produce end results.
- Steps range from simple tasks, like reading and writing data, to complex ones like splitting/combining/pruning data, transforming data with XSLT or XQuery, and validating data.
- Within a pipeline you can work with variables, create branches and loops, catch errors, etc. All of this processing is based on the data flowing through the pipeline.
- XProc pipelines are not limited to a linear succession of steps. They can fork and merge.
- XProc allows you to create custom steps by combining other steps. These custom steps can be used just like any other step. Custom steps can be collected into libraries.
- XProc supports housekeeping functions such as inspecting directories, reading documents from zip files, writing data to disk, etc.
- There is software—XProc processors—that can execute these pipelines.

Why and when would these capabilities be useful? In the physical world, pipelining and working in specialized steps is not unusual. For instance, an oil refinery takes crude oil as input and, through a series of steps and intermediate products, produces petrol/gasoline, kerosene, diesel, etc. Refineries take the word pipeline literally.

Another classic example of working in pipelines (although not literal) with specialized steps is a factory producing cars. This usually consists of a conveyor belt (the main pipeline) that takes the cars-to-be from one specialized assembly station to the next (the steps). There will probably be sub-conveyor belts (subpipelines) for parts like the engine, the cabling, the interior, etc. At the end you have a complete and functioning car.

Yet another example is the UNIX pipe. A command produces some output and you pipe that output to another command—for example `grep` or `tail`—which does further processing to get the desired result. The character used for chaining steps, `|`, is even called the "pipe" character.

So why do this in the world of information and document processing? One of the main reasons is that data is often not in the format you need it to be. Here are some examples:

- You have XML coming from some data source but need HTML for your website.
- You have data coming from multiple weather stations that needs to be merged into a single consolidated view. From this you produce a map with the information nicely laid out.
- Word processors produce zip files with lots of XML documents inside (most word processors do nowadays). You need the text in some other format so you have to inspect the zip file, combine the XML documents inside, and transform the result into what you need.

For straight transformation of XML data you can use languages such as XSLT and XQuery. But often tasks such as chaining, splitting, or merging are more complex than can be handled in a single transformation. For such tasks, you may need to perform housekeeping functions such as determining where to read from or write to, inspecting directories, creating zip files, or writing logs. Also, from a software engineering point of view, it is often better to work in small steps to get more legible and maintainable code. XProc is designed to make it easier for you express complex combinations of tasks.

A first example

As a relatively simple first example, consider the following use case: an off-the-shelf web-shop application produces a verbose XML document that contains order data. The data itself is complete (everything you need is in there) but its format is not directly usable. Since it is XML you cannot send it directly to the customer as an invoice. You need to convert it first. You may also need to feed your accounting system with order information in a completely different XML format.

To do this, you need to accomplish the following steps:

- Filter the verbose input document into something smaller and more to the point.
- Take the filtered output and create XML for the accounting system.
- Create an XHTML version of the invoice to display on the customer website.
- Create a PDF version of the invoice to e-mail to the customer. This takes two steps: transform the XHTML to XSL-FO then transform the XSL-FO to PDF.

In this example, all the heavy work—the transformations—is done by XSLT, which I don't show. For this example, I concentrate on the XProc pipeline (see Figure 1.1).

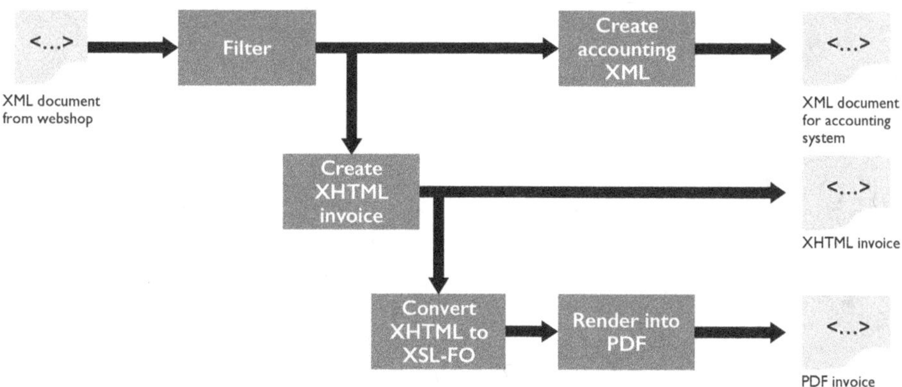

Figure 1.1 – First example pipeline

Example 1.1 shows how this pipeline could be expressed in XProc.

Example 1.1 – First example pipeline, expressed in XProc

```
<p:declare-step xmlns:p="http://www.w3.org/ns/xproc"  version="3.0">

  <!-- ================================================================== -->
  <!-- PROLOG: -->

  <p:input port="source" primary="true">
    <p:documentation>This is where the XML document from the webshop
      comes in</p:documentation>
  </p:input>
```

```
  <p:output port="result" primary="true" pipe="result@create-accounting-xml">
    <p:documentation>Our primary output will be the XML document for the
      accounting system</p:documentation>
  </p:output>

  <p:output port="xhtml-invoice" primary="true" pipe="result@create-xhtml-invoice">
    <p:documentation>This is where our XHTML invoice comes out</p:documentation>
  </p:output>

  <p:option name="pdf-filename" required="true">
    <p:documentation>This is the location where we'll write the PDF version
      of the invoice</p:documentation>
  </p:option>

  <!-- ============================================================== -->
  <!-- BODY: -->

  <p:xslt name="filter-input">
    <p:with-input port="stylesheet" href="path/to/filter-webshop-xml.xsl"/>
  </p:xslt>

  <p:xslt name="create-accounting-xml">
    <p:with-input port="stylesheet"
                  href="path/to/create-accounting-system-xml.xsl"/>
  </p:xslt>

  <!-- - - - - - - - - - - - - - - - - - - - - - - - - - - - - - - - - - -->
  <!-- subpipeline for creating the XHTML invoice: -->

  <p:xslt name="create-xhtml-invoice">
    <p:with-input port="source" pipe="result@filter-input"/>
    <p:with-input port="stylesheet" href="path/to/create-xhtml-invoice.xsl"/>
  </p:xslt>

  <!-- - - - - - - - - - - - - - - - - - - - - - - - - - - - - - - - - - -->
  <!-- subpipeline for creating the PDF invoice: -->

  <p:xslt name="create-fo-invoice">
   <p:with-input port="stylesheet" href="path/to/create-xsl-fo-from-xhtml.xsl"/>
  </p:xslt>

  <p:xsl-formatter/>
  <p:store href="{$pdf-filename}"/>

</p:declare-step>
```

Of course, this is not the only way to write this pipeline. Syntax variations are possible, as will be shown in the coming chapters.

The language specification, step library, and this book

The XProc specification (http://spec.xproc.org) consists of two main parts:

- The core language specification (*XProc 3.0: An XML Pipeline Language*)
- The step library (*XProc 3.0: Standard Step Library* and several additional documents listed at http://spec.xproc.org).

For this book, I chose to focus on the language and not the steps. This means I describe in depth how to call steps, provide options, connect ports, and handle all the other things required to create a pipeline. I re-interpret the XProc specification, which was written primarily for language implementers, with users in mind.

But XProc is not worth a penny without its step library. You can't do anything without it. However, experience from XProc 1.0 shows that the biggest learning curve for XProc is the language. Once you master this, finding and using the right steps is relatively easy.

Because steps are so important, I include a short overview of the available steps (Chapter 8) and include two appendices that list them in full (Appendix A and Appendix B). However, instead of re-writing this information, I generated these appendices from the original specifications (using an XProc pipeline). You can find the same information online, but I added it to the book so that you can refer to it easily.

A little history

Ideas for something, some programming language, for processing XML were there right from the beginnings of XML at the end of the twentieth century. But it was not until the end of 2005 that the W3C (The *World Wide Web Consortium*), which develops standards for the web, started a working group called the *XML Processing Model Working Group*.

After a lot of debate the working group created a recommendation for XProc 1.0, titled *XProc: An XML Pipeline Language*, dated May 11, 2010. The editors were Norman Walsh, Alex Milowski, and Henry Thompson.

There were various attempts to create working XProc 1.0 processors. But as far as I'm aware, XML Calabash[1] and MorganaXProc[2] are the only two that implement the full 1.0 standard and are also currently available as open source products.

After the release of version 1.0, the XProc working group continued debating a next version. Ideas were raised for version 2.0, which was based on a non-XML syntax. This didn't raise a lot of support from the community. As things happen, the enthusiasm and energy in the working group became less and less, and in 2016 it ceased to exist.

However, as it turned out, there were still people interested in creating a new XProc version. In June 2017, the *XProc Next Community Group* was founded and started working on a new version, now completely XML based. Because this was a completely different approach from the 2.0 initiative, the version number was increased to 3.0.

Here are some links to check out if you want more information on the history of XProc (see also the section titled "Additional resources" (p. xvii)):

- The W3C: https://www.w3.org/
- The XML Processing Model Working Group: https://www.w3.org/XML/Processing/
- The final W3C recommendation for XProc 1.0: https://www.w3.org/TR/xproc/
- The XProc Next Community Group on the W3C: https://www.w3.org/community/xproc-next/

---

1 https://xmlcalabash.com/
2 https://www.xml-project.com/morganaxproc/

Who is using XProc and for what?

Here are some examples of projects using XProc:

le-tex (https://www.le-tex.de/en)

> Under the label of transpect,[3] le-tex publishing services developed (and open sourced) a large collection of XProc steps for publishing pipelines. Applications include conversion from docx (Word), IDML (InDesign), and xlsx (Excel) to XML vocabularies such as JATS, TEI, DocBook, and HTML and conversions from these vocabularies to EPUB, LaTeX, IDML, xlsx, and docx.
>
> These libraries are used by many publishers and service vendors to turn hundreds of thousands of manuscript pages per year into typesetting system formats or to turn archival XML into new e-books or editable manuscript files. le-tex is arguably the largest user and developer of XProc pipelines worldwide.

DAISY Consortium (http://www.daisy.org/)

> The DAISY Consortium is a registered not-for-profit global collective of organizations that contributes to mainstream publishing standards, develops guidelines to promote best practices, raises awareness of accessible reading systems, and supports open standards for inclusive publishing.
>
> The DAISY Consortium uses XProc at the heart of its DAISY Pipeline project. The DAISY Pipeline is an open-source, cross-platform framework for the conversion of digital publications to various formats, with accessibility in mind. The framework is used by DAISY member organizations and others to convert DAISY digital talking books into Braille, EPUB with synchronized text and audio, and other accessible formats.
>
> Most of these digital publishing formats are based on XML and HTML. Using XProc to orchestrate XSLT transformations and other steps allows the DAISY Consortium to implement efficient, declarative, flexible, and heavily-modularized conversion workflows. This project features more than a hundred different XProc steps. They have also created a tool called XProcSpec that tests XProc pipelines.

[3] https://transpect.github.io

Noordhoff Uitgevers (https://www.noordhoffuitgevers.nl/)

Noordhoff Uitgevers is a large Dutch educational publisher. They use XProc to convert XML coming from their content management system into ready-to-process packages suitable for consumption by website front-end applications. Their system supports conversion, splitting, merging, and packaging of XML.

Xatapult (http://www.xatapult.com)

Xatapult is Dutch company, specialized in content engineering and XML processing. Among its many activities is spreading the XML gospel, for instance by writing books about XProc (guess which one). The processing for this book used an XProc-based tool chain that merges DocBook text, XML structure descriptions, and parts of the original XProc 3.0 specification into a coherent and complete DocBook 5 document, ready for publication.

Alternatives

Creating pipelines using XProc is certainly not the only way to approach these kinds of problems. Here are some alternatives:

Script files

A classic approach to pipelining is using languages such as UNIX shell scripts, Windows batch files, make, or Ant. With these languages, steps read and write from/to disk using temporary files.

The main drawback to this approach is the performance impact of reading and writing temporary files and creating separate processes for each step. XML is parsed and serialized over and over again and code is cluttered with a lot of housekeeping.

Chaining in XSLT

Sometimes all you do in a pipeline is chain XSLT transformations, one after the other. This can also be done in a single XSLT (V2.0 or higher) stylesheet, using variables to store intermediate results and modes to separate templates from each other.

The drawbacks of this approach are heavy memory use to store intermediate results, even after they are no longer needed, and the legibility of the stylesheet. I personally find it much harder to debug XSLT chains than XProc pipelines.

Using another language

Of course it is possible to write pipelines in another programming language, such as Java or C#. The XProc processors described in this book are written in Java and Scala, and if they can do it, so can you.

Whether you want to go this way is a matter of tastes and preferences: if you master programming language XYZ, but not XProc, it can be tempting to express the pipeline in XYZ. No need to learn another language.

But I think there is something to be said for using the right tool for the right job. Being able to express a pipeline at the correct level of abstraction, in a language that was designed for doing so, makes code more understandable and maintainable. Housekeeping (which will clutter your other programming language code) is taken care of by the XProc processor. Lots of XML processing steps (inserting/deleting/wrapping/unwrapping elements, handling attributes, XPath expressions, etc.) are native to XProc, but require extensive coding to implement in another language.

CHAPTER 2

Getting started with XProc

This chapter guides you through your first steps with XProc. There are two XProc processors you can use for this, XML Calabash and MorganaXProc, and I introduce them first. The main part of this chapter contains a short introductory 101 course that will help you take your first XProc bites and get a taste of what it can do.

Installing and using an XProc processor

There were two open source XProc 3.0 processors available at the time this book was published: XMLCalabash and MorganaXProc. Both products have existed for quite some time already, and they both have versions that implement V1.0.

XML Calabash

XML Calabash is an open source XProc processor developed by Norman Tovey-Walsh.

When this book was published the processor wasn't completely finished. Therefore, I cannot provide you with accurate details about how to install the processor and get it up and running. Please check the XML Calabash website[1] for installation information.

MorganaXProc

MorganaXProc is an open source XProc processor developed and maintained by `<xml-project/>`. The 3.0 version is officially branded MorganaXProc-III.

As with XML Calabash, MorganaXProc-III wasn't completely finished when this book was published. Please consult the MorganaXProc website[2] for more information on how to install it.

---

[1] http://xmlcalabash.com

[2] http://www.xml-project.com

Hello XProc world

The code examples (see the section titled “Using and finding code examples” (p. xvii)) contain a small, simple pipeline (Example 2.1) that you can use to test your installation.

Example 2.1 – Hello XProc world pipeline (`$SOURCES/hello-xproc/hello-xproc.xpl`)

```
<p:declare-step xmlns:p="http://www.w3.org/ns/xproc" version="3.0">

  <p:output port="result" primary="true" sequence="false"/>

  <p:identity>
    <p:with-input>
      <hello-xproc timestamp="{current-dateTime()}"/>
    </p:with-input>
  </p:identity>

</p:declare-step>
```

Command line for running this example

Assumptions: `$SOURCES/hello-xproc` is your current working directory, and the command to run the processor is on the system’s path.

XML Calabash

```
calabash hello-xproc.xpl
```

MorganaXProc-III

```
morgana hello-xproc.xpl
```

Integration in oXygen

The oXygen XML Editor (http://www.oxygenxml.com) is a popular XML IDE in professional XML circles. One of the many XML programming languages it supports is XProc 1.0, using the XML Calabash processor out of the box or the MorganaXProc processor through a plug-in.

By the time you read this, it is possible that oXygen now also supports XProc 3.0. If you’re an oXygen user, it’s worth a check.

XProc 101

And now a real first taste of XProc 3.0. Or, using another analogy: we're going to do some supervised paddling in the shallow pool before encouraging you to dive in the deep parts.

All code examples are in an accompanying GitHub repository. See the section titled "Using and finding code examples" (p. xvii) for details.

The problem in this 101 section is beautifying and publishing documents. Assume you have a lot of documents that look like Example 2.2.

Example 2.2 – Basic 101 input document example
(`$SOURCES/101/documents/example-contents-1.xml`)

```
<document>
  <title>My 101 publication</title>

  <div class="sect1">
    <title>First part</title>

    <div class="sect2">
      <title>My first chapter</title>
      <para>The text for the first chapter...</para>
      <para>More text</para>
    </div>

    <div class="sect2">
      <title>My second chapter</title>
      <para>The text for the second chapter...</para>
      <para>More text</para>
    </div>

  </div>

</document>
```

I made up this particular XML format for the sake of these examples. However, it is not uncommon to have all kinds of weird and non-standards-conforming XML documents to process. As long as you're using a single editing-and-publishing system you're fine, every part of the tool chain speaks the same language. But breaking out of the content silo created by these almost-but-not-quite-standard documents can be a nightmarish experience.

This 101 course assumes you have a lot of documents marked up like Example 2.2 that need to be published on a website. Let's convert them to HTML and do some other nifty tricks.

When this book was published, both of the available XProc processors had not finished implementing XProc 3.0. However, based on preliminary information from the implementors, the format of the command line parameters is known and will, hopefully, not change when the processors are finished. You will find example command lines at the end of each 101 sub-section. Consult the websites for XML Calabash and MorganaXProc for the latest information on installation and operation.

While playing around with examples you might get error messages that use puzzling references like `!1.m.n` (for instance `!1.4.5`). These messages refer to default step names. See the section titled "Default step names" (p. 124) for more information.

Converting to HTML

The first step is to convert the document to HTML. If you're coming from an XSLT background, your instincts will probably tell you to grab your favourite XSLT editor and start hacking. Nothing wrong with that. In fact, we're going to do just that.

If converting to HTML was the *only* task, a single XSLT would be the preferred way to do the job. No need for XProc at all. However, there are some additional requirements in this case that make XProc a more suitable candidate for solving the problem. So, let's continue.

Basic conversion

The basic conversion of this document to HTML can indeed be done with a simple XSLT stylesheet. However, let's place the stylesheet inside an XProc pipeline so we can enhance the example later (see Example 2.3).

Example 2.3 – Basic conversion pipeline
(`$SOURCES/101/01-basic-conversion/basic-conversion.xpl`)

```
<!-- 1. Pipeline document: -->
<p:declare-step xmlns:p="http://www.w3.org/ns/xproc" version="3.0">

  <!-- 2. Pipeline port declarations: -->
  <p:input port="source" primary="true"/>
  <p:output port="result" primary="true"/>

  <!-- 3. Convert document to HTML: -->
  <p:xslt>
    <p:with-input  port="stylesheet" href="xsl/basic-conversion.xsl"/>
  </p:xslt>

</p:declare-step>
```

1. The XProc pipeline starts with a `<p:declare-step>` element. This is always the root element of a pipeline. The `p` namespace-prefix is bound to the `http://www.w3.org/TR/xproc/` namespace. The mandatory `version` attribute is set to the XProc version, `3.0`.

2. Next, declare the pipeline's input and output ports. A port is a connector through which documents flow in or out. In Example 2.3 there are two ports:
   - An *input port* called `source`
   - An *output port* called `result`

   Both are *primary* ports (`primary="true"`). Primary ports perform a bit of magic based on the layout of the pipeline: for adjacent steps primary ports automatically connect.

   `source` and `result` are, by convention, the preferred names for primary input and output ports. You can name them differently, but I don't recommend this.

3. Then, call an XProc step called **`<p:xslt>`**. This starts an XSLT processor with the given stylesheet. The document from the `source` input port will be fed to this step as the document to convert. The conversion result will flow out of the `result` output port of the step.

Example 2.3 does nothing but wrap a single XSLT inside an XProc pipeline. Not very useful in itself but it's a good starting point. The XSLT in Example 2.4 creates the right structure, unwraps the `<div>` sections, turns `<div>` titles into `<h...>` elements, and translates `<para>` into `<p>`.

Example 2.4 – Basic conversion XSLT
($SOURCES/101/01-basic-conversion/xsl/basic-conversion.xsl)

```
<xsl:stylesheet version="3.0" xmlns:xsl="http://www.w3.org/1999/XSL/Transform"
  xmlns:xs="http://www.w3.org/2001/XMLSchema" exclude-result-prefixes="#all">

  <xsl:output method="xml" indent="yes" encoding="UTF-8"/>
  <xsl:mode on-no-match="shallow-copy"/>

  <xsl:template match="/document">
    <html>
      <head>
        <title>
          <xsl:value-of select="title"/>
        </title>
      </head>
      <body>
        <xsl:apply-templates select="* except title"/>
      </body>
    </html>
  </xsl:template>

  <xsl:template match="div">
    <!-- Unwrap the div elements from each other: -->
    <xsl:copy>
      <xsl:copy-of select="@*"/>
      <xsl:apply-templates select="* except div"/>
    </xsl:copy>
    <xsl:apply-templates select="div"/>
  </xsl:template>

  <xsl:template match="div/title">
    <!-- Find out how deep this div is nested to get the right heading level: -->
    <xsl:variable name="nesting-level" as="xs:integer"
                  select="count(ancestor::div)"/>
    <xsl:element name="h{$nesting-level}">
      <xsl:apply-templates select="@* | node()"/>
    </xsl:element>
  </xsl:template>

  <xsl:template match="para">
    <p>
      <xsl:apply-templates select="@* | node()"/>
    </p>
  </xsl:template>

</xsl:stylesheet>
```

The `<xsl:mode on-no-match="shallow-copy">` at the beginning of Example 2.4 invokes an identity transform for all unrecognized content. I will rely on this later.

After the conversion, our input document from Example 2.2 now looks like the straightforward and simple HTML in Example 2.5.

Example 2.5 – The 101 input document after basic conversion (`$SOURCES/101/documents/example-contents-1-converted.xml`)

```
<html>
   <head>
      <title>My 101 publication</title>
   </head>
   <body>
      <div class="sect1">
         <h1>First part</h1>
      </div>
      <div class="sect2">
         <h2>My first chapter</h2>
         <p>The text for the first chapter...</p>
         <p>More text</p>
      </div>
      <div class="sect2">
         <h2>My second chapter</h2>
         <p>The text for the second chapter...</p>
         <p>More text</p>
      </div>
   </body>
</html>
```

Command line for running this example

Assumptions: `$SOURCES/101/01-basic-conversion` is your current working directory, and the command to run the processor is on the system's path. The command lines in the examples below consist of multiple lines, but you need to enter them on a single line.

XML Calabash

```
calabash
  -i source=../documents/example-contents-1.xml
  basic-conversion.xpl
```

Add `-o result=path-to-output-file` to the command line to catch the result in a file.

MorganaXProc-III

```
morgana basic-conversion.xpl
  -input:source=../documents/example-contents-1.xml
```

Add `-output:result=path-to-output-file` to the command line to catch the result in a file.

Adding additional header information

Suppose that, on gathering the requirements for this conversion, you hear the website designers say that the header information for the HTML documents is not yet complete. In particular, they have not yet determined which JavaScript and CSS files need to be loaded.

So you persuade them to deliver these specifications in a small XML file that contains the additional header contents (see Example 2.6).

Example 2.6 – Additional header information input
(`$SOURCES/101/documents/additional-header-contents.xml`)

```
<additional-header-contents>
  <link rel="stylesheet" type="text/css" href="style-1.css"/>
  <link rel="stylesheet" type="text/css" href="style-2.css"/>
  <script type="text/javascript" src="javascript-1.js"/>
  <script type="text/javascript" src="javascript-2.js"/>
</additional-header-contents>
```

Now you have to insert the children of the root element of Example 2.6 into the `<head>` element of the HTML created in the previous section. Now you could do this as part of the stylesheet in Example 2.4, but instead, let's adjust the XProc pipeline. Assume for now that the file with the additional header information is stored at some fixed location (probably a shared directory between you and the website designers). Example 2.7 shows how you can load and insert this additional information.

Example 2.7 – Adding the additional header information from a fixed location
(`$SOURCES/101/02-adding-header-info/adding-header-info-1.xpl`)

```
<p:declare-step xmlns:p="http://www.w3.org/ns/xproc" version="3.0">

  <p:input port="source" primary="true"/>
  <p:output port="result" primary="true"/>


  <!-- 1. Define filename in variable: -->
  <p:variable name="additional-header-info-file"
    select="'../documents/additional-header-contents.xml'"/>

  <p:xslt>
    <p:with-input port="stylesheet" href="xsl/basic-conversion.xsl"/>
  </p:xslt>

  <!-- 2. The p:xslt step and the p:insert step implicitly connect -->

  <!-- 3. Insert the additional information: -->
  <p:insert match="/html/head" position="last-child">
    <p:with-input port="insertion" select="/*/*">
      <p:document href="{$additional-header-info-file}"/>
    </p:with-input>
  </p:insert>

</p:declare-step>
```

1. For code maintainability reasons I defined the name of the file in a variable called `additional-header-info-file` at the top of the pipeline. The path provided here (`../documents/additional-header-contents.xml`) points to the example document for this 101 course, so the example will run.

   To provide an absolute path, always prefix it with the file protocol specifier: `file:///path/to/my-document.xml`. To help you with this, XProc has a built-in function called `p:urify()` that helps you create correct URIs for the OS you're running on (see the section titled "Other functions" (p. 197)).

2. When steps are adjacent in the pipeline, like **`<p:xslt>`** and **`<p:insert>`** here, in most cases they're *implicitly connected*. This means that the results of the **`<p:xslt>`** step flow into the **`<p:insert>`** step.

   To be a bit more precise: **`<p:xslt>`** has a *primary output port* called `result` and **`<p:insert>`** has a *primary input port* called `source`. A primary input port automatically connects to the primary output port of the step before it (you can override this behavior). Most built-in steps have primary input and output ports defined. If you design your own steps with a primary input and output port, these will auto-connect as well. More information about this in the section titled "Connecting or binding ports" (p. 48).

3. XProc's built-in **`<p:insert>`** step inserts XML in the middle of some other XML. Let's dissect what's happening:
   - As described above, the output of the **`<p:xslt>`** step flows into the **`<p:insert>`** step.
   - The XPath expression in the `match="/html/head"` attribute tells the **`<p:insert>`** step to work on this element (or element*s* if it occurs more often, which in our case it won't).
   - The `position="last-child"` attribute tells **`<p:insert>`** to insert content after all other child elements of `/html/head`. Other possible values include `first-child`, `before`, and `after`.
   - **`<p:insert>`** has an additional (non-primary) input port called `insertion` from which the content to insert is read. The `<p:with-input>` element identifies the additional information.
   - The `select="/*/*"` attribute selects only the child elements of the root element in Example 2.6 (not the root element). To insert the whole document, omit the `select` attribute.

- The `<p:document>` child element of `<p:with-input>` tells XProc to load what will appear on this port from a specific URI.[3]
- The document name is defined in a variable and referenced in the `href` attribute using an Attribute Value Template (AVT): `href="{$additional-header-info-file}"` (see the section titled "Attribute and Text Value Templates" (p. 68)). The part between curly braces is treated as an XPath expression and evaluated.

The result is the HTML created by the XSL conversion with the additional header information inserted at the end of the `/html/head` element (see Example 2.8).

Example 2.8 – The additional header information inserted in the converted document (`$SOURCES/101/documents/example-contents-1-converted-additional.xml`)

```
<html>
  <head>
    <title>My 101 publication</title>
    <link rel="stylesheet" type="text/css" href="style-1.css" />
    <link rel="stylesheet" type="text/css" href="style-2.css" />
    <script type="text/javascript" src="javascript-1.js"></script>
    <script type="text/javascript" src="javascript-2.js"></script>
  </head>
  <body>
    <div class="sect1">
      <h1>First part</h1>
    </div>
    <div class="sect2">
      <h2>My first chapter</h2>
      <p>The text for the first chapter...</p>
      <p>More text</p>
    </div>
    <div class="sect2">
      <h2>My second chapter</h2>
      <p>The text for the second chapter...</p>
      <p>More text</p>
    </div>
  </body>
</html>
```

[3] As syntactic sugar you could have left out the `<p:document>` element and specified the `href` attribute directly on `<p:with-input>`. This is how it was done for the `stylesheet` port on the **`<p:xslt>`** step. Here it doesn't matter how you do this, but `<p:document>` has some additional options that might be useful in other cases. See the section titled "Reading external documents: `<p:document>`" (p. 139).

Command line for running this example

Assumptions: `$SOURCES/101/02-adding-header-info` is your current working directory, and the command to run the processor is on the system's path. The command lines in the examples below consist of multiple lines, but you need to enter them on a single line.

XML Calabash

```
calabash
  -i source=../documents/example-contents-1.xml
  adding-header-info-1.xpl
```

Add `-o result=path-to-output-file` to the command line to catch the result in a file.

MorganaXProc-III

```
morgana adding-header-info-1.xpl
  -input:source=../documents/example-contents-1.xml
```

Add `-output:result=path-to-output-file` to the command line to catch the result in a file.

Example 2.7 is not the only way to do this. In the following four sub-sections, I go over some variations that yield roughly the same results:

- Using an option instead of a variable.
- Getting the additional information from an extra input port.
- Supplying default connections for the input ports.
- Indenting the result XML by changing the `result` port's serialization.

Using an option instead of a variable

In Example 2.7 the name of the file to load was defined using a variable. However, you can also do this using an *option*. An option is a named value you pass to your pipeline; it is equivalent to parameters you pass to functions or methods in other programming languages.

```
<p:option name="additional-header-info-file"
  select="'../documents/additional-header-contents.xml'"/>
```

The (optional) `select` attribute holds the default value that is used when the option is not set on the step's invocation. So with this you have the original file location as a default, which you can *override* by explicitly setting the option's value.

The additional single quotes inside the double quotes in value of the `select` attribute are required. This is because the value of a `select` attribute is an XPath expression, which is a string constant that must be placed between quotes. Otherwise, the expression will be evaluated at the wrong time, yielding an unpredictable result.

You can set options in one of two ways:

- When this step is the outermost step, you have to set the option on the command line, which is processor dependent. For an example, see the "Command lines for running this example" sidebar below.
- When this step is invoked from within another step, use `<p:with-option>` or an attribute on the step (the section titled "Setting options: `<p:with-option>` (or by attribute)" (p. 128)).

To invoke a step from inside another step, the invoked step must be known to the invoking step. There are several ways you can do this:

- The step can be declared/defined inside the invoking step, using a nested `<p:declare-step>` element. See the section titled "Declaring a step: `<p:declare-step>` " (p. 80).
- If the step is specified in a document of its own (with a `<p:declare-step>` root element), it can be imported using the `<p:import>` element. See the section titled "Importing steps and step libraries: `<p:import>` " (p. 108).
- The step can also be part of an XProc step library. See the section titled "Building step libraries: `<p:library>` " (p. 109). Libraries must be imported using the `<p:import>` element.

Command line for running this example

Assumptions: `$SOURCES/101/02-adding-header-info` is your current working directory, and the command to run the processor is on the system's path. The command lines in the examples below consist of multiple lines, but you need to enter them on a single line.

XML Calabash

```
calabash
  -i source=../documents/example-contents-1.xml
  -o
additional-header-info-file=../documents/additonal-header-contents.xml
  adding-header-info-2.xpl
```

Add `-o result=path-to-output-file` to the command line to catch the result in a file.

MorganaXProc-III

```
morgana adding-header-info-2.xpl
  -input:source=../documents/example-contents-1.xml

-option:additional-header-info-file=../documents/additonal-header-contents.xml
```

Add `-output:result=path-to-output-file` to the command line to catch the result in a file.

Loading from another input port

Another way of loading the additional header information would have been through an *additional input port* on the pipeline (some people might consider this more XProc-ish).

Example 2.9 – Adding the header information using an additional input port (`$SOURCES/101/02-adding-header-info/adding-header-info-3.xpl`)

```
<!-- 1. Provide a name for the step: -->
<p:declare-step xmlns:p="http://www.w3.org/ns/xproc" version="3.0"
  name="html-conversion-pipeline">

  <p:input port="source" primary="true"/>
  <p:output port="result" primary="true"/>

  <!-- 2. Define additional input port -->
  <p:input port="header-info"/>

  <p:xslt>
    <p:with-input port="stylesheet" href="xsl/basic-conversion.xsl"/>
  </p:xslt>

  <p:insert match="/html/head" position="last-child">
    <p:with-input port="insertion" select="/*/*">
      <!-- 3. Connect the insertion port of p:insert to the header-info
        port of the step: -->
      <p:pipe step="html-conversion-pipeline" port="header-info"/>
    </p:with-input>
  </p:insert>

</p:declare-step>
```

1. To be able to refer to the additional input port, give the step a name using the `name="html-conversion-pipeline"` attribute on the root element.

2. Then declare the additional input port called `header-info`.

3. The additional input port must be connected using an *explicit connection* (there is no way to implicitly connect to the right input). The `<p:pipe>` child element of `<p:with-input>` does this. The `step="html-conversion-pipeline"` attribute refers to the `name` attribute of `<p:declare-step>` (i.e., the pipeline as a whole). The `port="header-info"` attribute connects to the input port declared in the `<p:input>` step.

A shortcut is to use a `pipe` attribute on the `<p:with-input>`:

```
<p:with-input port="insertion" select="/*/*"
  pipe="header-info@html-conversion-pipeline"/>
```

To use this construction you, of course, have to connect something to the `header-info` port on the step's invocation. This can be done in two ways:

- When this step is the outermost step, use the command line (see below).
- When this step is called from within another step, use `<p:with-input>` (the section titled "Connecting input ports: `<p:with-input>` " (p. 125)).

Command line for running this example

Assumptions: `$SOURCES/101/02-adding-header-info` is your current working directory, and the command to run the processor is on the system's path. The command lines in the examples below consist of multiple lines, but you need to enter them on a single line.

XML Calabash

```
calabash
  -i source=../documents/example-contents-1.xml
  -i header-info=../documents/additonal-header-contents.xml
  adding-header-info-3.xpl
```

Add `-o result=path-to-output-file` to the command line to catch the result in a file.

MorganaXProc-III

```
morgana adding-header-info-3.xpl
  -input:source=../documents/example-contents-1.xml
  -input:header-info=../documents/additonal-header-contents.xml
```

Add `-output:result=path-to-output-file` to the command line to catch the result in a file.

Supplying defaults for input ports

You can enhance the example by supplying default connections for the input ports. These connections kick in when you invoke this pipeline without supplying a connection for these ports. Example 2.10 shows two different ways of supplying a default.

Example 2.10 – Supplying default connections for the input ports
(`$SOURCES/101/02-adding-header-info/adding-header-info-4.xpl`)

```
<p:declare-step xmlns:p="http://www.w3.org/ns/xproc" version="3.0"
name="html-conversion-pipeline">

  <!-- 1. Make a default connection for the source input port to a document: -->
  <p:input port="source" primary="true">
    <p:document href="../documents/example-contents-1.xml"/>
  </p:input>
  <p:output port="result" primary="true"/>

  <!-- 2. Supply a fixed default document for the header-info port: -->
  <p:input port="header-info">
    <p:inline>
      <additional-header-contents>
        <link rel="stylesheet" type="text/css" href="style-1.css"/>
        <script type="text/javascript" src="javascript-1.js"/>
      </additional-header-contents>
    </p:inline>
  </p:input>

  <p:xslt>
    <p:with-input port="stylesheet" href="xsl/basic-conversion.xsl"/>
  </p:xslt>

  <p:insert match="/html/head" position="last-child">
    <p:with-input port="insertion" select="/*/*">
      <p:pipe step="html-conversion-pipeline" port="header-info"/>
    </p:with-input>
  </p:insert>

</p:declare-step>
```

1. For the `source` port, the default connection to the example contents document is created using the `<p:document>` child element. A shortcut would have been to leave out the `<p:document>` and put the `href` attribute directly on `<p:input>`. See the section titled "Reading external documents: `<p:document>`" (p. 139) for more information.

2. For the `header-info` port, a default connection is created to a *fixed* document. This document is stated inline in the XProc pipeline itself, using the `<p:inline>` element. This can be shortened, too. You can leave out the `<p:inline>` and state the document as a direct child of `<p:input>`. See the section titled "Specifying documents inline: `<p:inline>`" (p. 143) for more information.

Command lines for running this example

Assumptions: `$SOURCES/101/02-adding-header-info` is your current working directory, and the command to run the processor is on the system's path. The command lines in the examples below consist of multiple lines, but you need to enter them on a single line.

XML Calabash

Using all the default port connections:

```
calabash adding-header-info-4.xpl
```

Making explicit port connections:

```
calabash
  -i source=../documents/example-contents-1.xml
  -o
additional-header-info-file=../documents/additonal-header-contents.xml
  adding-header-info-4.xpl
```

Add `-o result=path-to-output-file` to the command line to catch the result in a file.

MorganaXProc-III

Using all the default port connections:

```
morgana adding-header-info-4.xpl
```

Making explicit port connections:

```
morgana adding-header-info-4.xpl
  -input:source=../documents/example-contents-1.xml

-option:additional-header-info-file=../documents/additonal-header-contents.xml
```

Add `-output:result=path-to-output-file` to the command line to catch the result in a file.

Indenting the result XML

The XML that flows out of the `result` port is not nicely indented. You might want to change this to make the output easier to interpret and verify. For this you have to change the port's serialization: The way the XML is written out to disk.

To change an output port's serialization you supply a `serialization` attribute whose value is an XPath `map` that specifies the serialization parameters as name/value pairs. For instance, you can turn on indentation as follows:

```
<p:output port="result" primary="true" serialization="map{ 'indent': true() }"/>
```

See the section titled "Specifying serialization" (p. 95) for more you can do with serialization.

Inserting additional data

Suppose the output HTML needs to include tables with data from yet another source, for instance a measurement instrument. In this example, I use some bogus weather data.

Example 2.11 – Additional data for inclusion in the resulting HTML (`$SOURCES/101/documents/additional-data.xml`)

```
<data>
  <weather city="Amsterdam" temperature="21" rain="drizzle"/>
  <weather city="Madrid" temperature="28" rain="none"/>
  <weather city="Stockholm" temperature="16" rain="heavy"/>
</data>
```

Suppose you want to display that data as shown in Table 2.1.

Table 2.1 – Output table with weather data

City	Temp (C)	Rain
Amsterdam	21	drizzle
Madrid	28	none
Stockholm	16	heavy

To specify where to insert this table, you need to make a small change to the input document, adding an `<add-additional-data>` element that uses the `source` attribute to point to the file that contains the additional data. In Example 2.12, the `<add-additional-data>` element is in the `<div>` with the title "My second chapter."

Example 2.12 – Input document with additional data location specified (`$SOURCES/101/documents/example-contents-2.xml`)

```
<document>
  <title>My 101 publication + additional data</title>

  <div class="sect1">
    <title>First part</title>

    <div class="sect2">
      <title>My first chapter</title>
      <para>The text for the first chapter...</para>
      <para>More text</para>
    </div>

    <div class="sect2">
      <title>My second chapter</title>
      <para>The text for the second chapter...</para>
      <add-additional-data source="additional-data.xml"/>
      <para>More text</para>
    </div>

  </div>

</document>
```

XProc has an instruction designed for this: **`<p:viewport>`** (the section titled "Acting on a part of a document: **`<p:viewport>`** " (p. 152)). A viewport takes part(s) of an XML document, usually an element and its descendants, and processes them in isolation. The result of this processing replaces the original without affecting the surroundings.

Example 2.13 shows how you can use **`<p:viewport>`** to process the `<add-additional-info>` element (based on the result of the section titled "Loading from another input port" (p. 24)).

Example 2.13 – Pipeline for processing the additional data
($SOURCES/101/03-insert-additional-data/insert-additional-data-1.xpl)

```
<p:declare-step xmlns:p="http://www.w3.org/ns/xproc" version="3.0"
  name="html-conversion-pipeline">

  <p:input port="source" primary="true"/>
  <p:output port="result" primary="true"/>

  <p:input port="header-info"/>

  <p:xslt>
    <p:with-input port="stylesheet" href="xsl/basic-conversion.xsl"/>
  </p:xslt>

  <p:insert match="/html/head" position="last-child">
    <p:with-input port="insertion" select="/*/*">
      <p:pipe step="html-conversion-pipeline" port="header-info"/>
    </p:with-input>
  </p:insert>

  <!-- 1. Add viewport to process the <add-additional-data> element -->
  <p:viewport match="add-additional-data">
    <!-- 2. Process the data into a table using an XSLT -->
    <p:xslt>
      <!-- 3. Get the data to convert, relative to the source document -->
      <p:with-input port="source" href="{resolve-uri(/*/@source, base-uri())}"/>
      <p:with-input port="stylesheet" href="xsl/convert-additional-data.xsl"/>
    </p:xslt>
  </p:viewport>
  <!-- 4. The <add-additional-data> element is replaced by the result of the
    <p:viewport>'s sub-pipeline -->

</p:declare-step>
```

1. The previous conversion result (which left the `<add-additional-data>` element untouched) flows into **`<p:viewport>`**. Again, the connection between **`<p:insert>`** and **`<p:viewport>`** is implicit because they're next to each other in the pipeline. The **`<p:viewport>`** triggers on the `<add-additional-info>` element, as specified in its `match` attribute. This particular example contains only one occurrence of this element, but it will trigger on all occurrences.

   The subpipeline inside **`<p:viewport>`** only sees this particular element and not the stuff surrounding it. To be more precise: the context-item inside a viewport becomes a document node with the element that triggered it as its root element.

A common mistake here is to assume that the element that triggered the viewport becomes the context-item and address the `source` attribute on the root element as `@source`. That will not work. Use `/*/@source` instead.

2. In Example 2.14, a simple XSLT transforms the data into HTML.

Example 2.14 – Stylesheet for converting the additional data (`$SOURCES/101/03-insert-additional-data/xsl/convert-additional-data.xsl`)

```
<xsl:stylesheet version="3.0" xmlns:xsl="http://www.w3.org/1999/XSL/Transform"
  xmlns:xs="http://www.w3.org/2001/XMLSchema" exclude-result-prefixes="#all">

  <xsl:template match="/">
   <table>
     <tr>
       <th>City</th>
       <th>Temp (C)</th>
       <th>Rain</th>
     </tr>
     <xsl:for-each select="/*/weather" expand-text="true">
       <tr>
         <td>{@city}</td>
         <td>{@temperature}</td>
         <td>{@rain}</td>
       </tr>
     </xsl:for-each>
   </table>
  </xsl:template>

</xsl:stylesheet>
```

3. The source data that needs to be converted is not what's flowing into the **`<p:viewport>`** directly (the `<add-additional-info>` element); it's the data pointed to by the `source` input port on the parent step (**`<p:declare-step>`**). So, you have to override the implicit connection of the **`<p:xslt>`**'s `source` port with an explicit reference to this file.

If I had used the `source` attribute's value directly (`href="{/*/@source}"`), it would have been resolved relative to the XProc document's location. However, relative paths in the content are meant to be relative to the content's location. XPath's `resolve-uri()` function, executed against the `base-uri()` of the original document, achieves this effect.

4. As a result, the <add-additional-data> element is replaced by the output of the **<p:viewport>** subpipeline: the required table structure.

Command line for running this example

Assumptions: `$SOURCES/101/03-insert-additional-data` is your current working directory, and the command to run the processor is on the system's path. The command lines in the examples below consist of multiple lines, but you need to enter them on a single line.

XML Calabash

```
calabash
  -i source=../documents/example-contents-1.xml
  -i header-info=../documents/additonal-header-contents.xml
  insert-additional-data-1.xpl
```

Add `-o result=path-to-output-file` to the command line to catch the result in a file.

MorganaXProc-III

```
morgana insert-additional-data-1.xpl
  -input:source=../documents/example-contents-1.xml
  -input:header-info=../documents/additonal-header-contents.xml
```

Add `-output:result=path-to-output-file` to the command line to catch the result in a file.

Generic data conversion to HTML

As the last part of this 101 course, let's make the last pipeline more generic. Assume you have more than one source of additional data, and each source emits a different XML structure. In that case it would be nice if you could not only specify the source of the data but also the stylesheet used to convert it. Fortunately, this is easy to do:

- First, amend the <add-additional-data> element with the name of the stylesheet:

```
<add-additional-data source="additional-data.xml"
  stylesheet="xsl/convert-additional-data.xsl"/>
```

- Second, tweak the pipeline to use this information. This only affects the **<p:xslt>** inside the **<p:viewport>**:

  ```
  <p:viewport match="add-additional-data">
    <p:xslt>
      <p:with-input port="source" href="{resolve-uri(/*/@source, base-uri())}"
      <p:with-input port="stylesheet" href="{/*/@stylesheet}"/>
    </p:xslt>
  </p:viewport>
  ```

  The name of the stylesheet to load is now read from the `stylesheet` attribute on `<add-additional-info>`. Its location is relative to the pipeline's location.

This will do the trick. Now you can add additional data sources to your content, converting them with tailored XSLT stylesheets into whatever HTML you need. The full pipeline can be found in `$SOURCES/101/03-insert-additional-data/insert-additional-data-2.xpl`.

Command line for running this example

Assumptions: `$SOURCES/101/03-insert-additional-data` is your current working directory, and the command to run the processor is on the system's path. The command lines in the examples below consist of multiple lines, but you need to enter them on a single line.

XML Calabash

```
calabash
  -i source=../documents/example-contents-1.xml
  -i header-info=../documents/additonal-header-contents.xml
  insert-additional-data-2.xpl
```

Add `-o result=path-to-output-file` to the command line to catch the result in a file.

MorganaXProc-III

```
morgana insert-additional-data-2.xpl
  -input:source=../documents/example-contents-1.xml
  -input:header-info=../documents/additonal-header-contents.xml
```

Add `-output:result=path-to-output-file` to the command line to catch the result in a file.

CHAPTER 3

XProc fundamentals

The previous chapter provides a first taste of XProc, but now it's time to go back to basics. What exactly is an XProc pipeline (or step) and what are the main concepts surrounding it?

This chapter, as the title implies, explains the fundamentals of XProc—the concepts you need to know and understand to work with it. It does not yet show much code, with the exception of a few illustrative examples. It's like looking at XProc from a helicopter. Don't worry, after this chapter we'll land and provide you with all the code you need.

Pipelines and steps

XProc is a pipeline language. A pipeline takes documents as input(s), does something with them using a series of steps, and produces output(s). Figure 3.1 shows a simple pipeline.

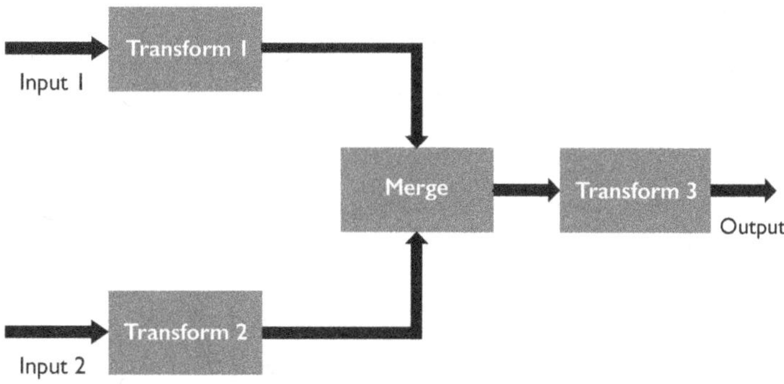

Figure 3.1 – A pipeline containing steps

Steps are the building blocks of XProc. A step takes documents as input(s), does something with those documents and produces output(s). Now that sounds familiar, doesn't it? On the outside, a step and a pipeline are indistinguishable. There is input, output, and document processing. If you don't know what's inside and consider it a black box, you wouldn't know the difference.

And that's exactly how XProc treats the two concepts: a pipeline is a step and steps are the XProc building blocks. Once you've written a pipeline, you can use it as a step somewhere else, just like any of the standard built-in steps.

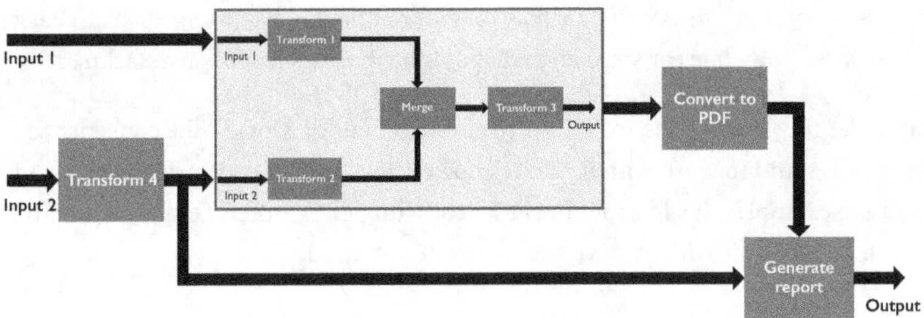

Figure 3.2 – A pipeline using another pipeline as a step

Up to now the word pipeline has been used in describing XProc. It's a concept that aids in understanding and explaining XProc. We all know pipes and stuff flowing through them, even if it's just the water pipes in our house. However, strange as it may sound for something defined as a pipeline language, XProc itself does *not* know pipelines as a separate concept, XProc works with *steps* (which can consist of steps, which can consist of... I think you get the picture).

This similarity between pipelines and steps is reflected in the language: to define a step, XProc has the `<p:declare-step>` element. It does not have a `<p:pipeline>` element.

The previous version of XProc did contain a `<p:pipeline>` element. It was syntactic sugar for a `<p:declare-step>` with the default input (`source`) and output (`result`) port pre-defined. It wasn't widely used and added complexity instead of simplifying things. Therefore, it was thrown out.

But what about the outermost step, the one you're executing directly with the XProc processor. Wouldn't you call that a pipeline? You could, but the difference would be rather artificial. Even that outermost step does exactly what a step is supposed to do: take input(s), process documents, produce output(s). So whether you execute a step directly from an XProc processor or use it as part of another step, it doesn't make a difference.

Therefore, from now on, I will use the words *step* and *pipeline* interchangeably.

Documents

XProc is a language for defining steps that process documents. But what exactly are these documents flowing through your steps?

Representations and properties

A document flowing through an XProc pipeline has two main parts: *representation* and *properties*. Both parts can be inspected, acted upon, and modified in XProc steps.

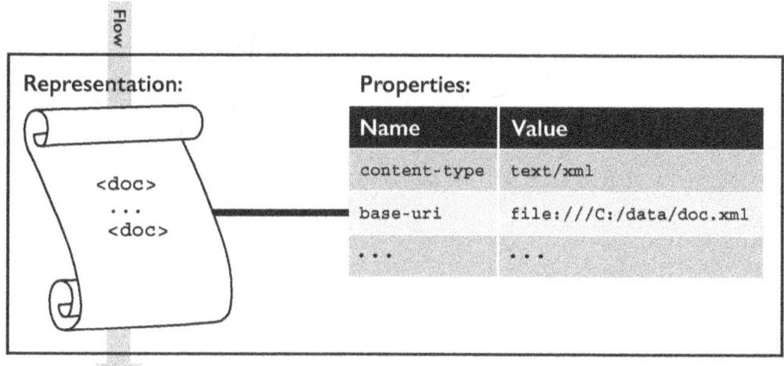

Figure 3.3 – Document consisting of a representation and properties flowing through a step

Representation
: The representation of a document is its contents. When you run an XML document through a step, its representation *is* the XML. For a binary format, such as jpeg, it's the binary contents.

  The reason for using the term *representation* and not, for instance, the *contents*, is that the XProc processor determines how to represent the document during processing. It might create a data structure in memory, load it as a BLOB (Binary Large Object), or leave it on disk. For the XProc user it doesn't matter.

Properties
: The document representation is always accompanied by a set of *properties*, a set of name/value pairs (technical details in the section titled "Document properties" (p. 63)). Properties can be inspected and modified by the XProc pipeline.

  You can also think of these properties as *metadata*, or, for a more physical analogy, the packing note attached to a package.

Document types

XProc distinguishes five principal document types: XML, HTML, JSON, text, and other. XML is the main, first-class document type with by far the most functionality available for processing. However, as you will see in the chapters to come, it is possible and useful to process non-XML documents using XProc.

XML Documents

Processing XML is what XProc was originally designed for, so it's no surprise that XProc treats XML as a privileged type. If you've worked with XML but never delved too deep into the standards surrounding it, you probably know it as a flexible but verbose data representation, using an awful lot of angle brackets. Opening an XML file in your favorite text editor will strengthen this idea (see Example 3.1).

Example 3.1 – An example XML document

```
<example id="123">
  <p>This is an <b>example</b>!</p>
  <p>Angle brackets all over the place.</p>
</example>
```

However, looks can be deceiving. What you see when opening an XML document like Example 3.1 is *data* in a certain *representation*. You could easily represent the same data in some other form. For instance, Example 3.2 shows the same content in JSON.

Example 3.2 – The same data as Example 3.1 but now in JSON format

```
{ "example": {
    "@id": "123",
    "p": [
      {
        "#text": [
          "This is an",
          "!"
        ],
        "b": "example"
      },
      "Angle brackets all over the place."
    ]
  }
}
```

These two examples contain the same data, but in two different formats. What we know as XML, with all those angle brackets, is just one of the possible *serializations* (that is, equivalent formats) of this data structure. Since the XML format is so common, most people don't consider other possible serializations. XML data can be serialized in many ways.

Connoisseurs will notice that Example 3.2 does not fully represent the XML. XML elements have an order in an XML document, but entries in a JSON object do not. However, this is what the common XML to JSON convertors come up with.

Then what is this XML data structure? XML is a *tree-shaped data structure* with nodes containing a document root, elements, attributes, text, and some others left out for now (see Figure 3.4).

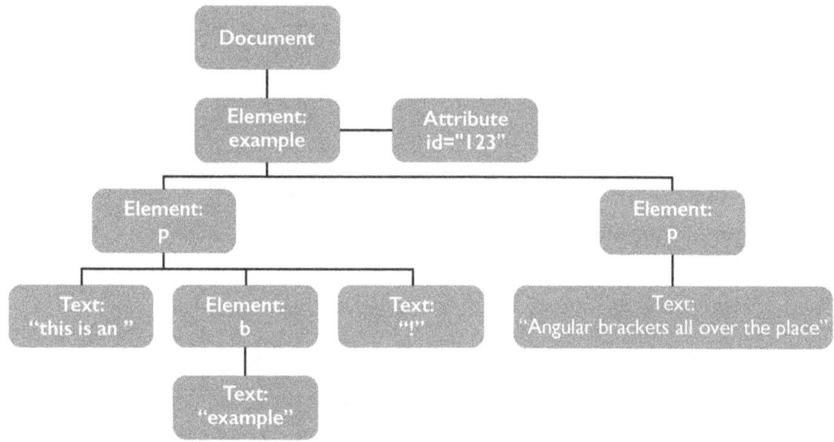

Figure 3.4 – The example document represented as a tree-shaped data structure

Programming languages, such as Java, Javascript or C#, use the well-known DOM (Document Object Model) for representing XML data. XML processors, such as XSLT, XQuery and XProc, use XDM (XQuery and XPath Data Model 3.1).[1] Figure 3.4 depicts a (simplified) XDM representation of Example 3.1 and Example 3.2.

[1] https://www.w3.org/TR/xpath-datamodel-31/

An XProc processor treats XML documents as tree-shaped data structures:

- Internally, an XProc processor does not work with content as text. It uses an XDM or XDM-like representation. This is much more efficient to handle than text, which must be parsed to process. XML documents flow through XProc steps as trees of data, not pieces of text.
- There are only two moments an XProc processor deals with XML in its serialized, usually angle bracketed, form:
  - When a document is loaded and parsed.
  - When a document is written (serialized).[2]
- You query XML documents using the XPath language (as in XSLT and XQuery). Understanding XPath becomes a lot easier if you think of XML documents as trees.

So, referring to the section titled "Representations and properties" (p. 37), the representation of an XML document inside the XProc processor is an XDM tree. Its source and destination serialization formats do not matter.

If you want to know more about the XDM data model, I recommend *XSLT 2.0 and XPath 2.0: Programmer's Reference* by Michael Kay, which contains a thorough and well written explanation of XDM (see the section titled "Additional resources" (p. xvii)).

HTML documents

HTML documents are not very different from XML documents; they're passed around as XDM, just like XML. The difference is in how they get in and out of the pipeline:

- HTML documents are usually not well-formed (in the XML sense). There can be unbalanced elements (e.g. a `<p>` without the corresponding `</p>`). Empty elements are not closed (writing a break as `<br>` rather than `<br/>`). XPath and XProc require well-formed documents.

  Therefore, an HTML document is parsed using the HTML5 parsing algorithm, which produces a tree that can be processed as if the input was a well-formed XML document.
- When serializing HTML documents, HTML serialization is used by default (the section titled "Specifying serialization" (p. 95)).

[2] XProc allows fine-grained control over serialization (see the section titled "Specifying serialization" (p. 95)).

JSON documents

JSON documents flow through the pipeline not as a tree but as a data structure. For instance the JSON document `{"a":"bla", "b":1}` will become a map with two entries: `map{"a":"bla", "b":1}` (see also the section titled "Map usage" (p. 60)).

This data structure is accessible and can be manipulated in the pipeline. Technical details can be found in the section titled "JSON documents" (p. 66) and code examples in the section titled "Working with JSON documents" (p. 204).

Text documents

Text documents flow through the pipeline as a very simple XDM tree: just the top document node and a single text node underneath (see Figure 3.5).

Figure 3.5 – A text document as an XDM tree

Examples of handling text documents can be found in the section titled "Working with text documents" (p. 210).

Other documents

XProc can handle other (a.k.a. binary) document types, like jpeg or zip files. How these are represented internally is completely implementation defined. It is not possible to do anything with binary content (unless there are specific steps for it, like for zip files). However, you can do things based on the document's content type. An example of this in the section titled "Working with other documents" (p. 212).

Steps

XProc's basic building block is the *step*. You can chain and re-use steps to make bigger, more complicated, steps. But what exactly constitutes a step and what kinds of steps are available?

Properties of a step

When you look at a step from the outside as a black box, it has the following main properties:

Type

A step can have a *type*. Examples include: `p:xslt`, `p:identity`, or `mysteps:mix-things-up`. You need a type to invoke/call the step from inside another step. It's analogous to the name of a function, method, or procedure in other programming languages.

A step's type must be a *qualified name*, with a mandatory, non-null, namespace. You cannot use the standard XProc namespace. A type usually has the format `xxx:yyy`, where `xxx` is a namespace prefix and `yyy` is the type's name.[3]

XProc's built-in steps all have types in the form `p:something`. The namespace prefix `p` must be bound to the namespace `http://www.w3.org/ns/xproc` (see Example 3.3).

Example 3.3 – Using the `p` prefix in XProc

```
<p:declare-step xmlns:p="http://www.w3.org/ns/xproc" ...>
  ...
  <p:xslt>
    ...
  </p:xslt>
  ...
</p:declare-step>
```

The namespace `http://www.w3.org/ns/xproc` is prescribed, but the namespace prefix `p` isn't. So you could use a prefix like `xproc` or even `bzzrgghl`. I strongly recommend against this: it obfuscates code and makes it much harder to interpret for other developers (or yourself in a few months). This book always uses the prefix `p` for the XProc namespace.

[3] There is another way to write qualified names (the `Q{}` notation), but this is seldom used.

If you have a step you want to use in another step, you have to give it a type. That is usually done by defining some namespace with a suitable prefix and using this in the `p:declare-step`'s `type` attribute, as shown in Example 3.4.

Example 3.4 – Defining the type of a step with a namespace of our own

```
<p:declare-step xmlns:p="http://www.w3.org/ns/xproc"
                xmlns:mysteps="http://my.own.url/ns/steps/or/whatever"
                type="mysteps:do-something" ...>
  ...
</p:declare-step>
```

Assuming this step is in a separate file, you can use the step in another step by first importing it and then calling/invoking it by its type, as shown in Example 3.5.

Example 3.5 – Using the typed step from Example 3.4 inside another step

```
<p:declare-step xmlns:p="http://www.w3.org/ns/xproc"
                xmlns:mysteps="http://my.own.url/ns/steps/or/whatever" ...>
  ...
  <p:import href="declaration-of-mysteps-do-something.xpl"/>
  ...
  <mysteps:do-something>
    ...
  </mysteps:do-something>
  ...
</p:declare-step>
```

More about defining and re-using your own steps in Chapter 5 and Chapter 6.

Ports

Although in theory you could have steps without ports, most steps have them. Ports are the *connectors* of a step, where documents flow in (input ports) or out (output ports). Ports are important, so there's a separate section about them, the section titled "Ports" (p. 45).

Options

Steps can have *options*. Options are name/value pairs that you can use to further determine a step's functionality. For instance, the **`<p:insert>`** step inserts one XML document into another. It has an option called `match` to determine *where* in the main document the other document must be inserted (e.g. `/*` or `/doc//sect1`). It also has an option called `position` to determine *how* this must be done (possible values: `first-child`, `last-child`, `before` or `after`).

There are several ways to pass options to steps. Example 3.6 shows how to do this using attributes:

Example 3.6 – Example passing the option `position` to a step using attributes

```
<p:declare-step xmlns:p="http://www.w3.org/ns/xproc" ...>
  ...
  <p:insert match="/*" position="first-child">
    ...
  </p:insert>
  ...
</p:declare-step>
```

Example 3.7 shows how to do this using `<p:with-option>`:

Example 3.7 – Example passing the option `position` to a step using `<p:with-option>`

```
<p:declare-step xmlns:p="http://www.w3.org/ns/xproc" ...>
  ...
  <p:insert>
    <p:with-option name="match" select="'/*'"/>
    <p:with-option name="position" select="'first-child'"/>
    ...
  </p:insert>
  ...
</p:declare-step>
```

Notice that the value of the `select` attribute of `<p:with-option>` is surrounded by single quotes. This is because the value is an XPath *expression*. If you don't quote the expression, it will be immediately interpreted by the processor and the result passed as the attribute value. You want the attribute value to be processed when the step is executed, not when it is declared. Therefore, it needs to be quoted. I discuss this in much more detail in the section titled "Setting options: `<p:with-option>` (or by attribute)" (p. 128).

Option value types can be anything that can be expressed in the XPath data model. This includes everything you might expect from other programming languages, including numbers, booleans, and strings. However, you can also use XML-related data types, like elements, attributes, or even complete documents. Options can be mandatory (a value has to be provided by the step's caller) or optional, in which case a default value applies if the option is missing. More about options in the section titled "Declaring options: `<p:option>`" (p. 102).

Kinds of steps

In working with XProc, it is useful to distinguish several kinds of steps.[4]

Core steps
: The core steps make up the XProc programming language. These steps handle functions such as looping (**`<p:for-each>`**), branching (**`<p:choose>`** or **`<p:if>`**), and error handling (**`<p:try>`**). Core steps are discussed in detail in Chapter 7.

Built-in steps
: XProc has built-in steps that provide you with out-of-the-box functionality to populate your pipelines. For instance, running an XSLT (**`<p:xslt>`**), processing an XInclude (**`<p:xinclude>`**), adding an attribute (**`<p:add-attribute>`**), etc. The built-in steps are listed in Chapter 8.

Self-defined steps
: Programming XProc *is* defining steps. How to write steps, in all its (in)glorious details, is the main subject of the chapters to come.

Extension steps
: XProc processors often add steps of their own for doing things which are not possible using the built-in steps. Consult the XProc processor's documentation to find out more about the extension steps it supports.

Ports

Ports are the *connectors* of steps. Documents flow in or out of a step through ports. Ports are the equivalent of the USB connectors on your computer or the network connectors on your router.

[4] The XProc specification uses a slightly different taxonomy to identify kinds of steps.

For instance, the **<p:xslt>** step has two input ports, one for the document and one for the stylesheet. It also has two output ports: one for the result of the XSLT transformation and one for the optional additional result documents (created with `<xsl:result-document>`).

Figure 3.6 – The **<p:xslt>** step with its input and output ports

Ports are defined with `<p:input>` and `<p:output>` elements. Example 3.8 shows simplified port declarations for the **<p:xslt>** step in Figure 3.6.

Example 3.8 – Simplified port declarations for the **<p:xslt>** step

```
<p:input port="source" primary="true" sequence="true"/>
<p:input port="stylesheet"/>
<p:output port="result" primary="true"/>
<p:output port="secondary" sequence="true"/>
```

Properties of ports

Ports have the following properties:

Port name

All ports have a name that identifies the port when you connect something to it. Port names are defined with the `port` attribute. By convention, the most important input port is called `source` and the most important output port `result`.

Most built-in steps have a `source` and `result` port. These ports are usually the *primary* input and output ports of the step. Primary ports play an important role in connecting steps. Port names follow the same rules as XML element/attribute names, with exception of colons. See below and the section titled "Connecting or binding ports" (p. 48) for more information.

Primary setting

One input and one output port (only one of each) can be identified as the step's *primary* input/output port. Primary ports auto-connect when you place steps next to each other. This makes pipelines much easier to write and, maybe even more important, to read and understand. More about this in the section titled "Connecting or binding ports" (p. 48).

To define a port as primary, add a `primary="true"` attribute to the port definition. When a step has a single input or output port, this is optional. By default, single input/output ports are primary unless overridden by the `primary="false"` attribute. The primary ports are, in most cases, called `source` and `result`.

Constraint settings

There are two attributes you can use to constrain the flow of documents for a port:

- `sequence`: Can the port handle/produce exactly one document, or can it handle zero-or-more documents?
- `content-types`: Which document MIME types can the port handle/produce?

If a constraint is violated, the processor will raise an error. See the section titled "Declaring input ports: `<p:input>`" (p. 86) for more.

Default connection

You can provide input ports with default connections or contents. The default is used when nothing is explicitly connected to the port. You can set the default to no input, to an inline XML document (inline means it's part of the XProc code) or to an external document. See the section titled "Declaring input ports: `<p:input>`" (p. 86) for more.

Connecting or binding ports

To make pipelines out of steps, you have to be able to connect or bind the ports of the individual steps. Documents must flow into input ports, whether they come from output ports of other steps, disk, the web, or elsewhere.

Ports can be bound in two ways:

Implicit bindings

This is the type of port connection you're going to use most. When one step follows another (and no explicit binding overrides this), the *primary output port* of the first step is automatically connected to the *primary input port* of the second step. No hassle, no fuss.

For instance, to connect two **`<p:xslt>`** steps together, so the result document of the first step becomes the source document for the second step, simply place them in sequence, as shown in Example 3.9. In this case, the output of the first step becomes the input of the second.

Example 3.9 – Implicit port binding for two `<p:xslt>` steps

```
<p:xslt>
  <p:with-input port="stylesheet" href="myxslt1.xsl"/>
</p:xslt>
<p:xslt>
  <p:with-input port="stylesheet" href="myxslt2.xsl"/>
</p:xslt>
```

This works because the **`<p:xslt>`** step has its source and result ports defined as primary ports (see Example 3.8). XProc uses this to automagically bind them.

Other implicit port bindings are:

- The primary input port of the pipeline connects to the primary input port of the very first step in the pipeline.
- The primary output port of the last step in your pipeline connects to the primary output port of the pipeline.

The following diagram illustrates this:

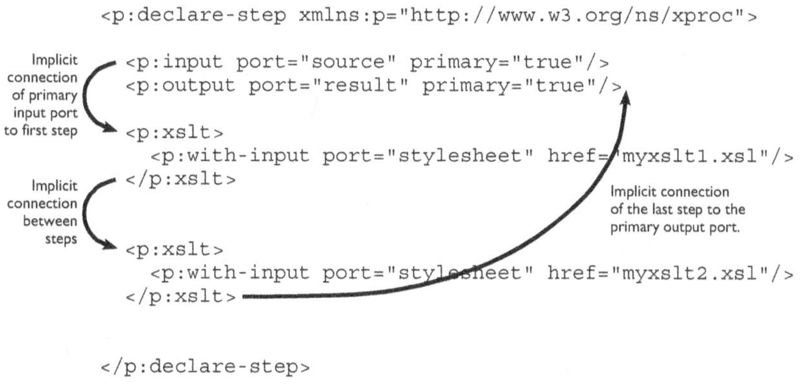

```
<p:declare-step xmlns:p="http://www.w3.org/ns/xproc">

  <p:input port="source" primary="true"/>
  <p:output port="result" primary="true"/>

  <p:xslt>
    <p:with-input port="stylesheet" href="myxslt1.xsl"/>
  </p:xslt>

  <p:xslt>
    <p:with-input port="stylesheet" href="myxslt2.xsl"/>
  </p:xslt>

</p:declare-step>
```


Figure 3.7 – Implicit connections in pipelines

I suggest that you use implicit connections whenever you can. Not only does this save you keystrokes during programming, it also makes the flow of documents intuitively clear. Documents flow from top to bottom through your XProc program.

Explicit binding

But not all ports are primary ports and, even for primary ports, the previous step is not always the right one. So XProc allows you to explicitly bind input ports. In fact we've already seen this. In Example 3.9, the `stylesheet` input ports of both **`<p:xslt>`** steps are explicitly bound to documents on disk using the `href` attribute.

Port binding is only done on input ports. You specify what an input port is connected to, not where an output port delivers its results. *Pull*, not push.

There are four things you can do to explicitly connect to an input port:

- You can connect it to a specific output port.
- You can provide an inline XML document as part of the XProc code itself.
- You can connect the port to an external document.
- You can specify "no input" (no documents will appear on the input port).

It is even possible to combine these, in which case multiple documents can appear on the port.

Figure 3.8 shows how you can explicitly connect the output of the first **<p:xslt>** to the input port of the second **<p:xslt>**.

```
<p:xslt name="first-xslt">
  <p:with-input port="stylesheet" href="myxslt1.xsl"/>
</p:xslt>

<p:xslt>
  <p:with-input port="source">
    <p:pipe step="first-xslt" port="result"/>
  </p:with-input>
  <p:with-input port="stylesheet" href="myxslt2.xsl"/>
</p:xslt>
```

Connect to another step by name

Connect to the result output port of this step by name

Figure 3.8 – Explicitly connect the result port of one step to the source port of another

To explicitly refer to a step, it must have a name, that's why the first **<p:xslt>** in Figure 3.8 has a `name="first-xslt"` attribute. You can use this name to bind the `source` input port of the second **<p:xslt>** step to the `result` output port of the first **<p:xslt>** step.

Figure 3.8 is not the only way to connect ports. XProc provides additional ways to specify connections, for example the `pipe` attribute. More about this in the section titled "Common connection constructs" (p. 139).

The following rules apply when connecting ports:

- Input ports must always be connected to something (even if it's to "no input"), you can't leave them dangling. This connection can be a default connection (specified in the step's declaration), an implicit connection (for primary ports), or an explicit connection.
- Output ports (including primary ones) can be left dangling. Any output appearing on non-connected output ports is discarded.

In XProc 1.0, all primary output ports had to be connected. If you didn't need the results, you had to connect the output port to a **<p:sink>** step (the section titled "p:sink" (p. 277)) to make things disappear. This restriction has been dropped. Now, unconnected output ports silently send their output into oblivion.

The Default Readable Port

Whether or not you override this with an explicit binding, a step will implicitly connect to a port called the *Default Readable Port* or DRP.

The DRP of a step is one of the following:

- The *primary* output port of the step directly before this step.
- For the first step in a pipeline, the primary input port of the pipeline itself.
- Undefined, for instance when the previous step did not define a primary output port.

The DRP concept plays an important role in the expansion of Attribute and Text Value Templates (see the section titled "Attribute Value Templates in the XProc code" (p. 69)).

CHAPTER 4

Programming concepts

This chapter runs through some of the more general concepts you need to program in XProc. This ranges from the underlying XPath language to Value Templates to common elements and attributes. It also delves into technical details of some of the concepts introduced in Chapter 3.

Some examples in this chapter use the **`<p:identity>`** step, which I haven't introduced, yet. This step does nothing. It passes what it receives on its (primary) `source` port to its (primary) `result` port. That doesn't sound very useful, but this simple behavior has applications. For instance, some examples in this chapter use it for initiating a pipeline with a fixed document:

```
<p:identity>
  <p:with-input port="source">
    <root>blablabla</root>
  </p:with-input>
</p:identity>
```

This will cause an XML document containing `<root>blablabla</root>` to flow out of the step's `result` port, ready for further processing. You can find more information about the **`<p:identity>`** step in the section titled "p:identity" (p. 258), and more applications of it can be found in the section titled "Using **`<p:identity>`** to clarify pipeline structure" (p. 199).

XPath in XProc

XML programming languages like XSLT and XQuery have their own syntax and semantics, but they use a common underlying language: XPath. XProc is no exception; it uses XPath 3.1 to specify elements and attributes in the XML and for expressions like the following:

- `/books/book`
- `/*/customers/customer[@id eq '1778090'][@status eq 'active']`
- `title[starts-with(., 'XProc')]`
- `1 + 2`
- `upper-case('xp') || 'roc'`

This book assumes that you have at least some background using XPath, probably in XSLT or XQuery, and I do not attempt to explain or teach it. For more information see the resources mentioned in the section titled "XProc and underlying standards" (p. xvii).

Example 4.1 shows a simple example of XPath at work in XProc. Imagine a document flowing through the pipeline and encountering this **<p:choose>** step, which checks the `status` attribute on the root element using an XPath expression in the `test` attribute.

Example 4.1 – An XPath expression inside a <p:choose> step

```
<p:choose>
  <p:when test="/*/@status eq 'final'">
    <!-- Do something with final documents… -->
  </p:when>
  <p:otherwise>
    <!-- Do something with non-final documents… -->
  </p:otherwise>
</p:choose>
```

Since XProc embraces XPath, it supports all of its data types. This is officially called the *XQuery and XPath Data Model* or XDM. This means you can work with all the usual suspects, such as numbers and strings, and with specific XML types such as elements, attributes, and documents. The newer data types, including maps and arrays, are supported as well.

Of course XProc supports variables. Example 4.2 shows how XProc declares and uses them.

Example 4.2 – Declaring and using variables in XProc

```
<p:variable name="path" as="xs:string" select="'/some/location/on/disk'"/>
<p:variable name="filename" as="xs:string"
       select="concat($path, '/', 'myxslt.xsl')"/>
…
<p:xslt>
  <p:with-input port="stylesheet" href="{$filename}"/>
</p:xslt>
```

Unfortunately, XProc cannot directly declare custom XPath functions (like `<xsl:function>` in XSLT or `declare function` in XQuery). However, if your processor supports it, you can import XSLT and XQuery function libraries and use them inside your XProc code. More about this in the section titled "Importing function libraries: `<p:import-functions>` " (p. 108).

Extension functions

XProc defines a set of extension functions for use in XPath expressions. Their capabilities range from retrieving information about the XProc processor (`p:system-property()`) to looping information (`p:iteration-position()` and `p:iteration-size()`) to working with document properties (for example, `p:document-property()`). You can find a list of extension functions in Chapter 9.

XPath expressions and step options

An important question to keep in the back of your mind when you're programming XProc is: *Who is going to interpret the expression?* Is it:

- The pipeline?
- The step?

So, why is this important? Some steps need expressions passed to them. An example is the **`<p:delete>`** step which deletes content from a document. It has an option called `match` that matches the item to be deleted. The value of this option must be a *string* containing a valid selection pattern (like in XSLT's `match` attribute). The step evaluates the match, *not* the surrounding pipeline. The *step* deletes content in the designated location(s). So you have to be sure this expression isn't accidentally evaluated by the pipeline.[1]

Confused? Let's illustrate this with an example. Assume you have a simple document flowing through your pipeline:

```
<html>
  <head/>
  <body>
    <p>Some text</p>
    <remark final="1">Remove this!</remark>
  </body>
</html>
```

[1] If you're not careful, this can cause frustration and headaches. It's such an important subject that I explain it again where you are likely to run into it: the section titled "Setting options: `<p:with-option>` (or by attribute)" (p. 128).

Suppose you want is to remove all `<remark>` elements with a `final="1"` attribute. The code in Example 4.3 will do the trick.

Example 4.3 – Remove all final remark elements

```
<p:delete>
  <p:with-option name="match" select="'remark[@final = 1]'"/>
</p:delete>
```

Notice that the `select` attribute in the example contains a *string value constant* (it is surrounded by apostrophes, `'...'`).

You must specify this option as a string because it has to be interpreted by the **`<p:delete>`** step and not by the pipeline. Let's figure out what would happen if you left out the apostrophes and specified it as follows:

```
<p:with-option name="match" select="remark[@final = 1]"/>
```

- The XProc processor encounters this `<p:with-option>`.
- It evaluates the XPath expression in the `select` attribute.
- This selects the `<remark final="1">` element and evaluates it, yielding `Remove this!`
- `Remove this!` will be passed to the **`<p:delete>`** step as the value of its `match` option.
- The **`<p:delete>`** step thinks the value of the `match` option is an selection pattern and starts evaluating `Remove this!` against the document.
- Since `Remove this!` is not a valid selection pattern, this will fail and result in an error.

An alternative for passing option values to steps is to specify them as option-attributes on the step invocation. Using this method, Example 4.3 can be rewritten as shown in Example 4.4.

Example 4.4 – Using an option-attribute to pass the `match` option's value

```
<p:delete match="remark[@final = 1]"/>
```

As you can see there are no more apostrophes in the option-attribute's value. This is because option-attribute values are (with two exceptions) treated as straight strings and not as expressions. The XProc processor will not attempt to evaluate them. Here are the exceptions:

The first exception is an expression between curly braces {…}. An Attribute Value Template (AVT) is an option-attribute containing an expression between curly braces that is evaluated by the XProc processor to construct its value (see the section titled "Attribute and Text Value Templates" (p. 68)).

For instance, you could assign the value you're comparing against to a variable and re-write Example 4.4 as shown in Example 4.5.

Example 4.5 – Specifying an option-attribute with an AVT

```
<p:variable name="final-value" as="xs:integer" select="1"/>
<p:delete match="remark[@final = {$final-value}]"/>
```

Because the `select` attribute of `<p:with-option>` is an expression that the pipeline can evaluate, you can use this to your advantage to construct the value of the **`<p:delete>`**'s `match` option as shown in Example 4.6.

Example 4.6 – Using an expression to construct an XPath expression in a `select` attribute

```
<p:variable name="final-value" as="xs:integer" select="1"/>
<p:delete>
  <p:with-option name="match"
    select="'remark[@final = ' || $final-value || ']'"/>
</p:delete>
```

The second exception to option-attributes being just strings is when the option's value is declared as a `map` or `array`. In that case the option-attribute's value is interpreted as an XPath expression (which must, of course, result in the appropriate data type).

For instance, the **`<p:xslt>`** step has an option called `parameters` which allows you to pass parameters to the stylesheet. Its data type is `map(xs:QName, item()*)`, and therefore, you can pass it a value as shown in Example 4.7.

Example 4.7 – Specifying a map as an option-attribute

```
<p:xslt parameters="map{ 'name': 'erik', 'language': 'XProc' }" ...>
```

Observant readers may notice that, despite the map's data type, its keys are strings, not QNames. This is QName magic in action, which will be discussed in the next section.

You can find much more about setting options, with or without using attributes, in the section titled "Setting options: `<p:with-option>` (or by attribute)" (p. 128).

QName magic

The datatype `xs:QName` (QName in short) stands for "Qualified Name," a name that might (or might not) be in some namespace. For instance, the names of XML elements and attributes are QNames. A QName has two parts:

- A *namespace* URI (which can be empty).
- A *local-name*. This is a non-empty string that must conform to the rules for element and attribute names (without a colon).

Constructing a QName in code can be done using the XPath function `QName()`. For instance, `QName('', 'my-element')` creates a QName with local-name `my-element` in no-namespace. `QName('http://my-domain.org/ns', 'my-element')` creates a QName in the `http://my-domain.org/ns` namespace.

QName's are used a lot in XProc. For instance, `p:add-attribute` has an option named `attribute-name` that holds the name of the attribute to add. The datatype for this option is `xs:QName`. Other examples are the keys in most of the maps used in XProc (which has a section of its own: the section titled "Map usage" (p. 60)).

Now in a world without magic you'd have to specify all these QNames as QNames, using the XPath function `QName()` over and over again. Especially for map construction (as we'll see later), this would be an chore. Therefore, the XProc designers waved their magic wands and sprinkled a touch of Hogwarts on the language: QName magic.

QName magic enables you to use simple strings instead of QNames in almost all situations where the datatype is `xs:QName`. For instance, without QName magic you'd always have to specify the name of an attribute to add (even if it wasn't in a namespace) as in Example 4.8.

Example 4.8 – Adding an attribute without QName magic

```
<p:add-attribute attribute-value="debug">
  <p:with-option name="attribute-name" select="QName((), 'status')"/>
</p:add-attribute>
```

There's nothing wrong with this (you can do this if you'd like to), but it would be cumbersome to use the `QName()` function all the time. With QName magic you can write it as in Example 4.9.

Example 4.9 – Adding an attribute with QName magic

```
<p:add-attribute attribute-value="debug">
  <p:with-option name="attribute-name" select="'status'"/>
</p:add-attribute>
```

Or, even better, you can use an option-attribute for the name as in Example 4.10.

Example 4.10 – Adding an attribute with QName magic using an option-attribute for the name

```
<p:add-attribute attribute-name="status" attribute-value="debug"/>
```

Namespace prefixes work the way you'd expect them to, using the namespace prefixes in scope as in Example 4.11.

Example 4.11 – Adding an attribute in a namespace with QName magic

```
<p:declare-step … xmlns:myns="http://my-domain.org/ns">
  …
  <p:add-attribute attribute-name="myns:status" attribute-value="debug"/>
  …
</p:declare-step>
```

The rules for specifying something that is a QName and its magic are as follows:

- If the value is already of type `xs:QName`, that value is used, unchanged.
- If the value is of type `xs:string` (or a type derived from this), an attempt is made to convert this into an `xs:QName`, using the XPath EQName production rules:[2]
  - Strings without colons, like `'invoice'` or `'gobbledygook'`, are converted to an `xs:QName` in no-namespace (*not* in the current default namespace, as you might expect).
  - Strings with a colon, like `'myns:my-elm'` or `'xsl:transform'`, are interpreted as usual. The namespace bindings (`xmlns:prefix="..."`) on the parent elements are used to find the right namespace for the given prefix, just like in plain vanilla XML.
  - Strings that use the `Q{}` notation, like `Q{http://docbook.org/ns/docbook}para` or `Q{http:/my-domain.org/ns}adacadabra` are interpreted as such. The result is an `xs:QName` with that namespace (the part between the curly braces) and local-name.

  Of course, the strings must follow the syntactic and semantic rules. For instance, a name in XML can contain only allowed characters, must not start with a digit, etc. Namespace prefixes must be defined. Any string that cannot be converted results in an error.
- A value that is neither a QName nor a string results in an error, unless it's a map's key. In that case the map's entry is silently discarded.

Map usage

XProc uses maps for a lot of functions, including passing parameters to transformations, working with document properties, and setting serialization properties.

[2] https://www.w3.org/TR/xpath-31/#doc-xpath31-EQName

Maps in XPath

One of the more recent additions to the XPath programming language is the map data type. A map is a collection of key/value pairs. The key must be an atomic data type (like string, number, etc.). The value can be anything, including atomic data types, elements, attributes, and documents. You can use the key to quickly and efficiently lookup the value. Here is an example of declaring a simple XProc variable with a map:

```
<p:variable name="days" as="map(xs:string, xs:string)" select="
    map {
      'Su' : 'Sunday',
      'Mo' : 'Monday',
      'Tu' : 'Tuesday',
      'We' : 'Wednesday',
      'Th' : 'Thursday',
      'Fr' : 'Friday',
      'Sa' : 'Saturday'
    }
  "/>
```

Given this declaration, you can look things up like `$days('We')` or even `$days?We`. There are special functions for maps, like `map:size($days)` (which returns `7`).

XProc also uses maps to pass parameters to steps like **`<p:xslt>`** and **`<p:xquery>`**. Both of these steps have an option called `parameters`, as shown below (notice the `xs:QName` datatype for the map's keys):

```
<p:option name="parameters" as="map(xs:QName, item()*)"/>
```

Why is the map key defined as a QName? It's not used often, so you might not be aware of this, but parameters in XSLT and XQuery are *qualified names*: they can be in a namespace. So you could have XSLT stylesheet parameters defined as shown in Example 4.12.

Example 4.12 – XSLT parameters with namespaces

```
<xsl:stylesheet xmlns:xsl="http://www.w3.org/1999/XSL/Transform"
  xmlns:myns="http://mydomain.com/ns/myns" …>
  …
  <xsl:param name="param1"/>
  <xsl:param name="myns:param2"/>
  …
</xsl:stylesheet>
```

In Example 4.12, the parameter `param1` is not in a namespace. However, `myns:param2` is in the `http://mydomain.com/ns/myns` namespace bound to the prefix `myns`. To pass a value to `myns:param2`, you must specify it with this namespace when passing parameters. Hence the `xs:QName` data type for the keys in the parameter-passing maps.

Having to do this whenever you have a QName in a namespace is inconvenient and verbose. Creating a map to pass values to the parameters in Example 4.12 requires you to use the XPath `QName()` function over and over again, as you can see in Example 4.13.

Example 4.13 – Using a map with `xs:QName` keys to pass parameters

```
<p:xslt>
  <p:with-input port="stylesheet" href="myxslt-with-qname-parameter.xsl"/>
  <p:with-option name="parameters" select="map{
        QName((), 'firstparam') : 'some value',
        QName('http://mydomain.com/ns/myns', 'secondparam') : 'some other value'
      }
    "/>
</p:xslt>
```

That's no fun, especially when you have a lot of parameters to take care of. Luckily, as we've already seen in the section titled "QName magic" (p. 58), XProc provides QName magic, which allows Example 4.13 to be rewritten as shown in Example 4.14, or you can use XPath's `Q{}` notation (see Example 4.15).

Example 4.14 – Using a map with `xs:string` keys to pass parameters

```
<p:xslt xmlns:myns="http://mydomain.com/ns/myns">
  <p:with-input port="stylesheet" href="myxslt-with-qname-parameter.xsl"/>
  <p:with-option name="parameters" select="map{
      'param1' : 'some value',
      'myns:param2' : 'some other value'
    }
    "/>
</p:xslt>
```

Example 4.15 – Using a map with `xs:string` keys in `Q{}` notation to pass parameters

```
<p:xslt>
  <p:with-input port="stylesheet" href="myxslt-with-qname-parameter.xsl"/>
  <p:with-option name="parameters" select="map{
      'param1' : 'some value',
      'Q{http://mydomain.com/ns/myns}param2' : 'some other value'
    }
    "/>
</p:xslt>
```

Clearly, Example 4.14 is much more convenient, intuitive, and easy to write than Example 4.13. And since QName magic is available throughout XProc, it applies to all options using maps with `xs:QName` keys (`as="map(xs:QName, …)"`), including options of type `map(xs:QName, …)` that you define in your own steps.

Document details

This section bundles the information you need to be aware of when you want to do more advanced things with documents.

Document properties

As introduced in the section titled "Representations and properties" (p. 37), every document flowing through an XProc pipeline is accompanied by a set of document properties. Technically, document properties are a map of type `map(xs:QName, item()*)`. In other words: the *keys* of the map are *qualified names* (names that might be in a namespace) and the *values* can be anything. XProc pre-defines three document properties: `content-type`, `base-url`, and `serialization`:

`content-type`

This property contains the MIME type of the document and will always be present. Example values are `text/xml` or `image/jpeg`. The XProc processor uses this property to determine what type of document it's dealing with, as you can see in Table 4.1 (see also the section titled "Document types" (p. 38)).

Table 4.1 – The relation between `content-type` and document type

Document type	MIME types	Examples

XML	`*/xml`
	`*/*+xml` except `application/xhtml+xml`
		`text/xml`
		`application/xml`
		`image/svg+xml`

HTML	`text/html` `application/xhtml+xml`	`text/html`
JSON	`application/json`	`application/json`
Text	`text/*` (not matching XML or HTML)	`text/plain` `text/csv`

Binary	Anything else	`image/jpeg`
		`application/octet-stream`
		`application/zip`

A `content-type` document property will always be present.

It is possible to limit the types of documents an input or output port will accept, based on the value of the document's `content-type` property. See the section titled "Specifying content types" (p. 99).

`base-uri`

This (optional) property holds the base URI of the document, usually the location it's loaded from or coming from, for instance `file:/my/doc.xml`. Not all documents have a base URI, and therefore, it does not need to be present.

A base URI *must* be absolute, and it must be valid according to RFC 3986.[3]

[3] https://tools.ietf.org/html/rfc3986

The XML, HTML, and text document types (see the section titled "Document types" (p. 38)) have a *document node* as their root (this concept is explained in the section titled "XML Documents" (p. 38)). For these document types, the value of the `base-uri` document property is always the same as the value returned by calling the XPath function `base-uri(/)`. So, assuming some XML, HTML, or text document flows through the pipeline, the following two variables will always be assigned the same value:

```
<p:variable name="base-uri-from-document-node"
  select="base-uri(/)"/>
<p:variable name="base-uri-from-document-properties"
  select="p:document-property(/, 'base-uri')"/>
```

`serialization`

This (optional) property holds the default serialization properties for the document. Serialization properties are used when a document is written back to disk (or somewhere else). They determine details like method (XML, HTML, etc.), character encoding, and indenting. More about this in the section titled "Specifying serialization" (p. 95).

Serialization properties within XProc are always specified as a map, and therefore, the value of the `serialization` document property *must* be of type `map(xs:QName, item()*)`.

The main reason this document property was introduced is that some steps, like **`<p:xslt>`** and **`<p:xquery>`**, allow you to specify serialization properties themselves (for instance using an XSLT `<xsl:output>` element). Some underlying XSLT and XQuery processors expose these properties and, if so, XProc remembers them.

If an XProc step that performs serialization has serialization properties specified (usually by using a `serialization` option), both sets of serialization properties are merged. Serialization properties specified on the step have precedence over serialization properties specified with the `serialization` document property.

XProc contains several mechanisms to work with the document properties:

- To access values in the document properties, use one of XProc's extension functions listed in the section titled "Document properties related functions" (p. 196). For instance, `p:document-properties()` gives you back the full map and `p:document-property()` the value of a single property.

- You can change document properties by using the `<p:set-properties>` step (the section titled "p:set-properties" (p. 276)). The only property you can't change is `content-type`, which is controlled by XProc.

See the section titled "Working with document-properties" (p. 202) for examples of code that works with document properties in a pipeline.

JSON documents

JSON documents flow through the pipeline as data structures. When JSON is parsed, the XProc processor decides which XDM data type is appropriate. The rules for this are the same as for the XPath `parse-json()` function[4] (see Table 4.2).

Table 4.2 – JSON and the XDM data type

JSON type	XDM type	JSON Example	XDM example
Object	`map(*)`	`{"a":"bla", "b":"x"}`	`map{"a":"bla", "b":"x"}`
Array	`array(*)`	`["a", 1, false]`	`["a", 1.0E0, false()]`
String	`xs:string`	`"a"`	`"a"`
Number	`xs:double`	`1`	`1.0E0`
Boolean	`xs:boolean`	`true`	`true()`
Null	Empty sequence	`null`	`()`

Once data flows into the pipeline, you can access these JSON-derived data structures using the familiar XPath context item dot operator (`.`). For example, assume the JSON document `{"status": "debug", ... }` is flowing through. Then you can write code like the following:[5]

```
<p:if test=".('status') eq 'debug'">
  ...
</p:if>
```

4 https://www.w3.org/TR/xpath-functions-31/#func-parse-json

5 You can find more JSON examples in the section titled "Working with JSON documents" (p. 204).

Documents and step results

Usually what flows out of a step is straightforward: one or more documents of some kind. But sometimes it's not clear. For instance, if you use the latest versions of XSLT or XQuery, they no longer require results to be XML documents; they can be anything, even a sequence of values with mixed data types. The result of such a transformation could be the following:

```
('Hello', 1, map{'world', 'Earth'}, true())
```

XProc has rules to deal with this:

- If a step emits a *sequence* of values, each value is converted into a *separate* document.
- Each value is inspected and, based on its XDM data type, handled as shown in Table 4.3.

Table 4.3 – Handling of output data types

XDM data type	Handling	Resulting content type
Single text nodes (`text()`)	The text node will be wrapped in a document node	`text/plain`
element (`element()`), comment (`comment()`), and processing instruction nodes (`processing-instruction()`)	The node will be wrapped in a document node	`application/xml`
Attribute nodes (`attribute()`)	Attribute nodes cannot be the output of a transform	N/A
document nodes (`document-node()`)	Pass on	`application/xml`
Map, array, or any other atomic value (string, number, boolean, etc.). This also applies to types that have no JSON equivalent, like dates and times.	Pass on	`application/json`

That maps, arrays, and atomic values always result in the content type `application/json` has a nasty side effect: a document that flows through the pipeline as `application/json` cannot always be serialized (written to disk)!

For instance, assume some step emits this map: `map{ 'a': (1, 2, 3) }`. Note that the (single) entry `'a'` in the map contains a value that is a *sequence* (in this case of the integers 1, 2, and 3). For this particular result, the last rule in Table 4.3 applies, so it will become a JSON document. But when the pipeline tries to serialize this document, it will fail because the JSON serialization rules do not know how to handle a sequence. More about serialization in the section titled "Specifying serialization" (p. 95).

Attribute and Text Value Templates

Attribute Value Templates (AVTs) and Text Value Templates (TVTs) are attributes and text nodes that are allowed to contain XPath expressions between curly braces {…}. These expressions are evaluated, and the expression is replaced by its result. For instance, Example 4.16.

Example 4.16 – Simple example of an AVT

```
<p:variable name="path" as="xs:string" select="'/my/path/to/something'"/>
...
<p:load href="{$path}/myfile.xml"/>
```

The `href` attribute is an AVT, so the `{$path}` part will expand into the value of the `$path` variable. After AVT processing the value of `href` will be: `/my/path/to/something/myfile.xml`.

Watch out, the definition of an AVT and TVT might differ from your expectations. Some people refer to Value Templates as the expression between curly braces, {…}, but that's not correct. An AVT is an attribute in which XPath expressions between curly braces are evaluated and expanded. A TVT is a text-node for which the same applies. The *whole* attribute/text-node is a value template, not just the curly braced expressions.

This also means that an attribute like `href` in Example 4.16 is, strictly speaking, an AVT, even if there's no curly brace.

AVTs have broad application in XProc pipelines, and you will find and use them in lots of places (the section titled "Attribute Value Templates in the XProc code" (p. 69)). However, TVTs are much rarer and can only be used inside inline content (the section titled "Value Template expansion in inline content" (p. 72)).

Some generic rules regarding Value Templates:

- To prevent curly braces from being interpreted as expression start/end characters, double them: write {{ or }} to represent a single bracket.
- Once inside an XPath expression in a Value Template, you don't have to do anything special. This extends to the first unmatched right curly bracket } that is not within a string literal or comment.
- An XPath expression in a value template must evaluate to a sequence of either atomic values (strings, numbers, etc.) or nodes (elements, attributes, etc.). If it doesn't, XProc won't know how to interpret the result. For example, there is no way a map can be represented if it shows up as the result of a Value Template.

Attribute Value Templates in the XProc code

Attribute values are considered an Attribute Value Template (AVT) in the following situations:

- When the XProc 3.0 specification explicitly defines an attribute as an AVT. This book marks these attributes with curly braces in their type description. For example: the `href` attribute on the `<p:with-input>` element (see the section titled "Connecting input ports: `<p:with-input>`" (p. 125)).
- When you set a step option by attribute instead of using `<p:with-option>` (for details see the section titled "Setting options: `<p:with-option>` (or by attribute)" (p. 128)).

  To illustrate this, assume you need to set an attribute on the root element of a document, and both the name and the value of the attribute are computed. Using `<p:with-option>`, you could do this as shown in Example 4.17.

Example 4.17 – Setting step option values using `<p:with-option>`

```
<p:variable name="prefix" as="xs:string" select="'myapp-'"/>
...
<p:set-attribute>
  <p:with-option name="match" select="'/*'"/>
  <p:with-option name="attribute-name" select="concat($prefix, 'att1')"/>
  <p:with-option name="attribute-value" select="...some other computed value..."/>
</p:set-attribute>
```

You can achieve the same result using AVTs (Example 4.18).

Example 4.18 – Setting the same step option values as in Example 4.17 using AVTs

```
<p:variable name="prefix" as="xs:string" select="'myapp-'"/>
...
<p:set-attribute match="/*"
                 attribute-name="{concat($prefix, 'att1')}"
                 attribute-value="{...some other computed value...}"/>
```

- In inline content (depending on certain conditions), see the section titled "Value Template expansion in inline content" (p. 72).
- Specific XProc processors might define extension attributes (see the section titled "Annotations" (p. 78)). Whether or not these attributes are AVTs is implementation defined.

Value Templates and the Default Readable Port

Value Templates are XPath expressions and can therefore reference the context item, like `{/*/@status}` or `{//sect[1]/title}`. So you need to understand what the expressions are evaluated against. XPath expressions in Value Templates are *always* evaluated against what appears on the *Default Readable Port* (DRP) (see the section titled "The Default Readable Port" (p. 51)). This is the case even when the step the Value Template is on doesn't use the DRP at all. For instance, have a look at the Figure 4.1.

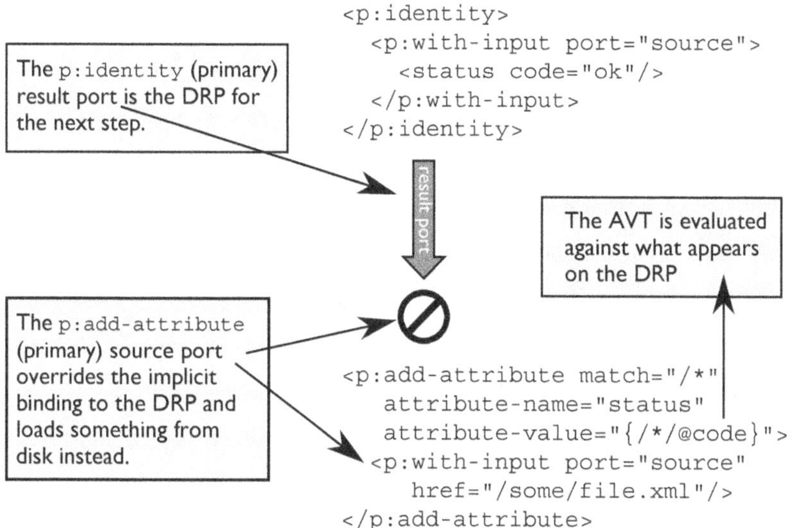

Figure 4.1 – Using the DRP to evaluate expressions in an AVT

- The primary output port of the **`<p:identity>`** step is the DRP for the **`<p:add-attribute>`** step, because **`<p:add-attribute>`** directly follows **`<p:identity>`** in the pipeline.
- The pipeline designer decided not to use the implicit binding to the DRP and explicitly bind the (primary) source input port of the **`<p:add-attribute>`** step to a document on disk.
- When evaluating `{/*/@code}`, you might erroneously expect it to be evaluated against what's on the step's primary input port. But no, it is always evaluated against the DRP, and therefore, its value will be `ok`.

A Value Template expression that reaches into the document on the DRP will fail when:

- The DRP emits multiple documents.
- The document, such as a jpeg image, cannot be handled by an XPath expression.

Expressions that do not reach into the document on the DRP (like `concat($a, $b)`) will always be fine. If you want or need to override the DRP's output as context item for such an expression, you have to use `<p:with-option>` to set the option's value (the section titled "Setting options: `<p:with-option>` (or by attribute)" (p. 128)).

Value Template expansion in inline content

Inline content is content inside `<p:inline>` elements or their shortcut version without a `<p:inline>` element (the section titled "Specifying documents inline: `<p:inline>` " (p. 143)). Inline content can contain both AVTs and TVTs (see Example 4.19).

Example 4.19 – Value Templates in inline content

```
<p:variable name="a" select="'AAA'"/>
<p:variable name="b" select="'BBB'"/>

<p:identity>
  <p:with-input port="source">
    <some-element id="{$a}">{$b}</some-element>
  </p:with-input>
</p:identity>
```

This will result in the following document appearing on the **`<p:identity>`** step's `result` port:

```
<some-element id="AAA">BBB</some-element>
```

Turning Value Templates on or off for inline content

Whether attributes and text nodes in inline content are considered Value Templates or not depends on the setting of the boolean `[p:]expand-text` and `p:inline-expand-text` attributes in the pipeline.

The square brackets (`[p:]`...) indicate that this attribute must sometimes be written without a `p:` prefix (that is, in no namespace) and sometimes in the XProc namespace (`p:`). See the section titled "The `[p:]` notation for attributes" (p. 75).

Example 4.20 – Value Templates in inline content turned off and then on again

```
<p:variable name="a" select="'AAA'"/>
<p:variable name="b" select="'BBB'"/>

<p:identity expand-text="false">
  <p:with-input port="source">
    <some-element id="{$a}">
      <value p:inline-expand-text="true">{$b}</value>
    </some-element>
  </p:with-input>
</p:identity>
```

In Example 4.20 the `expand-text="false"` attribute on the **`<p:identity>`** step turns Value Templating off for inline content, so the `id` attribute is not considered an AVT. The `p:inline-expand-text="true"` on `<value>` turns Value Templating on again, and therefore, the text-node containing `{$b}` is expanded. The result is as follows:

```
<some-element id="{$a}">
  <value>BBB</value>
</some-element>
```

The `p:inline-expand-text` attribute has disappeared, because it was interpreted by the XProc processor. The exact rules for this are as follows:

- To determine whether Value Templating in inline content is on or off, the XProc processor looks at the value of the following attributes in the nearest (ancestor):
  - `p:inline-expand-text` attribute in the inline content itself, or
  - `[p:]expand-text` attribute in the surrounding XProc code (not in the inline content)
- The `[p:]expand-text` attribute can appear on any element in your XProc pipeline. A `[p:]expand-text` attribute *inside* inline content has no special meaning and is simply considered part of the inline content.
- For even more nitty-gritty control of Value Templating, you can turn it on or off *inside* inline content using the `p:inline-expand-text` attribute. Since this attribute is interpreted, it is not considered part of the inline content itself and will not be part of its result.
- Value Template expansion in inline content is on by default.

Please note that `[p:]expand-text` and `p:inline-expand-text` turn both TVT *and* AVT expansion on/off.

When you use `<p:inline>` to represent literal JSON, make sure `expand-text` is set to `false` (it's `true` by default). Or, if you have masochistic tendencies, double *every* curly brace in your inline content (of which JSON happens to contain an awful lot).

TVT expansion in inline content

A TVT in inline content will expand just like an AVT, with one big difference: curly braced expressions in an AVT always evaluate to a string, but in a TVT they don't! They evaluate into whatever type the XPath expression results in.

For instance, assume the following document is flowing through the pipeline:

```
<document>
  <path>/my/path/to/something</path>
</document>
```

- AVT curly braced expressions will expand into a string:

  ```
  <p:load href="{/*}/myfile.xml"/>
  ```

  The `href` attribute's value will become:

  ```
  /my/path/to/something/myfile.xml
  ```

- In contrast, the same expression in a TVT expands into the `<document>` element:

  ```
  <p:identity>
    <p:with-input port="source">
        <root>{/*}</root>
    </p:with-input>
  </p:identity>
  ```

  This will become (on the **`<p:identity>`** step's `result` port):

  ```
  <root>
    <document>
      <path>/my/path/to/something</path>
    </document>
  </root>
  ```

If you're used to TVTs in XSLT (introduced in version 3.0), please note that XProc treats them differently: in XSLT, curly braced expressions in a TVT always result in a string (like in an AVT). But as explained above, in XProc this will become whatever type the expression evaluates to. It's more like it is in XQuery. This also means that TVTs must result in a well-formed document. For instance, when your TVT expression evaluates to one or more attributes, it must be placed directly after an element.

Common attributes

This section explains a number of attributes that can appear (almost) everywhere. Therefore, I will describe them here rather than repeating the description everywhere they appear.

The `[p:]` notation for attributes

Some of the common attributes use the `[p:]`... notation, e.g. `[p:]use-when`. This notation signifies that sometimes these attributes must be in the `p:` XProc namespace and sometimes they don't have to be. That may sound confusing, but the rules are clear and easy:

- Use the variant *without* the `p:` prefix on elements that are in the XProc namespace. For instance on built-in step invocations:

  ```
  <p:load use-when="$debug" … >
  ```

- Use the variant *with* the `p:` prefix on elements that are *not* in the XProc namespace. For instance, when you invoke a step you've defined yourself:

  ```
  <myns:mystep p:use-when="$debug" … >
  ```

See the section titled "Invoking steps" (p. 120) for more attributes that use the `[p:]` notation.

The `[p:]expand-text` attribute

The `[p:]expand-text` attribute determines whether Value Templates in inline content are on or off (see the section titled "Value Template expansion in inline content" (p. 72)).

The `[p:]use-when` attribute

The value of the `[p:]use-when` attribute is an XPath expression that can be evaluated statically. The expression is evaluated when the pipeline is compiled. If the resulting boolean value is `false` this removes the element the `[p:]use-when` attribute is on (and all its children) from the code. Since the expression is evaluated statically, it cannot refer to documents, options, ports, or anything else that was not available before the pipeline starts running. It can, however, reference *static* options (the section titled "Static options" (p. 105)). It can also use the environment information from the `p:system-property()` extension function and act on it.

The `xml:base` attribute

The `xml:base` attribute can appear anywhere. It sets the base URI against which relative URIs are resolved.

For example: if you have to refer to lot of documents in the `/my/docs` directory, set an `xml:base="file:///my/docs` somewhere on an encompassing element. You can then refer to the documents using a relative path.

The `xml:id` attribute

The `xml:id` attribute can appear anywhere and sets the identifier of the element. However XProc currently does nothing with this information.

Documentation and annotations

XProc has special mechanisms for documenting and annotating your code (I explain the difference in the sections to come). You can use these almost anywhere, so I will not mention them again in the XProc element descriptions.

Documentation

As everyone knows, documenting your code is important. Not only for other people but also for yourself as you stare terribly confused at your own code three months later. You can use XML comments (`<!-- ... -->`), but XProc has a specific element for this: `<p:documentation>`. The advantage of using `<p:documentation>` is that you can use markup as well as text, so you can, for instance, use HTML and later extract it with a documentation generator pipeline. But just using it for human-only processable text is also fine.

Here is a simple example that uses `<p:documentation>` elements:

Example 4.21 – Documenting a pipeline with `<p:documentation>` elements

```
<p:declare-step xmlns:p="http://www.w3.org/ns/xproc" …>

  <p:documentation>
    This step does the following …
    <b>Watch out:</b> In case of …
  </p:documentation>

  <p:input port="source" primary="true">
    <p:documentation>This input port expects a document that …</p:documentation>
  </p:input>
  …

</p:declare-step>
```

`<p:documentation>` elements can appear (almost) anywhere in your XProc code. They carry no special meaning for the processor and are completely ignored.

The only exception is when a `<p:documentation>` element is part of the contents of an `<p:inline>` element or an explicit inline (see the section titled "Specifying documents inline: `<p:inline>`" (p. 143)). These contain literal XML, and therefore, a `<p:documentation>` element becomes part of the XML.

There is no hard and fast rule for when to use XML comments and when to use `<p:documentation>`. You have to develop a convention of your own. Here's mine:

- Put comments that describe the interface of a step (like the declaration of options and ports) inside `<p:documentation>`. This in the hope that one day I'll come around to writing (or finding) code that generates step documentation (something like Javadoc).
- All other commenting is done in straight XML comments.

Annotations

Sometimes *annotations* are needed: ancillary information and instructions for the XProc processor. XProc itself says nothing about this; it is implementation defined. A processor might, for example, use annotations to identify some particular aspect of an implementation, to request additional non-standard features, to describe parallelism constraints, etc.

XProc offers two mechanisms for adding annotations to your code:

Extension attributes
: Besides the standard attributes, you can place additional extension attributes on any XProc element in your pipeline. The only rule is that these attributes must be in a different, non-null namespace.

The `<p:pipeinfo>` element
: You can place `<p:pipeinfo>` elements (almost) anywhere in your code. The contents can be anything.

: As with the `<p:documentation>` element, the only place where a `<p:pipeinfo>` has no special meaning is inside a `<p:inline>` element or an explicit inline.

Whatever mechanism you use, processors that do not understand annotations ignore them. Only processors they're meant for will act on them.

Here is a completely made up example of annotations for the fictitious XYZ XProc processor:

Example 4.22 – Annotations in an XProc step

```
<p:declare-step xmlns:p="http://www.w3.org/ns/xproc"
  xmlns:pxyz="http://www.xprocxyz.org/ns/extensions" ...>

  <p:input port="source" primary="true">
    <p:pipeinfo>parse=special</p:pipeinfo>
  </p:input>
  ...

  <p:xslt pxyz:process="parallel">
    <p:input port="stylesheet">
      <p:document href="do-something.xsl"/>
    </p:input>
  </p:xslt>
</p:declare-step>
```

CHAPTER 5
Defining steps: Prolog

This chapter dives into the details of defining steps. The main element you use to define steps is `<p:declare-step>`. Although not official XProc terminology, the contents of this element can be thought of as consisting of two parts:

Prolog
: The step's *prolog* defines its *interface* or *signature*: how it looks from the outside. This includes its type, input and output ports, options, imports, and various other details. The prolog is the subject of this chapter.

Body
: The *body* of the step contains the implementation of the pipeline; it defines its *functionality*: what's happening inside. The XProc specification calls this the *sub-pipeline*. This part is handled in Chapter 6.

Example 5.1 contains the prolog and body of a step.

Example 5.1 – An XProc step divided into a prolog and a body

```
<p:declare-step xmlns:p="http://www.w3.org/ns/xproc" ...>

  <!-- Step's prolog: -->
  <p:input port="source" primary="true"/>
  <p:output port="result" primary="true"/>
  <p:option name="debug" as="xs:boolean" required="false" select="false()"/>
  ...

  <!-- Step's body: -->
  <p:xslt>
    <p:with-input port="stylesheet" href="do-something.xsl"/>
  </p:xslt>
  ...

</p:declare-step>
```

Declaring a step: <p:declare-step>

You declare a step (a.k.a. pipeline) using <p:declare-step>. This section dives into its details.

Since this is the first XML element description in this book, here is a reminder of a few noteworthy things:

- How to read and interpret an element description is explained in the section titled "Explaining XML structures" (p. xiv).
- Attributes are fitted with an XPath data type, like `xs:string`, or a special data type, like `XPathExpr` (see the section titled "Special data types" (p. xvi)).
- Some attributes can appear (almost) everywhere. Their meaning is explained in the section titled "Common attributes" (p. 75). These attributes are not mentioned in the descriptions in this chapter.
- You can use <p:documentation>, <p:pipeinfo>, and extension attributes almost anywhere in your code. This is explained in the section titled "Documentation and annotations" (p. 76). These attributes are not mentioned in the descriptions in this chapter.

Here is what <p:declare-step> looks like:

```
<p:declare-step name? = xs:NCName
                type? = xs:QName
                psvi-required? = xs:boolean
                xpath-version? = xs:decimal
                exclude-inline-prefixes? = xs:string
                version? = xs:decimal
                visibility? = "public" | "private" >
  ( <p:import> |
    <p:import-functions> )*
  ( <p:input> |
    <p:output> |
    <p:option> )*
  <p:declare-step>*
  <!-- Step's body... -->
</p:declare-step>
```

Table 5.1 – Attributes of <p:declare-step>

Attribute	#	Type	Description
`name`	?	`xs:NCName`	The name of this step. You need this name to refer to its ports (from within the step itself).
`type`	?	`xs:QName`	The value of the `type` attribute is used to invoke/call this step. A step's type *must* be in a namespace. Therefore, it *must* either use a declared namespace prefix, or be written using the Q{} notation (e.g., `Q{http://mynamespace}mystep`). The XProc namespace is not allowed for step types.
`psvi-required`	?	`xs:boolean`	Default: `false` Is PSVI ("Post Schema Validation Infoset") support required or not. PSVI allows you to carry type information with your XML document. PSVI information is added when validating documents against a schema. Advanced XSLT and other transformations can use this to make decisions based on the type of something. If your XProc transformation requires PSVI support, set this attribute to `true`, so non-PSVI-supporting processors won't execute them.

Attribute	#	Type	Description
`xpath-version`	?	`xs:decimal`	Default: `3.1` The XPath version that must be used to evaluate XPath expressions. XProc 3.0 processors are only required to support `3.1`. You cannot specify a version lower than `3.1`. XProc processors can support higher values.
`exclude-inline-prefixes`	?	`xs:string`	Defines what to do with inline namespace definitions in your documents (see the section titled "Excluding namespace prefixes" (p. 145)).
`version`	?	`xs:decimal`	Fixed value: `3.0` The XProc version for your pipeline. **Important:** This attribute is mandatory on `<p:declare-step>` elements that are the root element of a document. It is optional on nested `<p:declare-step>` elements (if not set, the value is inherited from their parent). If specified, the value *must* be `3.0`. Specifying a different value is an error.

<table>
<tr><th>Attribute</th><th>#</th><th>Type</th><th>Description</th></tr>
<tr><td><code>visibility</code></td><td>?</td><td><code>xs:string</code></td><td>Default: <code>public</code>

Controls whether this step is visible to the importing pipeline when part of a library (<code><p:library></code>, see the section titled “Building step libraries: <code><p:library></code> ” (p. 109)). If this step is not part of a library the attribute is ignored.

<table>
<tr><th>Value</th><th>Description</th></tr>
<tr><td><code>public</code></td><td>The step is visible to the importing pipeline</td></tr>
<tr><td><code>private</code></td><td>The step is invisible to the importing pipeline and can only be used in the library itself.</td></tr>
</table>
</td></tr>
</table>

The elements in the prolog of a `<p:declare-step>` are about:

- Imports of external XProc pipelines, libraries, or XPath function libraries.
- Declarations of input ports, output ports, and/or options.
- Declarations of locally defined steps.

Table 5.2 – Child elements of <p:declare-step>

Child element	#	Description
`p:import`	*	Imports a step from an external source. See the section titled "Importing steps and step libraries: `<p:import>` " (p. 108). You can also use this element to import step *libraries*. See the section titled "Building step libraries: `<p:library>` " (p. 109).
`p:import-functions`	*	Imports function libraries (alas, not their global variables) from another language so they can be used inside the XPath expressions in your pipeline. The most common ones are XSLT and XQuery libraries, but other languages are not ruled out. See the section titled "Importing function libraries: `<p:import-functions>` " (p. 108). Whether importing functions is supported is implementation specific.
`p:input`	*	Declares an input port for this step. See the section titled "Declaring input ports: `<p:input>` " (p. 86).
`p:output`	*	Declares an output port for this step. See the section titled "Declaring output ports: `<p:output>` " (p. 89).
`p:option`	*	Declares an option for this step. See the section titled "Declaring options: `<p:option>` " (p. 102).

Child element	#	Description
p:declare-step	*	Use nested <p:declare-step> elements to declare steps that are local to the encompassing step. The effect is the same as for steps imported by a <p:import> element (the section titled "Importing steps and step libraries: <p:import> " (p. 108)). You may also use this element to declare an *atomic step*, see the section titled "Declaring an atomic step" (p. 85).

Declaring an atomic step

XProc processors usually allow you to add steps written in other programming languages; these are called *atomic steps*. How to create and add an atomic step is implementation defined, so I won't discuss that here.

To use an atomic step in your pipeline, the XProc processor must know its interface: its signature. To define the signature for the processor, you declare an atomic step by adding a <p:declare-step> element with only a prolog, no body.

Atomic step declarations may not import other pipelines and may not declare additional steps. In other words, the content of an atomic step declaration consists exclusively of <p:input>, <p:output>, and <p:option> elements.

Declaring ports

You declare the input and output ports of a step with the <p:input> and <p:output> elements. Input and output ports are not required. In fact it's normal to have steps that lack either input or output ports (and in rare cases even both). For instance, a step that reads from a zip file might want to specify this file as an option (by URI) to the step instead of providing it on an input port. Steps that write a zip (or other binary) file might want to do likewise, without using an output port. However, in most cases you want to specify ports, which is what this section is about.[1]

Declaring input ports: <p:input>

You declare an input port with the <p:input> element. XProc computes default connections for <p:input> statically, so they cannot depend on anything dynamic in your pipeline. Thus you cannot give <p:input> a default port connection (<p:pipe> or pipe attribute).

XProc 1.0 used <p:input> both for declaring *and* connecting a port. This was rather confusing, so <p:with-input> was invented for the latter function (the section titled "Connecting input ports: <p:with-input> " (p. 125)).

```
<p:input port = xs:NCName
         sequence? = xs:boolean
         primary? = xs:boolean
         content-types? = ContentTypes
         href? = { xs:anyURI }
         select? = XPathExpr
         exclude-inline-prefixes? = xs:string >
  ( <p:empty> |
    <p:document> |
    <p:inline> )*
  <!-- Or use any other element(s) (or plain text) as alternative for
       wrapping it in a <p:inline> -->
</p:input>
```

[1] <p:input> and <p:output> have attributes and child elements for connections that are used repeatedly. See the section titled "Common connection constructs" (p. 139) for details.

Table 5.3 – Attributes of <p:input>

Attribute	#	Type	Description
`port`	1	`xs:NCName`	The name of the port.
`sequence`	?	`xs:boolean`	Default: `false` When `true`, a *sequence* of documents (zero or more) is allowed to appear on the port. When `false`, *exactly one* document must appear on the port.
`primary`	?	`xs:boolean`	When `true`, this port is the *primary* input port of this step. The default value depends on the number of declared input ports: ■ When this is the only input port, the default is `true`. In other words: when a step has only one input port, it is automatically primary unless you set `primary` to `false`. ■ When there are multiple input ports, the default is `false`. You have to set `primary="true"` to select the primary port. A step can have only a single primary input port. By convention, the primary input port is called `source`.

Attribute	#	Type	Description
`content-types`	?	`ContentTypes`	Default: `*/*` Specifies the content types allowed to appear on the port (see the section titled "Specifying content types" (p. 99)).
`href`	?	`{ xs:anyURI }`	The URI of a default document to appear on this port. This is shorthand for a `<p:document>` child element with the same `href` attribute. (see the section titled "Specifying connections for input and output port declarations" (p. 93) and the section titled "Reading external documents: `<p:document>` " (p. 139)). Use either an `href` attribute *or* child elements, but not both, to specify defaults.
`select`	?	`XPathExpr`	If present, this XPath expression is applied to the default input of the port. It is applied only when a default connection is used (as specified in this input port declaration). It is ignored if a connection is provided on the step's invocation.
`exclude-inline-prefixes`	?	`xs:string`	Exclude namespace declarations in inline contents (see the section titled "Excluding namespace prefixes" (p. 145)).

The child elements of <p:input> define default connections or documents for the port, to be used when no connection is provided on step usage. See also the section titled "Specifying connections for input and output port declarations" (p. 93).

Table 5.4 – Child elements of <p:input>

Child element	#	Description
p:empty	*	Use the empty sequence as the default input for this port (see the section titled "Specifying nothing: <p:empty> " (p. 139)).
p:document	*	Use a document read from an URI as the default input for this port (see the section titled "Reading external documents: <p:document> " (p. 139)).
p:inline	*	Use the children of this element as the default input for this port (see the section titled "Specifying documents inline: <p:inline> " (p. 143)). If you only have a single <p:inline> child element, you can leave it out and state your inline document as direct children of <p:input>.

Declaring output ports: <p:output>

Declaring an output port is done with the <p:output> element:

```
<p:output port = xs:NCName
          sequence? = xs:boolean
          primary? = xs:boolean
          content-types? = ContentTypes
          serialization? = map(xs:QName, item()*)
          href? = { xs:anyURI }
          pipe? = xs:string
          exclude-inline-prefixes? = xs:string >
  ( <p:empty> |
    <p:document> |
    <p:pipe> |
    <p:inline> )*
  <!-- Or use any other element(s) (or plain text) as alternative for
       wrapping it in a <p:inline> -->
</p:output>
```

Table 5.5 – Attributes of <p:output>

Attribute	#	Type	Description
`port`	1	`xs:NCName`	The name of the port.
`sequence`	?	`xs:boolean`	Default: `false` When true, a *sequence* of documents (zero or more) can appear on the port. When false, *exactly one* document must appear on the port.
`primary`	?	`xs:boolean`	When true, this port is the *primary* output port of this step. The default value for this attribute depends on the number of declared output ports: ■ When there is only one output port, the default is `true`. In other words: When a step has only one output port, it is automatically primary unless you set `primary` to `false`). ■ When there are multiple output ports, the default is `false`. You have to set `primary="true"` to select the primary port. A step can have only a single primary output port. By convention, the primary output port is called `result`.

Attribute	#	Type	Description
`content-types`	?	`ContentTypes`	Default: `*/*` A specification of the content types allowed to appear on the port (see the section titled "Specifying content types" (p. 99)).
`serialization`	?	`map(xs:QName, item()*)`	Any parameters to be used when the contents appearing on this port is serialized (usually: written to disk) (see the section titled "Specifying serialization" (p. 95)). If no serialization is taking place (when this output port is connected to an input port of another step), the serialization parameters are ignored.
`href`	?	`{ xs:anyURI }`	The URI of a fixed default document to appear on this port. Shorthand notation for a `<p:document>` child element with the same `href` attribute (see the section titled "Reading external documents: `<p:document>`" (p. 139)). Use either an `href` attribute *or* child elements to specify defaults. The combination is not allowed.

Attribute	#	Type	Description
pipe	?	xs:string	Explicitly connect this output port to some output port of a step in this pipeline. This is a shortcut for <p:pipe> child elements (see the section titled "Explicitly connecting to another port: <p:pipe>" (p. 142)). Use either an href attribute, a pipe attribute *or* child elements to specify what appears on the port. Any combination is not allowed.
exclude-inline-prefixes	?	xs:string	Exclude namespace declarations in your inline contents (see the section titled "Excluding namespace prefixes" (p. 145)).

The child elements of <p:output> define what is to appear on this port. See also the section titled "Specifying connections for input and output port declarations" (p. 93).

Use either an href attribute, pipe attribute *or* child elements to specify defaults. The combination is not allowed.

Table 5.6 – Child elements of <p:output>

Child element	#	Description
`p:empty`	*	Causes the empty sequence (a.k.a. nothing) to appear on this port (see the section titled "Specifying nothing: `<p:empty>` " (p. 139)).
`p:document`	*	Read a document from an external source and use this as the document presented on the output port (see the section titled "Reading external documents: `<p:document>` " (p. 139)).
`p:pipe`	*	Connect this output port to an output port of a step somewhere in your pipeline (see the section titled "Explicitly connecting to another port: `<p:pipe>` " (p. 142)).
`p:inline`	*	The children of this element will appear on this port (see the section titled "Specifying documents inline: `<p:inline>` " (p. 143)). If you only have a single `<p:inline>` child element, you can leave it out and state your inline document as direct children of `<p:output>`.

If this is a primary port and you don't specify any implicit connection, this output port is implicitly, automatically, connected to the primary output port of the last step in your pipeline. See also the section titled "Connecting or binding ports" (p. 48).

Specifying connections for input and output port declarations

The previous two sections show that you can define connections for both input and output. You can, for instance, connect them to an external document using the `href` attribute or `<p:document>`, or you can specify fixed content using `<p:inline>`.

But, **watch out!** `<p:inline>` acts differently for input and output ports:

- If you specify connections when declaring an *input port*, you specify its *default connections*. These connections are used when nothing is explicitly or implicitly connected to this port. For instance:

  ```
  <p:input port="source" primary="true">
    <p:inline>
      <BLURB/>
    </p:inline>
  </p:input>
  ```

  In this example, when nothing is connected to the `source` input port, a single `<BLURB/>` document will appear on it. When you do connect something or the connection is implicit, `<BLURB/>` will never appear.

- If you specify connections when declaring an *output port*, you specify *what will appear on it, no matter what*. For instance:

  ```
  <p:output port="result" primary="true">
    <p:inline>
      <BLURB/>
    </p:inline>
  </p:output>
  ```

  This means that the `result` output port will *always* emit a `<BLURB/>`. Probably not a very useful result.

Why? This has everything to do with the way ports are connected to each other. As explained in the section titled "Connecting or binding ports" (p. 48), ports are connected by the input ports. Input ports pull, output ports don't push. Now consider the step you're declaring:

- Input ports want to pull something. When there's nothing connected, the default applies.

- Output ports *must* deliver something when connected. Where do they get this from? They get it from the connections defined when they are declared.

And in practice?

Now this might all sound complicated (and maybe it is), but how do you use it in practice? I've been programming XProc for several years, and the pattern I see is the following:

- Input ports rarely have a default specified.
- Output ports are usually explicitly connected to the primary output port of the last step in the pipeline. Sometimes they are connected somewhere else (in XProc 1.0 you had to use a `<p:pipe>`, now you can also use the `pipe` attribute).
- Output ports are never connected to something fixed or to an external document.

Of course, other programmers do different things, and there are use cases for defaults or fixed output documents. But usually your input and output port declarations will be simple.

Specifying serialization

Sometimes content in your pipeline must be written somewhere, usually to disk. This process is called *serialization*. Serialization is controlled by *serialization properties*: a list of name/value pairs encoded in a map of type `map(xs:Qname, item()*)` (see also the section titled "Map usage" (p. 60)).

Serialization properties come from two sources:

- The `serialization` attribute on the `<p:output>` element (see Example 5.2).

  Example 5.2 – Specifying serialization properties

```
<p:output port="result" primary="true"
  serialization="map{
      'method'                 : 'xml',
      'encoding'               : 'UTF-8',
      'omit-xml-declaration'   : false(),
      'indent'                 : true()
   }"
/>
```

- If present, the value of the `serialization` document property (see the section titled "Document properties" (p. 63)).

Both sets of serialization properties are merged. Serialization properties specified in the `serialization` attribute have precedence over serialization properties in the document property.

When serializing non-XML, the list of serialization properties is implementation defined.

For serializing XML, you have properties available. You can find a full definition in the *XSLT and XQuery Serialization 3.1*[2] specification. Table 5.7 contains a summary:

Table 5.7 – XML serialization properties

Property	Type/Values	Description
`byte-order-mark`	`xs:boolean`	Whether or not to add a byte order mark to the output (If you don't know what this is, you can probably ignore it, but for more information, go to Wikipedia[3] or W3C site[4] for much more detail). If it's not specified, the default varies by encoding: for `UTF-16` it's `true`, for all others, it's `false`.
`cdata-section-elements`	`xs:QName+`	Output the contents of these elements as a CDATA section.
`doctype-public`	`xs:string`	Output a DTD declaration with this as the public document type.
`doctype-system`	`xs:anyURI`	Output a DTD declaration with this as the system document type.
`encoding`	`xs:string`	The character encoding to be used. Usually (and by default) UTF-8.

[2] https://www.w3.org/TR/xslt-xquery-serialization-31/
[3] https://en.wikipedia.org/wiki/Byte_order_mark
[4] https://www.w3.org/International/questions/qa-byte-order-mark

<table>
<tr><th>Property</th><th>Type/Values</th><th>Description</th></tr>
<tr><td>escape-uri-attributes</td><td>xs:boolean</td><td>Whether to escape URI values for HTML and XHTML. URI escaping translates characters with special meanings in %... sequences. For instance space is %20.</td></tr>
<tr><td>include-content-type</td><td>xs:boolean</td><td>Whether to add a <meta> element inside <head> to specify the character encoding used for HTML and XHTML.</td></tr>
<tr><td>indent</td><td>xs:boolean</td><td>Whether to indent serialized XML.

In the absence of schema information, a processor cannot always be sure where spacing is significant. Use with care and at your own risk.</td></tr>
<tr><td>media-type</td><td>xs:string</td><td>Specifies the MIME content type for the serialized output. If not specified, the default is derived from the method parameter:

<table>
<tr><th>Method</th><th>Default media type</th></tr>
<tr><td>xml</td><td>application/xml</td></tr>
<tr><td>html</td><td>text/html</td></tr>
<tr><td>xhtml</td><td>application/xhtml+xml</td></tr>
<tr><td>text</td><td>text/plain</td></tr>
<tr><td>Any other</td><td>Implementation defined</td></tr>
</table></td></tr>
</table>

Property	Type/Values	Description
method	"xml" "html" "xhtml" "text" (or implementation defined)	The type of serialization to apply.
normalization-form	"NFC" "NFKC" "NFKD" "fully-normalized" (or implementation defined)	The normalization form for Unicode characters.
omit-xml-declaration	xs:boolean	Whether an XML declaration must be part of the serialization. The XML declaration is the <?xml version="..." encoding="..."?> line that you find at the top of most XML documents.
standalone	"true" "false" "omit"	The value (or omission) of the standalone declaration in the XML declaration.
undeclare-prefixes	xs:boolean	Undeclare the namespace prefix definitions in use so the document can declare its own.

Property	Type/Values	Description
`version`	`xs:string`	The XML version to use. In 99.99...% this is (default) `1.0`. Currently the only other value allowed is `1.1`.

Specifying content types

Both the `<p:input>` and the `<p:output>` port declaration elements accept an (optional) `content-types` attribute. This attribute specifies the allowed content types of documents on this port. If some other document arrives on, or is produced by, this port, an error will be raised. The content type of a document is determined by the value of its `content-type` document property (see the section titled "Document properties" (p. 63)).

The `content-types` attribute accepts a whitespace-separated list of content type specifications. Each content type specification in this list must have one of the following forms:

- A MIME type written as `type/subtype+ext`. The `type` and `subtype` parts are mandatory, `+ext` is optional. For instance: `application/xml` or `application/xhtml+xml`.

  All three parts can be specified as `*` meaning *any*.

- The same as above but preceded by a minus (`-`) sign. This indicates that the specified type is forbidden.

- To make life a little easier, you can use one of the shortcuts shown in Table 5.8.

Table 5.8 – Shortcuts for specifying content types

Keyword	Meaning	Expands to
`xml`	Any XML document	`application/xml text/xml */*+xml -application/xhtml+xml`
`html`	Any (X)HTML document	`text/html application/xhtml+xml`
`text`	Any text document	`text/* -text/html -text/xml`
`json`	Any JSON document	`application/json`
`any`	Any document	`*/*`

Here are some examples:

Content type	Description
`content-types="*/*"`	Accept any document on the port. If you don't specify a `content-types` attribute, this is the default.
`content-types="text/plain"`	Accept only plain text documents on the port.
`content-types="text/*"`	Accept any kind of text document on the port, also `text/html` and `text/xml`.
`content-types="*/*+xml"`	Accept XML documents on the port (but not `application/xml`).
`content-types="text/* */*+xml"`	Accept text and XML documents on the port.
`content-types="xml -html"`	Accept any XML but no (X)HTML documents.

Content type allowance rules

The exact rules for determining whether the content type of a document is allowed or not are somewhat complex, but turn out to be rather intuitive in practice. You probably don't need to understand them in detail, but if you do, here they are:

- The content type of a document (the value of its `content-type` document property) is held against all separate (whitespace separated) MIME type specifications in the `content-types` attribute.
- These MIME type specifications are inspected left to right (their order is significant!).
- If there is no match, the specification is ignored.
- If there is a match with an allowed specification, the document is considered acceptable.
- If there is a match with a forbidden specification (one that starts with a minus sign), the document is considered forbidden.
- A document is allowed if there is at least one acceptable match and the last match was not forbidden.

For example:

- A document with content type `image/svg` is allowed if `content-types="image/* application/xml"`, but not if `content-types="image/* -image/svg"`.
- Order matters, the document above would be allowed if `content-types="-image/svg image/*"`.
- In the particular case of shortcut values, note that `application/xhtml+xml` is allowed if `content-types="xml html"`, but not if `content-types="html xml"`.

Declaring options: <p:option>

Options are parameters you can pass into steps. The step can then act on those parameters by, for instance, changing the path through the step, turning specialized output on/off, passing them on to XSLT or XQuery transformations, and so forth. They're the equivalent of global parameters in XSLT stylesheets.

Here is what an option declaration looks like:

```
<p:option name = xs:QName
          as? = XPathType
          values? = xs:string
          required? = xs:boolean
          select? = XPathExpr
          static? = xs:boolean
          visibility? = "public" | "private" />
```

Table 5.9 – Attributes of <p:option>

Attribute	#	Type	Description
`name`	1	`xs:QName`	The name of the option.
`as`	?	`XPathType`	Default: `item()*` The data type of the option.
`values`	?	`xs:string`	A list of acceptable values for this option, expressed as an XPath sequence, for instance `('one', 'two', 'three')`. See the section titled "Specifying an option's acceptable values" (p. 104).
`required`	?	`xs:boolean`	Default: `false` Whether setting this option is required. When `false` you may specify a `select` attribute to provide a default value.

<table>
<tr><th>Attribute</th><th>#</th><th>Type</th><th>Description</th></tr>
<tr><td><code>select</code></td><td>?</td><td><code>XPathExpr</code></td><td>Default: <code>()</code>

If the option is not required (<code>required="false"</code>) you may specify a default value with the <code>select</code> attribute. Its value is an XPath expression that will be evaluated only when no value for this option is provided.</td></tr>
<tr><td><code>static</code></td><td>?</td><td><code>xs:boolean</code></td><td>Default: <code>false</code>

Whether this option is static. See the section titled “Static options” (p. 105) for more information.</td></tr>
<tr><td><code>visibility</code></td><td>?</td><td><code>xs:string</code></td><td>Default: <code>public</code>

Controls whether this option is visible for an importing pipeline when part of a step-library (<code><p:library></code>, see the section titled “Building step libraries: <code><p:library></code> ” (p. 109)). If this option is not part of a step-library, the attribute is ignored.

<table>
<tr><th>Value</th><th>Description</th></tr>
<tr><td><code>public</code></td><td>The option is visible to the importing pipeline</td></tr>
<tr><td><code>private</code></td><td>The option is invisible to the importing pipeline and can only be used in the step-library itself.</td></tr>
</table>
</td></tr>
</table>

In your step you can reference options like you reference variables: by prefixing their name with a $ sign. For instance, see Example 5.3.

Example 5.3 – Referring to an option

```
<p:option name="debug" as="xs:boolean" required="false" select="false()"/>
...

<!-- Use an option to change the flow of things in your pipeline: -->
<p:if test="$debug">
  ...
</p:if>

<!-- Or pass it on to an XSLT stylesheet: -->
<p:xslt>
  <p:with-input port="stylesheet" href="myxslt1.xsl"/>
  <p:with-option name="parameters" select="map{ debug : $debug }"/>
</p:xslt>
```

Specifying an option's acceptable values

Using the `values` attribute of `<p:option>`, you can specify a fixed list of acceptable values, specified as an XPath sequence. For example:

```
<p:declare-step xmlns:p="http://www.w3.org/ns/xproc" ...>

  <p:option name="validation-type" as="xs:string" values="('strict', 'lax')"
      select"'strict'"/>
  <p:option name="some-boolean" as="xs:anyAtomicType"
      values="(true(), false(), 'yes', 'no', 0, 1)" select="true()"/>

  ...
</p:declare-step>
```

Make sure that the values you specify are compatible with the type specified in the `as` attribute. For example:

```
<p:option name="multiplier" as="xs:integer" values="(1.5, 'pi')"/>
```

This `<p:option>` is invalid because none of the values is compatible with the stated data type: `xs:integer`.

Static options

Yes, options can be static, a somewhat unintuitive and confusing concept. Options are there to allow you to run your pipeline with different settings, so how on earth can they be static? Let's start with why they're here anyway. There are several reasons and use cases:

- A typical use case is debugging. Suppose you have debugging code that you want to keep in your source but turn off for production. It would be useful to have a `debug-on` option.

  To turn code completely on or off, XProc has the `[p:]use-when` attribute (the section titled "The `[p:]use-when` attribute" (p. 75)):

  ```
  <!-- Only write the intermediate result on debug: -->
  <p:store href="/some/path/intermediate.xml" use-when="$debug-on"/>
  ```

  Expressions in a `[p:]use-when` attribute are evaluated statically (during analysis/compilation of the pipeline) and, therefore, cannot depend on anything dynamic. Normal options are dynamic; their value is unknown until the pipeline runs. So you're stuck.

  Enter static options. A static option is an option whose value *must* be known during the analysis/compilation phase that occurs before running the pipeline—before the data starts flowing through. A value for a static option comes from one of the following:

  - The option's declaration `select` attribute, which sets the option's default value.
  - An implementation-defined mechanism, such as a command line option or parameter file.
- Something was needed to allow you to define values in the prolog of a step. Take, for instance, a set of serialization parameters (which is a map in XProc) that you want to define once but use for multiple output ports. Example 5.4 shows how you can do this.

Example 5.4 – Using a static option in the prolog to define a serialization map

```
<p:option name="serialization-map" static="true"
  select="map{
    'method'                 : 'xml',
    'encoding'               : 'UTF-8',
    'omit-xml-declaration'   : false(),
    'indent'                 : true()
  }"/>
<p:output port="result" primary="true" serialization="$serialization-map"/>
<p:output port="another-result" serialization="$serialization-map"/>
```

Or you may want to give a logical name to some data value to make your code more understandable (see Example 5.5).

Example 5.5 – Using a static option in the prolog to define a logical name

```
<p:option name="default-product-id" static="true" select="'12345'"
<p:option name="product-id" select="$default-product-id"/>
```

- In XProc you can define steps within steps (using nested `<p:declare-step>` elements). Static options defined in the parent step(s) are visible in the child step(s). This can be useful to prevent re-definition. For an example, see Example 5.6.

Example 5.6 – Using a static option in a nested step

```
<p:declare-step xmlns:p="http://www.w3.org/ns/xproc"
  xmlns:myns="http://www.myexampledomain.org/ns/steps" ...>

  ...
  <p:option name="smurf-basher" select="'Gargamel'" static="true"/>
  ...

  <!-- Define a step within a step: -->
  <p:declare-step type="myns:nested-step" ...>
    ...
    <!-- Refer to the static option defined in the parent step: -->
    <p:if test="/*/@person eq $smurf-basher">
      ...
    </p:if>
    ...
  </p:declare-step>

  ...
  <p:add-attribute attribute-name="person" attribute-value="{$smurf-basher}"/>
  <myns:nested-step/>
  ...

</p:declare-step>
```

You could of course do the same thing by passing the values to the inner step explicitly as non-static options, but this provides a nice, clean mechanism for constants.

- Sometimes you want to define a (constant) value only once and re-use it in multiple pieces of code: names, magic numbers, encryption keys, etc. For this, XProc allows you to declare static options in step libraries. When you import a step library, its public static options will be available to the importing pipeline or step library. See the section titled "Building step libraries: `<p:library>` " (p. 109) for an example.

An option in a step library is considered public static when:

- It's declared at the top level of the step library, so it must be a direct child of the `<p:library>` root element.

- Its `visibility` attribute is *not* set to `private` (so either absent or `public`).

Visibility of options

Visibility (or, as it's officially called, *scoping*) determines where in your code something is visible and therefore useable/accessible. The visibility/scoping rules for options are different for normal and static options:

- A normal (non-static) option is visible/useable after its declaration. This includes nested elements, such as code inside steps like **`<p:for-each>`** or **`<p:if>`**.

  The exception here is nested pipeline declarations (a `<p:declare-step>` inside a `<p:declare-step>`): a normal option is *not* visible inside a nested step declaration.

- The visibility rules for static options (the section titled "Static options" (p. 105)) are, unfortunately, somewhat more complicated:

  - Like normal, non-static options, they're visible after their declaration, including inside nested elements.

  - They're also visible inside nested pipeline declarations to any depth (`<p:declare-step>` elements inside `<p:declare-step>` elements).

  - Public static options in an imported step library (the section titled "Building step libraries: `<p:library>` " (p. 109)) are visible to the importing pipeline or step library.

  Another important thing to take into account for static options is that *visible static options may never be shadowed* (redeclared). This means that wherever a static option is visible, you're not allowed to use its name again for another (static or non-static) option or variable. This is different from normal options and variables, which can be shadowed.

Importing steps and step libraries: `<p:import>`

You can import other steps and step libraries using the `<p:import>` element:

```
<p:import href = xs:anyURI />
```

Table 5.10 – Attributes of <p:import>

Attribute	#	Type	Description
`href`	I	`xs:anyURI`	The URI of the step or library to import.

The `href` attribute must point to an XML document with root element either `<p:declare-step>` (the section titled "Declaring a step: `<p:declare-step>` " (p. 80)) or `<p:library>` (the section titled "Building step libraries: `<p:library>` " (p. 109)).

When you import a step library, the global (top-level) static options declared in this library are also imported.

Imports bubble up: if your main pipeline imports `library1.xpl`, and `library1.xpl` subsequently imports `library2.xpl`, then the declarations in `library2.xpl` are available in the main pipeline.

To further support this, an XProc processor will attempt *not* to import the same library twice, which allows for better structuring of code in separate modules. For instance: assume your main pipeline imports `library1.xpl` and `library2.xpl`, but `library1.xpl` needs `library2.xpl` as well. Then its safe (and even advisable) to add an `<p:import href="library2.xpl">` to `library1.xpl`, even though this library is now included twice.

Importing function libraries: `<p:import-functions>`

XProc does not provide a mechanism to define your own XPath functions, like in XSLT (`<xsl:function>` and XQuery (`declare function`). However, it does provide a way to import functions from another programming language. But whether this is supported is, unfortunately, implementation defined.

The reason for not making this feature—whose usefulness is undisputed—mandatory is that it proved very hard to implement. So this function was made optional to reduce the already high burden on implementers and to avoid delay in the availability of working processors.

```
<p:import-functions href = xs:anyURI
                    namespace? = xs:anyURI
                    type? = xs:string />
```

Table 5.11 – Attributes of <p:import-functions>

Attribute	#	Type	Description
href	1	xs:anyURI	The URI of the library to import.
namespace	?	xs:anyURI	If necessary (like for XQuery) the namespace of the imported functions.
type	?	xs:string	The MIME type of the library. Likely values are application/xslt+xml or application/xquery. If you don't specify this its value is implementation defined.

Building step libraries: <p:library>

You can combine steps into a library, which can be imported with the <p:import> element. To create a step library, wrap all the step declarations in a <p:library> element and make this a separate document:

```
<p:library psvi-required? = xs:boolean
           xpath-version? = xs:decimal
           exclude-inline-prefixes? = xs:string
           version = xs:decimal >
  ( <p:import> |
    <p:import-functions> )*
  ( <p:option> |
    <p:declare-step> )*
</p:library>
```

The attributes of <p:library> are a subset of the attributes of <p:declare-step> (the section titled "Declaring a step: <p:declare-step> " (p. 80)). More detailed information about their meaning and values can be found there.

Table 5.12 – Attributes of <p:library>

Attribute	#	Type	Description
`psvi-required`	?	`xs:boolean`	Default: `false` Whether or not PSVI ("Post Schema Validation Infoset") support is required.
`xpath-version`	?	`xs:decimal`	Default: `3.1` The XPath version that must be used for evaluating the XPath expressions within the pipeline.
`exclude-inline-prefixes`	?	`xs:string`	Defines what to do with inline namespace definitions in your documents (see the section titled "Excluding namespace prefixes" (p. 145)).
`version`	1	`xs:decimal`	This identifies the XProc version for your pipeline. Its value is fixed: `3.0`

Table 5.13 – Child elements of <p:library>

Child element	#	Description
`p:import`	*	Import a step or step-library on which this library is dependent (see the section titled "Importing steps and step libraries: `<p:import>` " (p. 108)).
`p:import-functions`	*	Imports function libraries from another language so these become useable inside the XPath expressions in this step-library. The most common ones are XSLT and XQuery libraries, but other languages are not ruled out. See the section titled "Importing function libraries: `<p:import-functions>` " (p. 108). Whether importing functions is supported is implementation specific.
`p:option`	*	Declares a global option. This *must* be a static option (the declaration must have the `static="true"` attribute set). See the section titled "Static options" (p. 105). Global static options in step-libraries are available to the steps that import them (unless visibility set to `private`).
`p:declare-step`	*	Define a step for this step-library (see the section titled "Declaring a step: `<p:declare-step>` " (p. 80)).

Example 5.7 shows how to define a step library.

Example 5.7 – Defining a step library

```
<p:library xmlns:p="http://www.w3.org/ns/xproc"
    xmlns:myns="http://www.myexampledomain.org/ns/steps" …>

  <!-- Define a global static option: -->
  <p:option name="magic-value" select="123456789" static="true"/>

  <!-- Define step 1: -->
  <p:declare-step type="myns:step1" …>
   …
  </p:declare-step>

  <!-- Define step 2 -->
  <p:declare-step type="myns:step2" …>
   …
  </p:declare-step>

</p:library>
```

Assuming this step library is stored in a document called `mysteps.xpl`, using it is simple (see Example 5.8).

Example 5.8 – Using a step library

```
<p:declare-step xmlns:p="http://www.w3.org/ns/xproc"
    xmlns:myns="http://www.myexampledomain.org/ns/steps" …>

  <p:import href="mysteps.xpl"/>
  …

  <!-- Use step 1: -->
  <myns:step1>
    …
    <!-- Use the global static option defined in the step-library: -->
    <p:variable name="extended-magic-value" select="$magic-value + 1"/>
    …
  </myns:step1>

  <!-- Use step 2: -->
  <myns:step2>
    …
  </myns:step2>

</p:declare-step>
```

Within a step library, steps and global static options can be declared `public` or `private` using the `visibility` attribute. Steps and global static options that are `public` (the default) are visible to the importing pipeline or step library. If they are declared `private`, they are visible only in this step library.

CHAPTER 6

Populating steps

The previous chapter explained how to set up a step by populating the step's *prolog* with subjects like defining ports, options, etc. This chapter dives into the details of writing a step's *body*: the part where the actual work is done.

A word upfront: understandable steps

One of the things you'll encounter sooner or later is that XProc programs do not look like pipelines at all. This is a hurdle you, unfortunately, have to take.

Thinking of pipelines, most of us probably see two- or three-dimensional networks of pipes before us, like Figure 6.1.

Figure 6.1 – Is this a pipeline I see in front of me? (image by isado[1] CC BY-ND 2.0[2])

[1] https://www.flickr.com/photos/18661853@N00

[2] https://creativecommons.org/licenses/by-nd/2.0

But XProc code, like all code, is *one dimensional.* Your code runs from top to bottom. As a consequence, the resulting flow of data is not immediately apparent when things get complicated.

Have a look at Figure 6.2. From some input document, two renditions are created (possibly for two different devices), using two separate XSLT stylesheets. The result is merged back together into some container document.

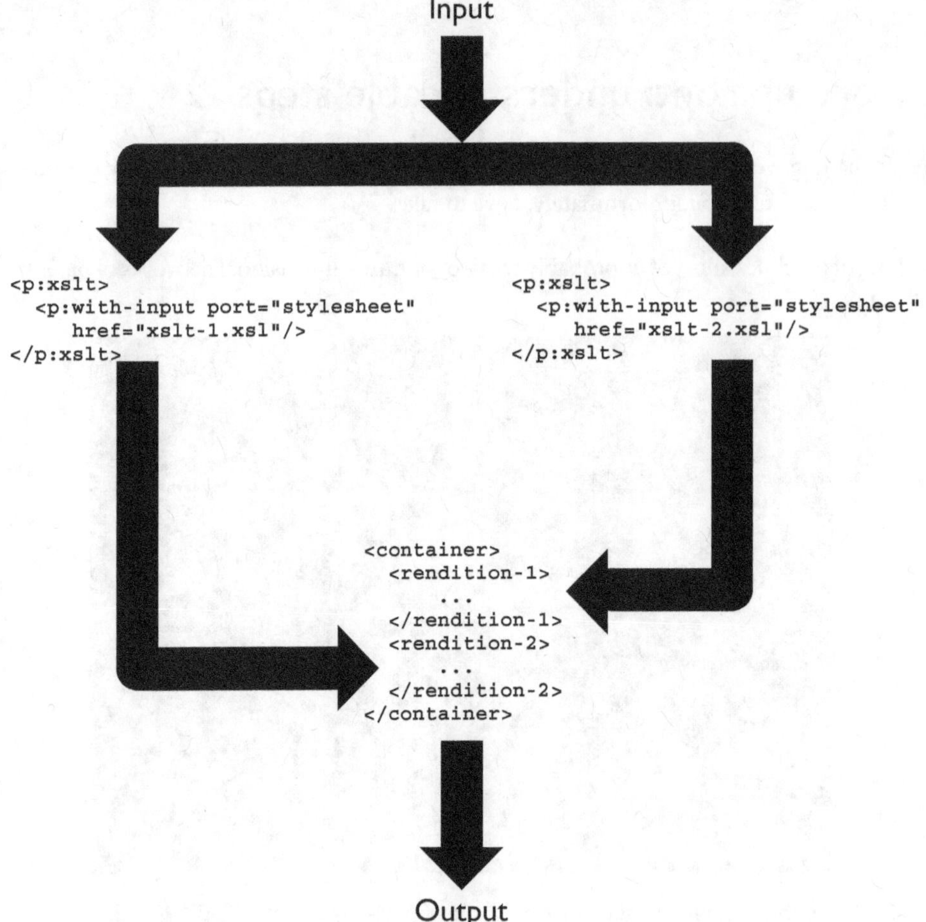

Figure 6.2 – A flow where the input document is transformed twice

Example 6.1 shows one way to realize this in XProc code.

Example 6.1 – XProc code for Figure 6.2

```
<p:declare-step xmlns:p="http://www.w3.org/ns/xproc" name="flow-example"
version="3.0">

  <p:input port="source" primary="true"/>
  <p:output port="result" primary="true"/>

  <!-- Transform the input (1): -->
  <p:xslt name="transform-1">
    <p:with-input port="stylesheet" href="xslt-1.xsl"/>
  </p:xslt>

  <!-- Transform the input (2): -->
  <p:xslt name="transform-2">
    <p:with-input port="source" pipe="source@flow-example"/>
    <p:with-input port="stylesheet" href="xslt-2.xsl"/>
  </p:xslt>

  <!-- Generate the container XML and put everything together: -->
  <p:insert match="/*/rendition-1" position="first-child">
    <p:with-input port="source">
      <container>
        <rendition-1/>
        <rendition-2/>
      </container>
    </p:with-input>
    <p:with-input port="insertion" pipe="result@transform-1"/>
  </p:insert>
  <p:insert match="/*/rendition-2" position="first-child">
    <p:with-input port="insertion" pipe="result@transform-2"/>
  </p:insert>

</p:declare-step>
```

Even for this simple example, you have to study carefully to find out what the flow of data is, whether there are subpipelines or not, what is connected to what, etc. It's not obvious, and that becomes even more apparent when it's drawn out (see Figure 6.3).

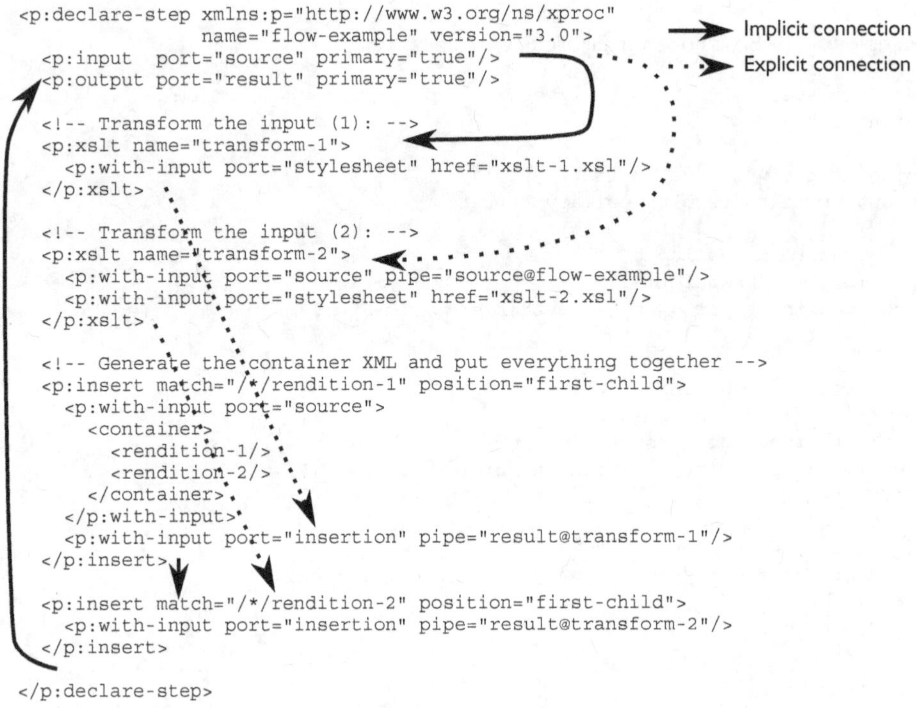

```
<p:declare-step xmlns:p="http://www.w3.org/ns/xproc"
                name="flow-example" version="3.0">
  <p:input  port="source" primary="true"/>
  <p:output port="result" primary="true"/>

  <!-- Transform the input (1): -->
  <p:xslt name="transform-1">
    <p:with-input port="stylesheet" href="xslt-1.xsl"/>
  </p:xslt>

  <!-- Transform the input (2): -->
  <p:xslt name="transform-2">
    <p:with-input port="source" pipe="source@flow-example"/>
    <p:with-input port="stylesheet" href="xslt-2.xsl"/>
  </p:xslt>

  <!-- Generate the container XML and put everything together -->
  <p:insert match="/*/rendition-1" position="first-child">
    <p:with-input port="source">
      <container>
        <rendition-1/>
        <rendition-2/>
      </container>
    </p:with-input>
    <p:with-input port="insertion" pipe="result@transform-1"/>
  </p:insert>

  <p:insert match="/*/rendition-2" position="first-child">
    <p:with-input port="insertion" pipe="result@transform-2"/>
  </p:insert>

</p:declare-step>
```

Implicit connection
Explicit connection

Figure 6.3 – Example 6.1 with all the connections drawn out

In Figure 6.3, the solid black lines are the implicit bindings—connections between ports the XProc processor makes without you having to declare them. The dotted lines are the explicit bindings—connections declared in the code (the section titled "Connecting or binding ports" (p. 48)).

Now look at the first **<p:xslt>** (`name="transform-1"`). It may look like the primary `result` port flows into the second `p:xslt` step. However, the second `p:xslt` explicitly connects its `source` port to the `source` port of the pipeline (`pipe="source@flow-example"`. This overrides the implicit binding between the first and second **<p:xslt>**.

To find out where the output of the first `<p:xslt>` goes, you have to find any references to it. In this example, it is connected to the `insertion` port of the first **<p:insert>**: `pipe="result@transform-1"`.

You can't do much about this complexity. Unfortunately, XProc processors do not (yet) take their input from drawings like Figure 6.2. The only thing you can do to help readers is to comment your code lavishly, use (comment) lines in between subpipelines to create visual breaks, etc.

A measure that I think improves readability of XProc steps is using `<p:identity>` steps to create connections and connectors in pipelines. See the section titled "Using **`<p:identity>`** to clarify pipeline structure" (p. 199) for more information.

Anatomy of a step's body

The body of a step consists of one or more of the following components:

- Calls to other steps. These steps can be:
  - Built-in steps, as listed in Chapter 8.
  - User-defined steps, which can be imported (the section titled "Importing steps and step libraries: `<p:import>` " (p. 108)) or declared in the step itself (the section titled "Declaring a step: `<p:declare-step>` " (p. 80)).

  The mechanism and syntax for invoking steps is the same in both cases and is explained in the section titled "Invoking steps" (p. 120).
- Core steps, as listed in Chapter 7.
- Variable declarations (with **`<p:variable>`**), as explained in the section titled "Declaring variables: `<p:variable>` " (p. 133).

The body of a step must always contain something, even if it's just **`<p:identity>`** (which does nothing). Example 6.2 uses all of the techniques listed above.

Example 6.2 – Prolog and body of a step

```
<p:declare-step xmlns:p="http://www.w3.org/ns/xproc">

  <!-- - - - - - - - - - - - - - - - - - - - - - - - - - - - - - - - - - - - -->
  <!-- PROLOG: -->

  <p:input port="source" primary="true"/>
  <p:output port="result" primary="true"/>

  <!-- - - - - - - - - - - - - - - - - - - - - - - - - - - - - - - - - - - - -->
  <!-- BODY: -->

  <!-- Set a variable based on what's in the input: -->
  <p:variable name="status" select="xs:boolean(/*/@status)"/>

  <!-- Do something based on the variable using a core step: -->
  <p:choose>
    <p:when test="$status eq 'normal'">
      <p:add-attribute attribute-name="normal" match="/*" attribute-value="true"/>
    </p:when>
    <p:otherwise>
      <p:identity/>
    </p:otherwise>
  </p:choose>

  <!-- Transform it a bit: -->
  <p:xslt>
    <p:input port="stylesheet">
      <p:document href="do-something.xsl"/>
    </p:input>
  </p:xslt>

</p:declare-step>
```

Invoking steps

Invoking a step is analogous to calling a method, function, or procedure in other programming languages. You invoke a step by using its *type* as XML element. To use a step you declared with `type="mysteps:do-something"`, write **`<mysteps:do-something>`**. To use the built-in step to add an attribute, you write **`<p:add-attribute>`**.

The difference between step types and names

Steps always have a *type* and optionally a *name*.

- A step's *type* is similar to a class name in an object-oriented programming language. It signifies what the step is going to do. In XProc pipelines you use the step's type as the name of the XML element when invoking the step:
  - Add an attribute: **`<p:add-attribute>`**
  - Insert something; **`<p:insert>`**
  - Your own step that deletes unused parts of some structure flowing through: **`<mysteps:delete-unused-parts>`**
- A step's *name* provides an identifier for a *specific invocation* of that step. You assign a name using the `name` attribute, for instance `<p:xslt name="transform-1" ...>`. Names must be unique within scope.

  The name identifies a specific step's invocation. You need to assign a name if you want to explicitly connect to the ports of this invocation. See Example 6.1 for this mechanism at work.

In traditional programming languages you pass parameters when calling something. In XProc you pass two things on a step's invocation:

- Connections to the input ports of the called step (the section titled "Connecting input ports: `<p:with-input>`" (p. 125)).
- Values for the options of the called step (the section titled "Setting options: `<p:with-option>` (or by attribute)" (p. 128)).

Here is what the invocation of a step looks like. Some attributes are specified using the `[p:]` notation. See the section titled "The `[p:]` notation for attributes" (p. 75) for more information.

```
<some-step name? = xs:NCName
           [p:]depends? = List of xs:NCName
           [p:]timeout? = xs:nonNegativeInteger
           [p:]message? = { xs:string }
           (option-value-attributes)? >
  ( <p:with-input> |
    <p:with-option> )*
</some-step>
```

Table 6.1 – Attributes of <some-step>

Attribute	#	Type	Description
name	?	xs:NCName	The name of this particular step invocation within this pipeline. You need this name to refer to this invocation to explicitly connect ports. If you don't provide a name, a default name is constructed. See the section titled "Default step names" (p. 124).
[p:]depends	?	List of xs:NCName	Declares additional dependencies on other steps for this step invocation. See the section titled "Step dependencies: [p:]depends attribute" (p. 125).
[p:]timeout	?	xs:nonNegativeInteger	Default: 0 A request to the pipeline processor to terminate this step invocation after the specified number of seconds (0 means no limit). It is implementation-defined whether a processor supports timeouts, and if it does, how precisely and precisely how the execution time of a step is measured. Check your processor's documentation.

Attribute	#	Type	Description
[p:]message	?	{ xs:string }	Specify (as an AVT) a (debug) message that will hopefully show up somehow, somewhere on some output channel (most probably stdout, stderr or a log file). Whether something will happen and how is implementation-defined. Check your processor's documentation.
(option-value-attributes)	?		Setting step options can be done both with <p:with-option> and, as a shortcut, by specifying them as an attribute here (the section titled "Setting options: <p:with-option> (or by attribute)" (p. 128)).

The child elements of a step invocation specify the connections for the input ports and set values for the options:

Table 6.2 – Child elements of <some-step>

Child element	#	Description
p:with-input	*	Explicitly connects something to an input port of this step. See the section titled "Connecting input ports: <p:with-input> " (p. 125).
p:with-option	*	Sets the value for an option of this step. See the section titled "Setting options: <p:with-option> (or by attribute)" (p. 128).

Default step names

If you don't provide an explicit name using the `name` attribute, the XProc processor manufactures a default name for you. A default name is formatted as `!1.m.n...`, for instance `!1.3.2`. All the numbers in between the dots are computed based on the relative position of the element in the XProc document. For instance have a look at Example 6.2 (p. 120).

- The root `<p:declare-step>` element will get the name `!1`
- The first element in the pipeline where a `name` attribute is allowed is **`<p:choose>`**, so this gets the name `!1.1`
  - The `<p:when>` gets the name `!1.1.1`
  - The `<p:otherwise>` gets the name `!1.1.2`
- The **`<p:xslt>`** following the **`<p:choose>`** gets the name `!1.2`

You may have noticed that the `name` attribute has an `xs:Qname` type, but default names do *not* conform to the rules for valid QNames (a QName cannot start with a `!`). As strange as it may sound, this is a deliberate design decision to keep XProc users from using the default step names for explicitly connecting steps. You must provide a name yourself if you want to do this.

So why are there default names (and why do you need to bother)? The main reason is that they pop-up in error messages. When an error message refers to a step that has no name, it uses the constructed default name.

Theoretically, you could take this `!1.m.n...` and find the erroneous step in your pipeline. Just follow the numbers, right? In practice, it's not easy to do. Following a name like `!1.5.2.4` is, at least for me, too much of an effort. The error message itself will usually be enough to know which step to look at.

Step dependencies: `[p:]depends` attribute

In most cases the order in which steps execute is perfectly clear: any step that depends on the output of another step is guaranteed to be run after that step. However, sometimes a step depends on another one in ways that are not apparent in the input and output connections. Consider, for example, a pipeline that interacts with two different web services. It may very well be the case that one web service has to run before the other, even though the latter does not consume any output from the former.

For these (rare) cases you can specify explicit dependencies using the `[p:]depends` attribute. Its value is a space separated list of the step names this step depends on.

Connecting input ports: `<p:with-input>`

You can connect input ports explicitly using `<p:with-input>`. The attributes and child elements of this element determine what the sources are and what will appear on the port.

If necessary you can attach *multiple sources* to an input port. You can, for instance, specify a direct document with `<p:inline>` *and* a connection to some output port with `<p:pipe>`. Everything you specify will appear on the port, in the order as specified. In practice, multiple sources are rarely necessary, usually there will be only a single source connected.

```
<p:with-input port? = xs:NCName
              select? = SelPattern
              href? = { xs:anyURI }
              pipe? = xs:string
              exclude-inline-prefixes? = ExcludePrefixes >
  ( <p:empty> |
    <p:document> |
    <p:pipe> |
    <p:inline> )*
  <!-- Or use any other element(s) (or plain text) as alternative for
       wrapping it in a <p:inline> -->
</p:with-input>
```

Table 6.3 – Attributes of <p:with-input>

Attribute	#	Type	Description
`port`	?	`xs:NCName`	The name of the port. If you don't specify a `port` attribute, the following applies: ■ On most steps it defaults to the primary input port. ■ On some of the core steps (Chapter 7) it has a special meaning which will be explained there.
`select`	?	`SelPattern`	If present, this XPath expression is applied to the input on port.
`href`	?	`{ xs:anyURI }`	The URI of the document to appear on this port. Shorthand notation for a `<p:document>` child element with the same `href` attribute. See the section titled "Reading external documents: `<p:document>`" (p. 139).
`pipe`	?	`xs:string`	Explicitly connect this input port to some output port of a step in this pipeline. This is a shortcut for `<p:pipe>` child elements (see the section titled "Explicitly connecting to another port: `<p:pipe>`" (p. 142)).
`exclude-inline-prefixes`	?	`ExcludePrefixes`	Exclude namespace declarations in your inline contents. See the section titled "Excluding namespace prefixes" (p. 145).

Use either an `href` attribute, a `pipe` attribute *or* child elements to specify what appears on the port. The combination is not allowed.

Table 6.4 – Child elements of <p:with-input>

Child element	#	Description
`p:empty`	*	Use the empty sequence (a.k.a. nothing) as the input for this port. See the section titled "Specifying nothing: `<p:empty>` " (p. 139).
`p:document`	*	Use a document read from a URI as the input for this port. See the section titled "Reading external documents: `<p:document>` " (p. 139).
`p:pipe`	*	Connect this input port to an output port of another step or an input port of the encompassing step. See the section titled "Explicitly connecting to another port: `<p:pipe>` " (p. 142).
`p:inline`	*	Use the children of this element as input for this port. See the section titled "Specifying documents inline: `<p:inline>` " (p. 143). If you only have a single `<p:inline>` child element, you can leave it out and state your inline documents as direct children of `<p:input>`.

The reason you cannot mix `href` and `pipe` attributes with child elements is *order*: the pipeline processor needs to know in which order the inputs must be offered. However, attributes have, according to the XML specification, no explicit order. When mixing input-definition attributes and child elements, the processor has no way to find out the intended order, and therefore their combination is forbidden.

Setting options: `<p:with-option>` (or by attribute)

Steps can have options (the section titled "Declaring options: `<p:option>`" (p. 102)). On a step's invocation, you can set these options in two ways:

- Using `<p:with-option>` child elements within the step's invocation. For instance:

Example 6.3 – Passing options using `<p:with-option>` elements

```
<p:load>
  <p:with-option name="href" select="'/some/document/on/disk.xml'"
</p:load>

<p:insert>
  <p:with-option name="match" select="'/*'"/>
  <p:with-option name="position" select="'first-child'"/>
  <p:with-input port="insertion">
    ...
  </p:with-input>
</p:insert>
```

- As an attribute, on the step's invocation element. For instance:

Example 6.4 – Passing options as attributes

```
<p:load href="/some/document/on/disk.xml"/>

<p:insert match="/*" position="first-child">
  <p:with-input port="insertion">
    ...
  </p:with-input>
</p:insert>
```

Examples 6.3 and 6.4 mean exactly the same thing, but if you study them closely, an interesting and noteworthy difference becomes apparent: Example 6.3 uses apostrophes around the option's values but Example 6.4 doesn't. Why is that?

- An XPath expression in the `select` attribute will always be interpreted by the pipeline. But you don't want it interpreted by the pipeline; it must be interpreted by the step! Therefore, make it a literal string by putting apostrophes around it.
- If you pass option values by attribute, the values are literals, no strings attached; additional apostrophes are unnecessary.

This is an important distinction and, therefore, is worth being explained twice. The other explanation, which takes things from a slightly different angle, can be found in the section titled "XPath expressions and step options" (p. 55).

The `<p:with-option>` element is defined as follows:

```
<p:with-option name = xs:QName
               as? = XPathType
               select = XPathExpr
               collection? = { xs:boolean }
               href? = { xs:anyURI }
               pipe? = xs:string
               exclude-inline-prefixes? = ExcludePrefixes >
  ( <p:empty> |
    <p:document> |
    <p:pipe> |
    <p:inline> )*
  <!-- Or use any other element(s) (or plain text) as alternative for
       wrapping it in a <p:inline> -->
</p:with-option>
```

Table 6.5 – Attributes of <p:with-option>

Attribute	#	Type	Description
`name`	1	`xs:QName`	The name of the option.
`as`	?	`XPathType`	The data type of the option.
`select`	1	`XPathExpr`	An XPath expression that determines the value of the variable.
`collection`	?	`{ xs:boolean }`	Default: `false` If `true` the XPath context item for setting this variable will be undefined. All documents are now available as the *default collection* (through the `collection()` function. See the section titled "Addressing multiple documents" (p. 137).
`href`	?	`{ xs:anyURI }`	The URI of a default document to base this variable on. Shorthand notation for a `<p:document>` child element with the same `href` attribute (see the section titled "Reading external documents: `<p:document>` " (p. 139)).
`pipe`	?	`xs:string`	Explicitly use what's appearing on this output port to compute the value for this option. This is a shortcut for `<p:pipe>` child elements (see the section titled "Explicitly connecting to another port: `<p:pipe>` " (p. 142)).

Attribute	#	Type	Description
exclude-inline-prefixes	?	ExcludePrefixes	Exclude namespace declarations in your inline contents (see the section titled "Excluding namespace prefixes" (p. 145)).

Use either an href attribute, a pipe attribute *or* child elements to specify what appears on the port. Combinations are not allowed.

Table 6.6 – Child elements of <p:with-option>

Child element	#	Description
p:empty	*	Use the empty sequence (a.k.a. nothing) as the input for this option. See the section titled "Specifying nothing: <p:empty> " (p. 139).
p:document	*	Use a document read from an URI as the input for this option. See the section titled "Reading external documents: <p:document> " (p. 139).
p:pipe	*	Use a connection to an output port of another step (or the input port of the step itself) as the input for this option. See the section titled "Explicitly connecting to another port: <p:pipe> " (p. 142).
p:inline	*	Use the children of this element as the input for this option. See the section titled "Specifying documents inline: <p:inline> " (p. 143). If you only have a single <p:inline> child element, you can leave it out and state your inline documents as direct children of <p:variable>.

There are some additional rules when you set options by attribute instead of using `<p:with-option>`:

- Option attributes are Attribute Value Templates (AVTs). See the section titled "Attribute Value Templates in the XProc code" (p. 69). Thus, passing an option like this:

  ```
  <mysteps:write-to-log>
    <p:with-option message="concat('Status value: ', /*/@status)"
  </mysteps:write-to-log>
  ```

  can also be written as:

  ```
  <mysteps:write-to-log message="{concat('Status value: ', /*/@status)}"/>
  ```

  or as:

  ```
  <mysteps:write-to-log message="Status value: {/*/@status}"/>
  ```

- With the exception of `map` and `array` typed options (see below), the contents of the attribute are taken as a string and then cast to the appropriate datatype. For instance, an option called `count` of type `xs:integer` can be given a value with `count="12{1 + 2}"`. This will first become the string `'123'`, which is then cast to the integer `123`.
- Making the value of an attribute a string also means that you can never specify a sequence of things using the option attribute mechanism. For instance, an option called `names` declared with `as="xs:string+"` cannot be given a sequence of values using constructs like:

  ```
  names="norm,achim,gerrit,erik"
  names="'norm','achim','gerrit','erik'"
  names="('norm','achim','gerrit','erik')"
  ```

  Whatever you specify in this `names` attribute, the `names` option will always get a single value: exactly the string value of the attribute. To pass a sequence to an option you have to use `<p:with-option>`. For instance:

  ```
  <p:with-option name="names" as="xs:string+"
    select="('norm','achim','gerrit','erik')"/>
  ```

- When the datatype of the option is `map` or `array`, the contents of the attribute *is* interpreted directly as an XPath expression (which must, of course, result in the appropriate data type). For instance, when you want to set the value for an option declared as:

  ```
  <p:option name="mymap" as="map(*)"/>
  ```

You can do this with the following attribute on the step's invocation:

```
mymap="map{ 'a': 'b', 12: 13 }"
```

- You cannot use the attribute mechanism for options called `name` (since `name` is a pre-defined attribute on a step's invocation). You have to use `<p:with-option>` in this (edge) case.
- You can only use the attribute mechanism for options that are not in a namespace.

  For instance, when you have an option called `myns:myoption`, you have to use `<p:with-option>`.

Declaring variables: `<p:variable>`

XProc allows you to declare variables that you can use in XPath expressions elsewhere in your pipeline. It's the equivalent of `<xsl:variable name="..." select="..."/>` in XSLT or a `let $... := ...` in XQuery. The syntax follows XSLT: you specify a variable *without* a `$` prefix (`<p:variable name="example-var" .../>`) and refer to it using a `$` prefix (`$example-var`).

The nice thing about XProc variables is that they're not "simple" declarations; they are part of the pipeline. Loosely speaking you could think of them as a `<p:identity>` step (which does next to nothing) with the side-effect of setting a variable. And that's useful: it allows you to inspect the documents flowing through the variable's declaration and use them. For instance, Example 6.5 shows how to read the value of an attribute on the root element and store it in a variable.

Example 6.5 – Storing the value of an attribute in a variable

```
<p:variable name="status" select="/*/@status"/>
```

Later on in your code you can use `$status` to retrieve this value.

The bad news is that this feature adds complexity. Because a `<p:variable>` can inspect documents, you'll also want to specify which documents are used for this. By default, these are the documents appearing on the Default Readable Port (the section titled "Value Templates and the Default Readable Port" (p. 70)). But what happens if this is a sequence of documents or if you want to base your variable on documents appearing somewhere else in the pipeline?

Assume, for instance, that in your pipeline you have a `<p:xslt>` step that emits a single additional document on its `secondary` port (because the stylesheet uses `<xsl:result-document>`). And somewhere deep in the pipeline you need the value of an attribute of this secondary document. Example 6.6 shows how you could do this.

Example 6.6 – Basing the value of a variable on something appearing elsewhere

```
<p:declare-step xmlns:p="http://www.w3.org/ns/xproc" version="3.0">

  <p:input port="source" primary="true"/>
  <p:output port="result" primary="true"/>

  ...

  <p:xslt name="xsl-step-with-secondary-output">
    <p:input port="stylesheet">
      <p:document href="xslt-producing-secondary-output.xsl"/>
    </p:input>
  </p:xslt>

  ...

  <!-- Determine the status of the secondary output: -->
  <p:variable name="secondary-status" select="/*/@status">
    <p:pipe step="xsl-step-with-secondary-output" port="secondary"/>
  </p:variable>

  ...

</p:declare-step>
```

Let one thing be absolutely clear: basing the value of a variable on something else, as in Example 6.6, does *not* change anything in the document flow and the implicit connections. So the step right behind the `<p:variable>` in Example 6.6 does *not* suddenly "receive" (i.e., have an implicit connection to) the output of the `secondary` port of the `xsl-step-with-secondary-output` step.

As should be familiar by now, you can also base a variable on other things, including: inline documents (`<p:inline>`) and external documents (`<p:document>`).

Here's the full specification for `<p:variable>`:

```
<p:variable name = xs:QName
            as? = XPathType
            select = XPathExpr
            collection? = { xs:boolean }
            href? = { xs:anyURI }
            pipe? = xs:string
            exclude-inline-prefixes? = ExcludePrefixes >
  ( <p:empty> |
    <p:document> |
    <p:pipe> |
    <p:inline> )*
  <!-- Or use any other element(s) (or plain text) as alternative for
       wrapping it in a <p:inline> -->
</p:variable>
```

Table 6.7 – Attributes of <p:variable>

Attribute	#	Type	Description
`name`	1	`xs:QName`	The name of the variable.
`as`	?	`XPathType`	The data type of the variable.
`select`	1	`XPathExpr`	An XPath expression that determines the value of the variable.
`collection`	?	`{ xs:boolean }`	Default: `false` If `true` the XPath context item for setting this variable will be undefined. All documents are now available as the *default collection* (through the `collection()` function. See the section titled "Addressing multiple documents" (p. 137).

Attribute	#	Type	Description
`href`	?	`{ xs:anyURI }`	The URI of a default document to base this variable on. Shorthand notation for a `<p:document>` child element with the same `href` attribute (see the section titled "Reading external documents: `<p:document>`" (p. 139)).
`pipe`	?	`xs:string`	Explicitly use what's appearing on this output port to compute the value for this variable. This is a shortcut for `<p:pipe>` child elements (see the section titled "Explicitly connecting to another port: `<p:pipe>`" (p. 142)).
`exclude-inline-prefixes`	?	`ExcludePrefixes`	Exclude namespace declarations in your inline contents (see the section titled "Excluding namespace prefixes" (p. 145)).

Use either an `href` attribute, a `pipe` attribute *or* child elements to specify what appears on the port. Using both attributes is not allowed.

Table 6.8 – Child elements of <p:variable>

Child element	#	Description
`p:empty`	*	Use the empty sequence as the input for this variable. See the section titled "Specifying nothing: `<p:empty>` " (p. 139).
`p:document`	*	Use a document read from a URI as the input for this variable. See the section titled "Reading external documents: `<p:document>` " (p. 139).
`p:pipe`	*	Use a connection to an output port of another step (or the input port of this step) as input. See the section titled "Explicitly connecting to another port: `<p:pipe>` " (p. 142).
`p:inline`	*	Use the children of this element as input. See the section titled "Specifying documents inline: `<p:inline>` " (p. 143). If you only have a single `<p:inline>` child element, you can leave it out and state your inline documents as direct children of `<p:variable>`.

Addressing multiple documents

Getting a value from an XML document into a variable is easy: simply use an XPath expression (for instance `select="/*/@status"`) to refer to it. However, this only works when there is a single document flowing through. In case of multiple documents or no document, the expression will fail and you'll end up with a runtime error.

But what if there are multiple documents flowing through, and you need to address a specific one? Or you need to combine information from several of these documents into your variable's value? In that case set `collection="true"`, which will cause several things to happen:

- There will no longer be a context against which expressions like `/*/@status` can be resolved. These kinds of expressions will now fail miserably.
- A default *collection* with all the documents flowing through will be created. This collection can be accessed using XPath's `collection()` function.

That sounds useful. Example 6.7 counts the number of documents flowing through.

Example 6.7 – Counting the number of documents flowing through

```
... (some steps that produce multiple documents)

<p:variable name="number-of-documents" as="xs:integer" collection="true"
  select="count(collection())"/>
```

But what if I want address a *specific* document? Here things get complicated because the `collection()` function is by (XPath) definition unordered. So you can *not* rely on the nth document in the pipeline being also the nth document in the collection (which would have been handy because you could address the nth document as `collection()[n]`).

So how *can* you get to a specific document?

- If you know the exact base URI of the document (the value of the document's `base-uri` property), you can address the document using `collection('/the/base/uri')`.
- If you know some other distinguishing thing, use that. For instance if you're sure there's only one document with root element `<singular>`, use `collection()/singular/`....
- The steps that produce this sequence of documents might add information to their document properties (see the section titled "Working with document-properties" (p. 202)). You can then use the `p:document-properties()` function (the section titled "Document properties related functions" (p. 196)) to base decisions on this.

Entries in the default collection for non-XML/HTML documents will return the internal representation of this document:

- For JSON the value that represents the document (see the section titled "JSON documents" (p. 66)). For instance, this can be a map or array.
- For text documents a document consisting of a single text node (see the section titled "Text documents" (p. 41)).
- For other (binary) documents it is unspecified.

Visibility of variables

Visibility (or, as it's officially called, *scoping*) determines where in your code something is visible and therefore useable/accessible. Variables are visible/useable after their declaration. This includes nested elements such as code inside steps like **`<p:for-each>`** or **`<p:if>`**.

Although considered bad practice, variables can shadow (redeclare) other variables and options, with the exception of static options (see the section titled "Static options" (p. 105)).

Common connection constructs

There are some common constructs for connecting that you'll find often in the XProc specification. These constructs are used to declare ports, connect ports, and set variables and options. To avoid duplicating information, I have collected the descriptions of these constructs in this section.

Specifying nothing: `<p:empty>`

A `<p:empty>` element simply specifies that nothing is connected to or will appear on the port. Its content model is extremely simple: no attributes and no child elements. That's all folks.

When you use `<p:empty>`, you cannot specify other connections to the port.

Reading external documents: `<p:document>`

To read external documents you use `<p:document>`. Such a document can come straight from disk or from other sources such as the web.

```
<p:document href = { xs:anyURI }
            content-type? = xs:string
            document-properties? = map(xs:QName, item()*)
            parameters? = map(xs:QName, item()*) />
```

Table 6.9 – Attributes of <p:document>

Attribute	#	Type	Description
`href`	1	`{ xs:anyURI }`	The URI of the document to read. Relative URI-s are made absolute against the base URI of the `<p:document>`. In most cases that will be the location of your XProc program but you might have overridden this using an `xml:base` attribute.
`content-type`	?	`xs:string`	The content type (MIME type) of the document to load.
`document-properties`	?	`map(xs:QName, item()*)`	This sets the properties for the document to load. See the section titled "Representations and properties" (p. 37). Special rules apply, see below.
`parameters`	?	`map(xs:QName, item()*)`	Contains optional parameters used when loading the data. See below.

The first thing the XProc processor needs to do is find out what it is supposed to load. To determine the content type (the content's MIME type), it looks at the following things (in this order):

- Is the `content-type` attribute specified, *or* does the map supplied in the `document-properties` attribute contain a `content-type` entry? If so, use this. It's an error to specify both.
- Is a protocol used that specifies the content type (for instance `http`, which tells you what content type it delivers)? If so, use this.
- In all other cases the content type is implementation defined.

If you load something from disk and don't set an explicit content-type, the result is implementation defined. You can't rely on the XProc processor treating, for instance, an XML document as XML. In practice, however, you can rely on the XProc processor to do the right thing. It will probably look at the file extension to determine the type.

After the XProc processor has determined the content-type, it will look at the `parameters` map for more information. Interpretation of this map depends on the content type:

XML data	The only parameter an XProc processor is required to understand is `dtd-validate`. When set to `true`, the document *must* have a DTD doctype declaration, and the processor will validate it. Any other parameter is implementation defined.
Text and binary data	All parameters are implementation defined.
JSON data	The only parameters an XProc processor is required to understand are the parameters for the XPath 3.1 `fn:parse-json()` function.[3] Any other parameter is implementation defined.

Here is an example of loading an XML file but forcing the processor to treat it as text. It also sets an additional property that you can act on in your pipeline later on:

```
<p:document href="somefile.xml"
   document-properties="map{ 'content-type' : 'text/plain',
                             'my-status-property' : 'very-important' }"/>
```

Here is an example that shows how you can set parameters (taken from the XPath 3.1 `fn:parse-json()` function) when loading JSON:

```
<p:document href="somefile.json"
            parameters="map{ 'liberal' : true(),
                             'duplicates' : 'use-first' }"/>
```

Shorthand notation

If you only need to load a single document *and* you don't have any requirements for the document properties or parameters, you can use the `href` attribute on the parent element instead of `<p:document>`. So this:

```
<p:with-input port="source" href="somefile.json"/>
```

is equivalent to this:

```
<p:with-input port="source">
  <p:document href="somefile.json"/>
</p:with-input>
```

[3] For more on this function, see https://www.w3.org/TR/xpath-functions-31/#func-parse-json.

Explicitly connecting to another port: `<p:pipe>`

As we've seen, ports are usually connected implicitly based on their location in the pipeline. But with subpipelines, everything stops being straight and linear, and you have to connect ports explicitly. This is done with `<p:pipe>`.

```
<p:pipe step? = xs:NCName
        port? = xs:NCName />
```

Table 6.10 – Attributes of <p:pipe>

Attribute	#	Type	Description
`step`	?	`xs:NCName`	The name of the step you want to connect to. If not specified, this defaults to the step it would connect to implicitly.
`port`	?	`xs:NCName`	The name of the port you want to connect to, on the step named in the `step` attribute. If absent, this defaults to its primary output port.

Shorthand notation

You can use a `pipe` attribute on the parent element as a shortcut for one or more `<p:pipe>` elements. Its value is a space-separated list of one or more step/port specifications:

- Use `port-name@step-name` to connect to a named port on a named step.
- Use `@step-name` (with a leading `@`) to connect to the primary output port of this step.
- Use `port-name` (without a trailing `@`) to connect to a port on the implicitly connected step.

Using the `pipe` attribute you could specify this:

```
<p:with-input port="source">
  <p:pipe step="step1" port="source"/>
  <p:pipe step="step2"/>
  <p:pipe port="special"/>
</p:with-input>
```

as this:

```
<p:with-input port="source" pipe="source@step1 @step2 special"/>
```

Specifying documents inline: `<p:inline>`

Using `<p:inline>`, you can specify input documents straight within your XProc pipeline. There are several situations where this is useful, for instance:

- You want to specify an XSLT transformation (on the `stylesheet` port of a `<p:xslt>` step) not as an external document but directly in your pipeline.
- The input to an XSLT transformation doesn't matter, and you just want to pass something like `<dummy/>` on its input port.
- You want to start your transformation with a template document that is filled in later.

The definition of the `<p:inline>` element is as follows:

```
<p:inline exclude-inline-prefixes? = ExcludePrefixes
          content-type? = xs:string
          document-properties? = map(xs:QName, item()*)
          encoding? = xs:string >
  Any element(s)) or plain text
</p:inline>
```

Table 6.11 – Attributes of <p:inline>

Attribute	#	Type	Description
`exclude-inline-prefixes`	?	`ExcludePrefixes`	Exclude namespace declarations in your inline contents. See the section titled "Excluding namespace prefixes" (p. 145) for more information.
`content-type`	?	`xs:string`	The content type (MIME type) of the inline document.
`document-properties`	?	`map(xs:QName, item()*)`	A `<p:inline>` results in documents flowing through the pipeline and documents always have document-properties attached (see the section titled "Representations and properties" (p. 37)). You can set these document-properties explicitly using this attribute.
`encoding`	?	`xs:string`	Only allowed for non-XML content: specify the *encoding* of the inline document. The only value XProc processors must acknowledge is `base64`. This means (of course) that the contents of the `<p:inline>` must be something base64 encoded. Other values are implementation defined.

Some nitty-gritty details on how the XProc processor treats the contents of a `<p:inline>`:

- First the content-type (MIME type) of the `<p:inline>` must be determined. This is done by looking at either the `content-type` attribute or the `content-type` entry in the map passed to the `document-properties` attribute. It's an error to specify both. If neither is found the content is assumed to be XML.
- If the content-type is XML, the content of the `<p:inline>` must be a *single document*. That is, it must have a single root element, optionally preceded or followed by comments and/or processing instructions.
- If the content is non-XML, the innards of the `<p:inline>` must be an XML text node. So straight text (with the special XML characters escaped as entities (`&` for `&`, `<` for `<`, etc.) or one or more CDATA sections.

Shorthand notation

In case you only want to use a straight and simple XML document inline, you can leave out the `<p:inline>` element and specify the XML document as a direct child of the parent element.

Excluding namespace prefixes

When you specify some XML using `<p:inline>`, it inherits all namespace definitions from the surrounding XProc code. You probably don't need these definitions (or at least not all of them). But they will show up in your end result if you just let them be. Although superfluous namespace definitions don't hurt, they clutter up your XML. Therefore you can exclude (or undefine) namespace definitions within your `<p:inline>`. Here are the rules:

- The XProc namespace itself (`http://www.w3.org/ns/xproc`) is excluded by default.
- Set the `exclude-inline-prefixes` attribute to:
  - `#all` to exclude all namespace prefixes.
  - To a space separated list of existing (in scope) namespace prefixes to exclude these specific namespace definitions. Use `#default` to exclude the default namespace.
- A namespace definition excluded on an ancestor of the `<p:inline>` is also excluded. You can, for instance, set `exclude-inline-prefixes="#all"` on the `<p:declare-step>` so this becomes the default for all your `<p:inline>` elements.

But what happens if you exclude a namespace but still use it in an `<p:inline>`? XML permits this, even though it seems dangerous. Luckily, XProc processors allow this, which means you can specify `exclude-inline-prefixes="#all"` and still use any of the namespace prefixes. However, the XProc processor is free to re-define this namespace using another prefix.

Here is an example from the specification. Suppose you have the pipeline in Example 6.8.

Example 6.8 – Pipeline that uses `exclude-inline-prefixes`

```
<p:declare-step xmlns:p="http://www.w3.org/ns/xproc" version="3.0">

  <p:output port="result"/>

  <p:identity xmlns:a="http://example.com/a"
              xmlns:b="http://example.com/b"
              xmlns:c="http://example.com/c">
    <p:with-input port="source">
      <p:inline exclude-inline-prefixes="a b">
        <doc>
          <b:part/>
        </doc>
      </p:inline>
    </p:with-input>
  </p:identity>

</p:declare-step>
```

The result *might* be:

```
<doc xmlns:c="http://example.com/c">
  <b:part xmlns:b="http://example.com/b"/>
</doc>
```

The namespace with prefix `c` is still there, even though it isn't used, because it wasn't excluded. The namespace with prefix `b` is there, even though it was excluded, because it was used. However, because you excluded `b`, the XProc processor can change the prefix, as shown here:

```
<doc xmlns:c="http://example.com/c">
  <ns1:part xmlns:ns1="http://example.com/b"/>
</doc>
```

CHAPTER 7

Core steps

This chapter handles XProc's core steps. These steps enable functions such as looping, branching, and error handling. In other words, they turn XProc from a language for just chaining steps into a full programming language.

Looping: `<p:for-each>`

The **`<p:for-each>`** step processes, one by one, the documents appearing on its input port. Or it can split up a document and loop over the separated parts.

Let's start with an example of the latter. Assume you have an XML document that must be split into sub-documents. Each sub-document must get an attribute that contains the date/time and must be stored on disk using a filename that contains a sequence number (first document 1, second document 2, etc.).

The incoming XML document looks like Example 7.1.

Example 7.1 – Example input document to split

```
<docs>
  <doc>
    <!-- Some contents for the first document... -->
  </doc>
  <doc>
    <!-- Some contents for the second document... -->
  </doc>
</docs>
```

Example 7.2 shows an XProc pipeline that splits the document in Example 7.1.

Example 7.2 – Pipeline to split the document from Example 7.1

```
<p:declare-step xmlns:p="http://www.w3.org/ns/xproc" version="3.0">

  <p:input port="source"/>
  <p:output port="result"/>

  <p:for-each>
    <!-- 1 - Selection using the p:for-each's anonymous input port: -->
    <p:with-input select="/*/doc"/>
    <!-- 2 - Add a timestamp attribute: -->
    <p:add-attribute attribute-name="timestamp" select="{current-dateTime()}"/>
    <!-- 3 - Write the result to disk: -->
   <p:store href="{concat('/some/path/doc-', p:iteration-position(), '.xml')}"/>
  </p:for-each>

  <!-- 4 - Discard the documents, just report a count: -->
  <p:count/>

</p:declare-step>
```

1. The subpipeline within a **<p:for-each>** has an *anonymous* input port that provides the documents the **<p:for-each>** iterates on. You can specify what should appear on this port using `<p:with-input>` as the first child of **<p:for-each>**. If you don't specify anything, the connection is implicit.

   Example 7.2 contains such a `<p:with-input>`:

   - This `<p:with-input>` does not specify a port connection, so it is an implicit connection to the primary (`source`) input port of the encompassing step.
   - However, it does specify a `select` attribute. This will select those portions of the input document that match the XPath expression in the `select` attribute (`/*/doc`).

     This XPath expression will match two `<doc>` elements in Example 7.1. The result is that the single input document with root element `<docs>` is split into a sequence of two documents, both with root element `<doc>`.

2. Within the **<p:for-each>**, the **<p:add-attribute>** element adds an attribute to each document the **<p:for-each>** iterates on: that is, each `<doc>` element in the original input.

3. The result is stored on disk. This is done by the **`<p:store>`** element, which computes the file name for each result and stores it as the value of the `href` attribute. The XProc extension function `p:iteration-position()` returns the number of the current iteration (see the section titled "Iteration related functions" (p. 195)). The resulting `href` values are `/some/path/doc-1.xml` and `/some/path/doc-2.xml`.

4. In addition to writing the two files, the **`<p:store>`** step also outputs the results. Therefore, because the **`<p:for-each>`** step loops twice, it outputs two documents as a sequence. In Example 7.2, this output is discarded and replaced with the output of **`<p:count>`**, which is the count of documents written.

   You can find more details about how the subpipeline in **`<p:for-each>`** connects to the **`<p:count>`** step in the section titled "The subpipeline's anonymous output port" (p. 170).

Using Example 7.1 as input, Example 7.2 writes two files to disk. The first one, `/some/path/doc-1.xml`, contains:

```
<doc timestamp="2019-01-18T09:08:22.189+01:00">
  <!-- Some contents for the first document... -->
</doc>
```

Of course the value of the `timestamp` attribute will differ, depending on when the pipeline was run. The contents of the second file you can probably guess.

The current date/time in a pipeline

Programming languages like XSLT and XQuery always return the *same* value for functions like `current-dateTime()`. Even when your stylesheet runs for hours the current date/time will always be reported as the date/time the processing started.

In XProc this behavior is processor dependent. Both XML Calabash and MorganaXProc return the actual date/time of the call to `current-dateTime()` (or `current-date()` or `current-time()`).

This is useful if you want to report the duration of a pipeline run. For instance, in the beginning of your pipeline, you can store the current date/time in a variable:

```
<p:variable name="start" as="xs:dateTime" select="current-dateTime()"/>
```

As one of the final steps, add a `duration` attribute to the root element of your result:

```
<p:add-attribute attribute-name="duration"
  attribute-value="{current-dateTime() - $start}"/>
```

This will construct a `duration` attribute expressed as an `xs:duration`, for instance `PT3.14S`.

The definition of **`<p:for-each>`** is as follows:

```
<p:for-each name? = xs:NCName >
  <p:with-input>?
  <p:output>*
  <!-- A subpipeline containing the steps to be taken on each iteration... -->
</p:for-each>
```

Table 7.1 – Attributes of <p:for-each>

Attribute	#	Type	Description
`name`	?	`xs:NCName`	The name of this **`<p:for-each>`** within this pipeline. You need this name to refer to it when you want or need to connect ports explicitly.

Table 7.2 – Child elements of <p:for-each>

Child element	#	Description
p:with-input	?	Explicitly defines what is to appear on the (anonymous) input port for the **<p:for-each>**. Each resulting document will cause an iteration. See the section titled "Connecting input ports: <p:with-input> " (p. 125). Do *not* use a name attribute (since the input port is anonymous).
p:output	*	Explicitly defines an output port for this <p:for-each>. What appears on this port is the sequence of documents produced for this port, from all the iterations, in order of appearance. See the section titled "Declaring output ports: <p:output> " (p. 89) and the section titled "Explicitly defining output ports in subpipelines" (p. 171).

Within the **<p:for-each>** an additional port called current is available. This port will provide the document the **<p:for-each>** currently iterates on. The first step within your **<p:for-each>** will implicitly connect to this port, so usually you don't need it (as is the case in Example 7.2). But if the processing within the **<p:for-each>** gets complicated you might.

For instance, Example 7.3 does some complicated processing and inserts the results back into the original document.

Example 7.3 – Insert the results of a computation into the original in a **<p:for-each>**

```
<p:for-each name="complicated-loop">

  … (do some complicated stuff)

  <p:identity name="complicated-results"/>

  <!-- Insert what we've computed into the original: -->
  <p:insert match="/*" position="last-child">
    <p:with-input port="source" pipe="current@complicated-loop"/>
    <p:with-input port="insertion" pipe="result@complicated-results"/>
  </p:insert>

</p:for-each>
```

Acting on a part of a document: <p:viewport>

The **<p:viewport>** step enables you to run a subpipeline on specific elements in the documents appearing on its input port. This is useful when you want to change only parts of your document and leave the rest as is.

As an example, assume you have an XHTML document and need to insert a <hr/> at the end of every <div class="chapter">, effectively separating each chapter with a horizontal line. Example 7.4 shows how you can do this using **<p:viewport>**:

Example 7.4 – Using <p:viewport> to separate chapters in HTML

```
<p:declare-step xmlns:p="http://www.w3.org/ns/xproc"
  xmlns:html="http://www.w3.org/1999/xhtml" version="3.0">

  <p:input port="source" primary="true"/>
  <p:output port="result" primary="true"/>

  <p:viewport match="html:div[@class eq 'chapter']">
    <p:insert position="first-child">
      <p:with-input port="insertion">
        <html:hr/>
      </p:with-input>
    </p:insert>
  </p:viewport>

</p:declare-step>
```

In Example 7.4, the **<p:viewport>** is implicitly connected to the primary input port `source` of the pipeline. The following will occur if you feed this pipeline an XHTML document that includes some <div class="chapter"> elements:

- The **<p:viewport>** will pass the input document through unchanged until it finds an element that matches the value of its `match` attribute (HTML <div class="chapter"> elements).
- When a match is found, the subpipeline inside the **<p:viewport>** runs with the matched element as its input. The result of the subpipeline replaces the original matched element (including all of its attributes and child elements).
- In Example 7.4, the subpipeline simply inserts <hr> at the end of the matched <div>, replacing the original <div>.

A useful feature of **<p:viewport>** is that the `match` attribute can contain references to variables and options. This gives you a lot of flexibility in expressing the match. For example, you could extend Example 7.4 to define the chapter class name in a variable, as shown in Example 7.5.

Example 7.5 – Using a variable reference in the **<p:viewport>**'s `match` attribute

```
<p:variable name="chapter-class-name" select="'chapter'"/>

<p:viewport match="html:div[@class eq $chapter-class-name]">
  ...
</p:viewport>
```

The definition of **<p:viewport>** is as follows:

```
<p:viewport name? = xs:NCName
            match = SelPattern >
  <p:with-input>?
  <p:output>?
  <!-- A subpipeline containing the steps to be taken for each match... -->
</p:viewport>
```

Table 7.3 – Attributes of <p:viewport>

Attribute	#	Type	Description
`name`	?	`xs:NCName`	The name of this **<p:viewport>** in this pipeline. You need this name to refer to it when you want or need to connect ports explicitly.
`match`	1	`SelPattern`	The selection pattern that matches the nodes to process in the subpipeline. The pattern must match an element or a whole document, anything else will result in an error. The `match` attribute may contain references to variables and options.

Table 7.4 – Child elements of <p:viewport>

Child element	#	Description
`p:with-input`	?	Explicitly defines what is to appear on the (anonymous) input port for the **`<p:viewport>`**. See the section titled "Connecting input ports: `<p:with-input>` " (p. 125). Do *not* use a `name` attribute (since the input port is anonymous).
`p:output`	?	Explicitly defines the output port of the subpipeline. See the section titled "Declaring output ports: `<p:output>` " (p. 89). If you don't specify an output port, the primary output port of the last step in the subpipeline is used.

`<p:viewport>` has an additional port called `current`. This port provides access to the document the **`<p:viewport>`** is currently working on (with the matched element as its root node). The first step within your **`<p:viewport>`** implicitly connects to this port, so you usually don't need it. Example 7.3 shows one place where the `current` port can be useful.

A common mistake is assuming that the matched content being processed in the **`<p:viewport>`** subpipeline is still connected to the full document it came from. Code that attempts to reach original parent nodes by, for instance, using XPath's `ancestor::` axis or `..` constructions will fail. The document processed by the subpipeline is a true stand-alone document with the matched element as its root node. The parent nodes it originated from are not accessible.

Making decisions: `<p:if>` and `<p:choose>`

There are two core steps you can use for making decisions:

- The **`<p:choose>`**/`<p:when>`/`<p:otherwise>` is similar to the `<xsl:choose>` in XSLT or the `case` statement in several other programming languages.
- The **`<p:if>`** allows only a single branch (no else), just like an `<xsl:if>` in XSLT.

Multiple decisions: `<p:choose>`

A **<p:choose>**, in cooperation with its child elements `<p:when>` and `<p:otherwise>`, allows you to specify multiple branches with subpipelines, of which one (and only one!) is chosen and executed. This is equivalent to an `<xsl:choose>` in XSLT.

Assume you have an input document with a `version` attribute on its root element. If `version="1"` or `version="2"` you want to validate the document. For other versions you don't want to bother. Here is an example that performs this trick:

Example 7.6 – Using **<p:choose>** for making decisions about validation

```
<p:declare-step xmlns:p="http://www.w3.org/ns/xproc" version="3.0">

  <p:input port="source" primary="true"/>
  <p:output port="result" primary="true"/>

  <p:choose>
    <p:when test="/*[@version eq '1']">
      <p:validate-with-xml-schema>
        <p:with-input port="schema" href="v1schema.xsd"/>
      </p:validate-with-xml-schema>
    </p:when>
    <p:when test="/*[@version eq '2']">
      <p:validate-with-xml-schema>
        <p:with-input port="schema" href="v2schema.xsd"/>
      </p:validate-with-xml-schema>
    </p:when>
    <p:otherwise>
      <p:identity/>
    </p:otherwise>
  </p:choose>

</p:declare-step>
```

- The **<p:choose>** is implicitly connected to the primary input port `source` of the pipeline. Assume it runs on a document with a `version` attribute on its root node.
- The `<p:when>` branches inside the **<p:choose>** test the `version` attribute and trigger validation with the appropriate schema.
- The `<p:otherwise>` doesn't do much (its subpipeline with only a `<p:identity>` just copies input to output). So when the `version` attribute is anything else then `1` or `2`, no validation will take place.

The definition of **<p:choose>** is as follows:

```
<p:choose name? = xs:NCName >
  <p:with-input>?
  <p:when>*
  <p:otherwise>?
</p:choose>
```

Table 7.5 – Attributes of <p:choose>

Attribute	#	Type	Description
name	?	xs:NCName	The name of this **<p:choose>** within this pipeline. You need this name when you want to connect ports explicitly.

Table 7.6 – Child elements of <p:choose>

Child element	#	Description
p:with-input	?	Explicitly defines what will appear on the (anonymous) input port for the **<p:choose>**. See the section titled "Connecting input ports: <p:with-input> " (p. 125). Do *not* use a name attribute (since the input port is anonymous).
p:when	*	For every <p:when> present, in the order in which they are stated, the expression in the test attribute is evaluated. The subpipeline for the *first* (and only the first) <p:when> where this expression evaluates to true is executed.
p:otherwise	?	When none of the <p:when> test expressions evaluates to true, the subpipeline in the <p:otherwise> is executed.

Some additional remarks:

- A **<p:choose>** must contain at least one `<p:when>` or a `<p:otherwise>`. In other words: a **<p:choose>** must have at least one child element.
- When you define a primary output port in one `<p:choose>`/`<p:otherwise>` branch, every other `<p:choose>`/`<p:otherwise>` subpipeline must have a primary output port with the same name.

What happens when none of the `<p:when>` branches is selected (none of the conditions in their `test` attributes evaluates to `true`) and there is no `<p:otherwise>`? In the vast majority of cases the **<p:choose>** will behave as a simple **<p:identity>** step. Therefore, in Example 7.6. you could omit the `<p:otherwise>` step since it contains only a **<p:identity>**.

In most cases you don't have to worry about this, but there are conditions that must be met: *All* the `<p:when>` branches must define a primary output port. A primary output port is defined if:

- The subpipeline inside the **<p:choose>** has an implicit primary output port (because its last step has one).
- You specify it explicitly with the `<p:output primary="true">` child element.

If a primary output port is not defined and no `<p:when>` is selected, the `<p:choose>` element will emit nothing.

p:when

The definition of `<p:when>` is as follows:

```
<p:when name? = xs:NCName
        test = XPathExpr
        collection? = { xs:boolean } >
  <p:with-input>?
  <p:output>*
  <!-- A subpipeline containing the conditional steps… -->
</p:when>
```

Table 7.7 – Attributes of <p:when>

Attribute	#	Type	Description
name	?	xs:NCName	The name of this <p:when>. You need this name when you want to connect ports explicitly.
test	1	XPathExpr	An XPath expression. When this expression evaluates to true, the subpipeline inside this <p:when> is executed.
collection	?	{ xs:boolean }	Default: false If true the XPath context item for the test expression will be undefined. All documents are now available as the *default collection* through the collection() function (see the section titled "Addressing multiple documents" (p. 137)).

Table 7.8 – Child elements of <p:when>

Child element	#	Description
p:with-input	?	The (anonymous) input port that explicitly defines against which document the expression in the test is evaluated. Do *not* use a name attribute (the input port is anonymous). If you don't specify this explicit anonymous input port, the test expression is evaluated against the input of the parent <p:choose>.
p:output	*	Explicitly defines an output port for this <p:when>. See the section titled "Declaring output ports: <p:output> " (p. 89) and the section titled "Explicitly defining output ports in subpipelines" (p. 171).

p:otherwise

The definition of <p:otherwise> is simple:

```
<p:otherwise name? = xs:NCName >
  <p:output>*
  <!-- A subpipeline containing the conditional steps... -->
</p:otherwise>
```

Table 7.9 – Attributes of <p:otherwise>

Attribute	#	Type	Description
name	?	xs:NCName	The name of this <p:otherwise>. You need this name when you want to connect ports explicitly.

Table 7.10 – Child elements of <p:otherwise>

Child element	#	Description
p:output	*	Explicitly defines an output port for this <p:otherwise>. See the section titled "Declaring output ports: <p:output> " (p. 89) and the section titled "Explicitly defining output ports in subpipelines" (p. 171).

Single decision: <p:if>

<p:if> is another, shorter way of writing a **<p:choose>** that has only a single <p:when>. There is no equivalent of an else clause, but when the test expression evaluates to `false`, it acts (almost, see below) like the **<p:identity>** step. Therefore, in most practical cases, you can use **<p:if>** as a convenient shorthand notation for:

```
<p:choose>
  <p:when test="...">
    ...
  </p:when>
  <p:otherwise>
    <p:identity/>
  </p:otherwise>
</p:choose>
```

The definition of `<p:if>` is as follows:

```
<p:if name? = xs:NCName
      test = XPathExpr
      collection? = { xs:boolean } >
  <p:with-input>?
  <p:output>*
  <!-- A subpipeline containing the conditional steps... -->
</p:if>
```

Table 7.11 – Attributes of <p:if>

Attribute	#	Type	Description
`name`	?	`xs:NCName`	The name of this `<p:if>` within this pipeline. You need this name when you want to connect ports explicitly.
`test`	1	`XPathExpr`	An XPath expression. When this expression evaluates to `true`, the subpipeline inside the `<p:if>` is executed.
`collection`	?	`{ xs:boolean }`	Default: `false` If `true` the XPath context item for the test expression will be undefined. All documents are now available as the *default collection* (through the `collection()` function. See the section titled "Addressing multiple documents" (p. 137).

Table 7.12 – Child elements of <p:if>

Child element	#	Description
`p:with-input`	?	The (anonymous) input port that explicitly defines against which document the expression in the `test` is evaluated. Do *not* use a `name` attribute (the input port is anonymous). If you don't specify this explicit anonymous input port, the test expression is evaluated against the input of **`<p:if>`**.
`p:output`	*	Explicitly defines an output port for this **`<p:if>`**. See the section titled "Declaring output ports: `<p:output>`" (p. 89) and the section titled "Explicitly defining output ports in subpipelines" (p. 171).

A few details (which, in most cases, you can forget):

- The **`<p:if>`** *must* specify a primary output port. This can be achieved in two ways:
  - By making sure that the subpipeline inside the **`<p:if>`** has an implicit primary output port (because its last step has one).
  - By specifying it explicitly with an `<p:output primary="true">` child element.
- If the test expression on the **`<p:if>`** evaluates to `false` (the *else* condition), the `<p:if>` will, for all practical purposes, act like a **`<p:identity>`** step and simply pass on its input(s).

Grouping: `<p:group>`

A **`<p:group>`** is a convenience wrapper for a collection of steps. It doesn't really do much.

A (very good) reason to use **`<p:group>`** is to clarify code. If you have a group of steps that strongly belong together, put a **`<p:group>`** around them to signify this. It helps in editing as well: most IDEs and XML Editors can collapse elements (reduce what is visible to a single line). Collapsing a **`<p:group>`** can make long and complicated code easier to read.

In XProc version 1.0, **<p:group>** had a practical purpose. You couldn't define variables just anywhere (like you can in version 3.0); you could only define them at the top of a (sub-)pipeline. So when you needed a variable in the middle of your code you had to use a **<p:group>**.

The definition of **<p:group>** is as follows:

```
<p:group name? = xs:NCName >
  <p:output>*
  <!-- A subpipeline… -->
</p:group>
```

Table 7.13 – Attributes of <p:group>

Attribute	#	Type	Description
`name`	?	`xs:NCName`	The name of this **<p:group>** within this pipeline. You need this name when you want to connect ports explicitly.

Table 7.14 – Child elements of <p:group>

Child element	#	Description
`p:output`	*	Explicitly defines an output port for this **<p:group>**. See the section titled "Declaring output ports: `<p:output>` " (p. 89) and the section titled "Explicitly defining output ports in subpipelines" (p. 171).

Error handling: <p:try>

Of course your code is flawless and no errors will ever occur. True? Of course not, exceptions can come from anywhere and even if *you* are a super programmer, the environment may wreak havoc. So every major programming language has some kind of try/catch construction and XProc is no exception.

Here is a skeleton **<p:try>**:

Example 7.7 – A skeleton **<p:try>**

```
<p:try>

  … the subpipeline that might produce an error

  <p:catch code="err:XD0011">
    … subpipeline that does something in case of error err:XD0010
  </p:catch>
  <p:catch>
    … subpipeline that does something in case of any other error
  </p:catch>
  <p:finally>
    … subpipeline with cleanup code that runs
      regardless of whether there were errors or not
  </p:finally>

</p:try>
```

The definition of **<p:try>** is as follows:

```
<p:try name? = xs:NCName >
  … the subpipeline that might produce an error
  <p:catch>*
  <p:finally>?
</p:try>
```

Table 7.15 – Attributes of <p:try>

Attribute	#	Type	Description
`name`	?	`xs:NCName`	The name of this **<p:try>** within this pipeline. You need this name when you want to connect ports explicitly.

Table 7.16 – Child elements of <p:try>

Child element	#	Description
`p:catch`	*	For every `<p:catch>` present, in the order in which they are stated, the error raised is matched against the list of errors in its `code` attribute. The subpipeline for the *first* (and only the first) `<p:catch>` with such a match is executed. A `code` attribute *must* be present on all but the last `<p:catch>`. A final `<p:catch>` without a `code` attribute serves as catch-all for errors not caught in previous `<p:catch>` elements.
`p:finally`	?	A subpipeline with code to be run, regardless of whether an error occurred or not. This usually contains cleanup code for, for instance, releasing resources.

<p:try> must contain *at least* one `<p:catch>` or a `<p:finally>`. In other words: **<p:try>** without at least a single branch is not allowed.

<p:try> catches only *dynamic* errors: errors that are produced while executing the pipeline. Static errors, errors produced before the pipeline is run, like syntax errors, cannot be caught.

In XProc 1.0, the subpipeline inside the **<p:try>** that might produce the error had to be enclosed in a **<p:group>**. That is no longer the case. Of course, nothing prevents you from doing this; **<p:group>** is totally valid.

p:catch

A `<p:catch>` catches either a list of specific errors (as stated in its `code` attribute) or any error (no `code` attribute). A catch-all `<p:catch>`, without a `code` attribute, can only occur as the last of the list of `<p:catch>` elements.

The definition of `<p:catch>` is as follows:

```
<p:catch name? = xs:NCName
         code? = list of xs:QName >
  <p:output>*
  <!-- A subpipeline containing the conditional steps... -->
</p:catch>
```

Table 7.17 – Attributes of <p:catch>

Attribute	#	Type	Description
name	?	xs:NCName	The name of this `<p:catch>` within this pipeline. You need this name when you want to connect ports explicitly. For instance, see Example 7.8.
code	?	list of xs:QName	A space separated list of error codes to be caught by this `<p:catch>`. See below.

Table 7.18 – Child elements of <p:catch>

Child element	#	Description
p:output	*	Explicitly defines an output port. See the section titled "Declaring output ports: `<p:output>` " (p. 89) and the section titled "Explicitly defining output ports in subpipelines" (p. 171).

Error codes listed in the `code` attribute are *qualified names* (must have a namespace component) and the namespace prefix(es) must be bound.

- For a list of dynamic errors produced by XProc itself, have a look at the formal specification. For instance, one of the errors it can produce is:

  err:XD0010: It is a dynamic error if the match expression on p:viewport matches an attribute or a namespace node.

  The `err:` prefix must be bound to `http://www.w3.org/ns/xproc-error`.

- You can define your own error codes with the **<p:error>** step (see the section titled "p:error" (p. 247)). This gives you full control over the error code produced:

```
<p:error code="MYERR42" code-prefix="myapp"
  code-namespace="http://my.own-namespace.org/ns/errors"/>
```

- Steps that execute programs in other programming languages (like XSLT or XQuery) can raise errors originating from that language or raised deliberately in code.

Probably the easiest way to find out what error codes are raised in what circumstances is to deliberately generate errors and look at the messages they produce.

In case of an error, the XProc processor cannot know where things went wrong or what was executed and what was not. Therefore, the subpipeline inside of <p:catch> cannot access any output ports or variables from the subpipeline of its parent **<p:try>**.

You can get information about the error(s) that caused this <p:catch> to execute. Every <p:catch> has a port available called `error` on which a document with error information appears. See the section titled "Error specification" (p. 167).

p:finally

Whatever happens inside the **<p:try>**, whether there were errors or not, the <p:finally> subpipeline is *always* evaluated. Use it for recovery and resource cleanup tasks.

```
<p:finally name? = xs:NCName >
  <p:output>*
  <!-- A subpipeline containing the final steps... -->
</p:finally>
```

Table 7.19 – Attributes of <p:finally>

Attribute	#	Type	Description
name	?	xs:NCName	The name of this <p:finally> within this pipeline. You need this name when you want to connect ports explicitly.

Table 7.20 – Child elements of <p:finally>

Child element	#	Description
p:output	*	Explicitly defines an output port for this <p:finally>. See the section titled "Declaring output ports: <p:output> " (p. 89) and the section titled "Explicitly defining output ports in subpipelines" (p. 171).

As with <p:catch>, you cannot access output ports and variables from the **<p:try>** subpipeline, but a port called error is available with additional information (if no error occurred, no document will appear on this port). See the section titled "Error specification" (p. 167).

Error specification

When a <p:catch> or <p:finally> executes, it has a port called error available. On this port a document with error information appears. The format of this document is always the same:

```
<c:errors>
  <c:error>*
</c:errors>
```

Table 7.21 – Child elements of <c:errors>

Child element	#	Description
c:error	*	Information about the error that occurred.

```
<c:error name? = xs:NCName
         type? = xs:QName
         code? = xs:QName
         href? = xs:anyURI
         line? = xs:integer
         column? = xs:integer
         offset? = xs:integer >
  <!-- Optional well-formed contents with more information about the error... -->
</c:error>
```

Table 7.22 – Attributes of <c:error>

Attribute	#	Type	Description
name	?	xs:NCName	The name of the step that failed. Either the value of its name or, on no name attribute, a generated name.
type	?	xs:QName	The type of the step that caused the error. For instance p:xslt or p:load.
code	?	xs:QName	The error code (if available). For instance err:XD0041.
href	?	xs:anyURI	If the error was caused by a specific document, or by the location of some erroneous construction in a specific document, this attribute holds its URI.
line	?	xs:integer	The line number in the document identified by the href attribute where the error occurred.
column	?	xs:integer	The column number in the document identified by the href attribute where the error occurred.
offset	?	xs:integer	The offset in the document identified by the href attribute where the error occurred.

The c namespace prefix is bound to the namespace http://www.w3.org/ns/xproc-step (xmlns:c="http://www.w3.org/ns/xproc-step").

The error location in a file identified with the href attribute is identified either with line and column attributes, or the offset attribute, usually not both.

Here's an example that sets the name of the error as an attribute on the root element:

Example 7.8 – Using the error specification

```
<p:try xmlns:c="http://www.w3.org/ns/xproc-step">

  … the subpipeline that might produce an error

  <p:catch name="catch-the-bloody-error">
    <p:add-attribute attribute-name="error-name" match="/*">
      <p:with-option name="attribute-value" select="/c:error/@name"
          pipe="error@catch-the-bloody-error"/>
    </p:add-attribute>
  </p:catch>

</p:try>
```

Output ports of subpipelines

Several (sub)elements of the core steps contain *subpipelines*:

- **<p:for-each>**
- <p:when> and <p:otherwise>
- **<p:if>**
- **<p:group>**
- <p:catch> and <p:finally>

A pipeline can have output ports. So how does this work for *sub*pipelines?

- If you don't explicitly define any output ports, in most cases there will be an *anonymous* output port. See the section titled "The subpipeline's anonymous output port" (p. 170).
- A subpipeline can explicitly define output ports. This is handled in the section titled "Explicitly defining output ports in subpipelines" (p. 171).

The subpipeline's anonymous output port

Let's revisit Example 7.2 (**<p:for-each>**). The subpipeline inside the **<p:for-each>** does not define an output port, but its output is still implicitly connected to the final **<p:count>** step. That's intuitively clear, but what exactly is happening here?

Assume you have a subpipeline, like Example 7.2, that meets these characteristics:

- It has not declared any explicit output ports (see the section titled "Explicitly defining output ports in subpipelines" (p. 171)).
- The last step in the subpipeline has a primary output port that is unconnected.

In that case the subpipeline will have an *anonymous* primary output port, connected to the last step's primary output port. The results of the subpipeline will appear on this port.

To illustrate this, have a look at the following (completely nonsensical) pipeline:

Example 7.9 – The subpipeline's anonymous output port in action

```
<p:declare-step xmlns:p="http://www.w3.org/ns/xproc"
  version="3.0" exclude-inline-prefixes="#all">

  <p:output port="result" sequence="true"/>

  <!-- 1 - Seed the pipeline with two documents: -->
  <p:identity>
    <p:with-input>
      <A/>
      <B/>
    </p:with-input>
  </p:identity>

  <!-- 2 - Loop over the documents, add an attribute: -->
  <p:for-each name="loop">
    <p:add-attribute attribute-name="x" attribute-value="y"/>
  </p:for-each>

  <!-- 3 - Explicitly connect to the loop's anonymous output port: -->
  <p:identity>
    <p:with-input pipe="@loop"/>
  </p:identity>

</p:declare-step>
```

1. The pipeline is seeded with two documents (`<A/>` and `<B/>`).

2. It loops over these documents using **`<p:for-each>`**. Its subpipeline, which consists of a single **`<p:add-attribute>`**, is very simple. But its final (and only) step has an unconnected primary output port.

3. The pipeline's final **`<p:identity>`** reads explicitly from the **`<p:for-each>`** subpipeline's anonymous primary output port using `<p:with-input pipe="@loop">`. That's fine, the output will be `<A x="y"/>` and `<B x="y"/>`. But if you try to connect to a *named* output port, for instance `pipe="result@loop"`, the processor will raise an error. There is no named output port, only an anonymous one.

In most cases you can forget about this anonymous port. Most of the time it is used silently. That's intuitive and fits the pattern of implicit port connections. You only need to be aware of this port when you explicitly connect to it or explicitly declare subpipeline output ports.

Explicitly defining output ports in subpipelines

Subpipelines, like the contents of **`<p:for-each>`**, can also explicitly define output ports. This feature gives you more control over what flows out of the step's primary port. For example, assume you have a **`<p:for-each>`** that ends with a **`<p:store>`** to store a result to disk (see Example 7.10).

Example 7.10 – **`<p:store>`** as the last step in a **`<p:for-each>`**

```
<p:for-each>
  …
  <p:store href="…"/>
</p:for-each>
```

What flows out of a **`<p:store>`**'s `result` port is the document that was stored, so the result of this **`<p:for-each>`** will be the sequence of stored documents.

`<p:store>` also defines another, non-primary, output port called `result-uri` on which a simple document appears containing the full URI where the document was stored (for instance `<c:result>file:/my/location/stored.xml</c:result>`).

Suppose you want the output of *this* port to appear as the result of the **<p:for-each>** step? Example 7.11 shows how to do this.

Example 7.11 – Using the `result-uri` port as the primary output of **<p:for-each>**

```
<p:for-each>
  <p:output pipe="result-uri@store-it"/>

  …
  <p:store name="store-it" href="…"/>
</p:for-each>
```

Example 7.11 defines the **<p:for-each>**'s anonymous primary output port and connects it to the **<p:store>**'s `result-uri` port.

Another application of explicitly defined output ports is to diversify the output of these steps. Suppose that somewhere in the middle of your subpipeline, you create something that should be available to steps outside of this core step). You can define additional output ports to take that output. The XProc specification provides this example (Example 7.12) for `<p:for-each>`.

Example 7.12 – Defining additional output ports in a **<p:for-each>**

```
<p:for-each name="chapters">
  <p:with-input select="//chapter"/>

  <p:output port="html-results">
    <p:pipe step="make-html" port="result"/>
  </p:output>
  <p:output port="fo-results">
    <p:pipe step="make-fo" port="result"/>
  </p:output>

  <p:xslt name="make-html">
    <p:with-input port="stylesheet" href="make-html.xsl"/>
  </p:xslt>

  <p:xslt name="make-fo">
    <p:with-input port="source" pipe="current@chapters"/>
    <p:with-input port="stylesheet" href="make-fo.xsl"/>
  </p:xslt>

</p:for-each>
```

- In Example 7.12, `<p:for-each>` receives a document with `<chapter>` elements. Each chapter must be turned into both HTML and XSL-FO, each of which goes to a different place.
- The `<for-each>` loop defines two additional output ports:
  - `html-results`, which takes its input from the `make-html.xsl` transformation
  - `fo-results`, which takes its input from the `make-fo.xsl` transformation
- On both ports a sequence of formatted documents appears.

Explicitly defining output ports for steps that have multiple subpipelines can lead to confusion: what happens when you create *different* output ports in each subpipeline, as in Example 7.13?

Example 7.13 – Creating different output ports in the sub-pipelines of a `<p:choose>`

```
<p:choose>

  <p:when test="/*/@status eq 'ok'">
    <p:output name="A">...</p:output>
    ...
  </p:when>

  <p:when test="/*/@status eq 'error'">
    <p:output name="A">...</p:output>
    <p:output name="B">...</p:output>
    ...
  </p:when>

  <p:otherwise>
    <p:output name="C">...</p:output>
    ...
  </p:otherwise>

</p:choose>
```

Does this mean that when `status="ok"` there is only output port `A`? And when `status="error"` there are output ports `A` and `B`? And otherwise you have only `C`? That would be strange, because you would run into errors if, for example, you tried to read from port `B` when `status="ok"`.

XProc's designers have taken this into account. All defined output ports are always available, no matter which branch actually executes. In Example 7.13, this means that ports `A`, `B` and `C` are always there. When the branch that defines a port doesn't execute, nothing will appear on that port.

CHAPTER 8

Built-in steps

XProc has lots of built-in steps that make your pipeline sing and dance. But there are so many that it will take you a while to get familiar with them. Appendix A, *Standard step library* and Appendix B, *Optional built-in steps overview* contain the full description of each built-in and optional step, copied from the specification.

However, I won't leave you completely at the mercy of the specification:

- Sprinkled through the book are examples of the most common built-in steps.
- The section titled "The standard step library" (p. 176) has a short description of each step.
- The section titled "Some commonly used steps" (p. 182) describes some often-used steps.
- The section titled "Common attributes" (p. 75) describes a set of common attributes that can appear on any step.
- The Step Index contains an index of all references in this book to steps (built-in and optional).

Classification of built-in steps

XProc divides its built-in steps into several categories:

- At the heart of XProc are the steps that every XProc processor *must* support: the *standard step library*. You can rely on these steps to be available, no matter what processor you use. An overview of these steps can be found in Appendix A.
- Optional steps are steps an XProc processor does not have to support. But if a processor does support an optional step, the implementation must conform to the specification.

For maintenance reasons, the optional step specifications are split into several sub-specifications.

When I wrote this book, the following sub-specifications were available:

Dynamic pipeline execution	A step for running a dynamically constructed pipeline from within another pipeline: `<p:run>` (the section titled "Dynamic pipeline execution" (p. 301)).
File steps	Steps for copying and deleting files, managing directories, etc. (the section titled "File steps" (p. 301)).
Operating system steps	Steps that interact with the processor's underlying operating system, for example, to get OS-specific information or run external commands (the section titled "Operating system steps" (p. 313)).
Mail steps	Steps (currently only one) that allow you to send email from within an XProc pipeline (the section titled "Mail steps" (p. 317)).
Paged media steps	Steps to produce paged media from XML. For instance: XSL-FO to PDF (the section titled "Paged media steps" (p. 318)).
Text steps	Steps for text handling; currently, this is just for converting Markdown to HTML (the section titled "Text steps" (p. 320)).
Validation steps	Steps for validating XML documents with XML schema, RelaxNG, or Schematron (the section titled "Validation steps" (p. 320)).

There is also a sub-specification for RDF/Semantic web steps, but it was undefined when I wrote this book. Appendix B contains descriptions of all of the optional steps.

The standard step library

The following table lists the standard built-in steps that XProc 3.0 always provides, no matter what. The observant reader will notice that the descriptions look remarkably like the ones in the specification. No surprise, they were *generated* from the specification using an XProc (1.0) pipeline (as are Appendix A and Appendix B).

Table 8.1 – The Standard Step Library

Step	Description	Page
p:add-attribute	The p:add-attribute step adds a single attribute to a set of matching elements. The input document specified on the source is processed for matches specified by the selection pattern in the match option. For each of these matches, the attribute whose name is specified by the attribute-name option is set to the attribute value specified by the attribute-value option.	229
p:add-xml-base	The p:add-xml-base step exposes the base URI via explicit xml:base attributes. The input document from the source port is replicated to the result port with xml:base attributes added to or corrected on each element as specified by the options on this step.	230
p:archive	The p:archive step outputs on its result port an archive (usually binary) document, for instance a ZIP file. A specification of the contents of the archive may be specified in a manifest XML document on the manifest port. The step produces a report on the report port, which contains the manifest, amended with additional information about the archiving.	231
p:archive-manifest	The p:archive-manifest creates an XML manifest file describing the contents of the archive appearing on its source port.	239
p:cast-content-type	The p:cast-content-type step creates a new document by changing the media type of its input. If the value of the content-type option and the current media type of the document on source port are the same, this document will appear unchanged on result port.	240
p:compare	The p:compare step compares two documents for equality.	244

Step	Description	Page
`p:compress`	The `p:compress` step serializes the document appearing on its `source` port and outputs a compressed version of this on its `result` port.	244
`p:count`	The `p:count` step counts the number of documents in the `source` input sequence and returns a single document on `result` containing that number. The generated document contains a single `c:result` element whose contents is the string representation of the number of documents in the sequence.	246
`p:delete`	The `p:delete` step deletes items specified by a selection pattern from the `source` input document and produces the resulting document, with the deleted items removed, on the `result` port.	246
`p:error`	The `p:error` step generates a dynamic error using the input provided to the step.	247
`p:filter`	The `p:filter` step selects portions of the source document based on a (possibly dynamically constructed) XPath select expression.	248
`p:hash`	The `p:hash` step generates a hash, or digital "fingerprint", for some value and injects it into the `source` document.	248
`p:http-request`	The `p:http-request` step allows authors to interact with resources over HTTP or related protocols. Implementations *must* support the `http` and `https` protocols. (Implementors are encouraged to support as many protocols as practical. In particular, pipeline authors may attempt to use `p:http-request` to load documents with computed URIs using the `file:` scheme.)	250
`p:identity`	The `p:identity` step makes a verbatim copy of its input available on its output.	258

Step	Description	Page
p:in-scope-names	The p:in-scope-names step exposes all of the in-scope variables and options as a set of parameters in a c:param-set document.	258
p:insert	The p:insert step inserts the insertion port's document into the source port's document relative to the matching elements in the source port's document.	259
p:json-join	The p:json-join step joins the sequence of documents on port source into a single JSON document (an array) appearing on port result. If the sequence on port source is empty, the empty sequence is returned on port result.	260
p:json-merge	The p:json-merge step merges the sequence of appearing on port source into a single JSON object appearing on port result. If the sequence on port source is empty, the empty sequence is returned on port result.	261
p:label-elements	The p:label-elements step generates a label for each matched element and stores that label in the specified attribute.	263
p:load	The p:load step has no inputs but produces as its result a document (or documents) specified by an IRI.	264
p:make-absolute-uris	The p:make-absolute-uris step makes an element or attribute's value in the source document an absolute IRI value in the result document.	266
p:namespace-delete	The p:namespace-delete step deletes all of the namespaces identified by the specified prefixes from the document appearing on port source.	267
p:namespace-rename	The p:namespace-rename step renames any namespace declaration or use of a namespace in a document to a new IRI value.	268

Step	Description	Page
`p:pack`	The `p:pack` step merges two document sequences in a pair-wise fashion.	270
`p:parameters`	The `p:parameters` step exposes a set of parameters as a `c:param-set` document.	271
`p:rename`	The `p:rename` step renames elements, attributes, or processing-instruction targets in a document.	273
`p:replace`	The `p:replace` step replaces matching nodes in its primary input with the top-level node(s) of the `replacement` port's document.	274
`p:set-attributes`	The `p:set-attributes` step sets attributes on matching elements.	275
`p:set-properties`	The `p:set-properties` step sets document properties on the source document.	276
`p:sink`	The `p:sink` step accepts a sequence of documents and discards them. It has no output.	277
`p:split-sequence`	The `p:split-sequence` step accepts a sequence of documents and divides it into two sequences.	277
`p:store`	The `p:store` step stores (a possibly serialized version of) its input to a URI. The input is copied to the `result` port. Additionally this step outputs a reference to the location of the stored document on the `result-uri` port.	278
`p:string-replace`	The `p:string-replace` step matches nodes in the document provided on the `source` port and replaces them with the string result of evaluating an XPath expression.	279

Step	Description	Page
`p:text-count`	The `p:text-count` step counts the number of lines in a text document and returns a single XML document containing that number.	280
`p:text-head`	The `p:text-head` step returns lines from the beginning of a text document.	280
`p:text-join`	The `p:text-join` step concatenates text documents.	281
`p:text-replace`	The `p:text-replace` step replaces all occurrences of substrings in a text document that match a supplied regular expression with a given replacement string.	282
`p:text-sort`	The `p:text-sort` step sorts lines in a text document.	283
`p:text-tail`	The `p:text-tail` step returns lines from the end of a text document.	284
`p:unarchive`	The `p:unarchive` step outputs on its `result` port specific entries in an archive (for instance from a zip file).	285
`p:uncompress`	The `p:uncompress` step expects on its `source` port a compressed document. It outputs an uncompressed version of this on its `result` port.	287
`p:unwrap`	The `p:unwrap` step replaces matched elements with their children.	288
`p:uuid`	The `p:uuid` step generates a UUID and injects it into the `source` document.	289
`p:wrap`	The `p:wrap` step wraps matching nodes in the `source` document with a new parent element.	290
`p:wrap-sequence`	The `p:wrap-sequence` step accepts a sequence of documents and produces either a single document or a new sequence of documents.	291

Step	Description	Page
p:www-form-urldecode	The p:www-form-urldecode step decodes a x-www-form-urlencoded string into a JSON representation.	292
p:www-form-urlencode	The p:www-form-urlencode step encodes a set of parameter values as a x-www-form-urlencoded string.	293
p:xinclude	The p:xinclude step applies XInclude processing to the source document.	293
p:xquery	The p:xquery step applies an XQuery query to the sequence of documents provided on the source port.	294
p:xslt	The p:xslt step invokes an XSLT stylesheet.	297

Some commonly used steps

This section describes a few of the more common XProc steps and provides some examples.

Doing nothing: <p:identity>

Full step description: the section titled "p:identity" (p. 258).

The **<p:identity>** step is a bit peculiar, it does nothing. For instance, suppose you have the following in your pipeline:

```
<p:identity/>
```

This has exactly zero effect. **<p:identity>** copies what it receives on its primary input port to its primary output port. That's it, nothing more, nothing less. How on earth can this be useful?

A common use case for **<p:identity>** is within **<p:choose>** (see the section titled "Multiple decisions: **<p:choose>** " (p. 155)), when you want nothing done on a branch (see Example 8.1).

Example 8.1 – Using **<p:identity>** in a **<p:choose>**

```
<p:choose>
  <p:when test="/*/@status eq 'production'">
    <p:identity/>
  </p:when>
  <p:when test="/*/@status eq 'test'">
    <p:add-attribute attribute-name="testmode"
      attribute-value="true"/>
  </p:when>
  <p:otherwise>
    <p:add-attribute attribute-name="timestamp"
      attribute-value="{current-dateTime()}"/>
  </p:otherwise>
</p:choose>
```

Another use case is selecting part of a document. This case (see Example 8.2) uses the `select` attribute of the `<p:with-input>`.

Example 8.2 – Using a **<p:identity>** to select part(s) of a document

```
<p:identity>
  <p:with-input select="/*/sect1"/>
</p:identity>
```

This will select every `<sect1>` element that is a child of the root node and output this on the `result` port. And yes, when there are multiple `<sect1>` elements this will split a single input document into a *sequence* of output documents.

Another example of this can be found in the section titled "Working with JSON documents" (p. 204), Example 10.8.

Some more raisons d'être for **<p:identity>** can be found in Chapter 10, the section titled "Using **<p:identity>** to clarify pipeline structure" (p. 199).

XSLT Transformation: `<p:xslt>`

Full step description: the section titled "p:xslt" (p. 297).

Most people I know who use XProc come from an XSLT background, so it's no surprise that XProc uses XSLT as a Swiss Army Knife for processing XML. With the **<p:xslt>** step you can run XSLT stylesheets on the documents flowing through your pipeline.

It's not unusual to have pipelines that consist entirely of **<p:xslt>** steps. Some problems that are hard to crack with a single stylesheet are much easier to solve by chaining XSLTs. So you may get pipelines that look like Example 8.3.

Example 8.3 – A chain of <p:xslt> steps

```
<p:declare-step xmlns:p="http://www.w3.org/ns/xproc" ...>

  <p:input port="source" primary="true"/>
  <p:output port="result" primary="true"/>

  <p:xslt>
    <p:with-input port="stylesheet" href="first-xslt.xsl"/>
  </p:xslt>

  <p:xslt>
    <p:with-input port="stylesheet" href="second-xslt.xsl"/>
  </p:xslt>

  ...

</p:declare-step>
```

The **<p:xslt>** step has two input ports and two output ports:

- The primary `source` input port receives the document to transform. Usually this will be what is flowing through the pipeline.
- The `stylesheet` port identifies the XSLT stylesheet. Usually the stylesheet is stored on disk, and its location is supplied in an `href` attribute or a `<p:document>` child element.
- The result of running the stylesheet appears on the primary `result` output port.
- The `secondary` output port emits the documents generated by the stylesheet in `<xsl:result-doument>` instructions.

If you need to use parameters in the stylesheet, you can do this by passing the `parameters` option a map (see the section titled "Map usage" (p. 60)). Example 8.4 passes something from an option value into the XSLT stylesheet.

Example 8.4 – Passing parameters to an XSLT stylesheet

```
<p:option name="parameter-to-pass-to-xslt"/>

...

<p:xslt>
  <p:with-input port="stylesheet" href="xslt-with-parameters.xsl"/>
  <p:option name="parameters"
    select="map { 'first-param'  : $parameter-to-pass-to-xslt,
                  'second-param' : 12345 }"
</p:xslt>
```

The `first-param` and `second-param` parameter are passed to the top-level stylesheet parameters. So for Example 8.4 to work, the stylesheet must contain something like:

```
<xsl:param name="first-param"/>
<xsl:param name="second-param"/>
```

Some additional things you can do in the **`<p:xslt>`** invocation include setting an initial mode or assigning an initial template to execute. See the section titled "p:xslt" (p. 297) for details.

One last thing that might be interesting for advanced stylesheet writers is what happens when *multiple documents* appear on the `source` port. An XSLT stylesheet can only process a single document, so something needs to be done. XProc solves this as follows:

- The *first* document appearing on the `source` port is used as the primary input document for the stylesheet.
- All documents (including the first one) are passed to the stylesheet as its default *collection* and can be accessed using the `collection()` function.

Adding attributes: `<p:add-attribute>` and `<p:set-attributes>`

Full step descriptions: the section titled "p:add-attribute" (p. 229) and the section titled "p:set-attributes" (p. 275).

If you need to add a single attribute to one or more elements, use the **`<p:add-attribute>`** step. Example 8.5 adds a class (passed as an option to the pipeline) to all `<h1>` elements.

Example 8.5 – Adding an attribute using the `<p:add-attribute>` step

```
<p:option name="class-value-for-h1-elements"/>

...

<p:add-attribute select="h1" attribute-name="class"
  attribute-value="{$class-value-for-h1-elements}"/>
```

The `match` option of **`<p:attribute>`** is used to find the matching elements in the document. If you don't specify it, the default value is `/*`, so your attributes will end up on the root element. There are additional options for setting the attribute's namespace and namespace prefix.

> Something I often do during development is add a *timestamp* to my output, like this:
>
> ```
> <add-attribute attribute-name="timestamp"
>   attribute-value="{current-dateTime()}"/>
> ```
>
> This allows me to easily verify that the output I'm looking at is indeed the latest output produced by the latest test run and not some cached or previously generated result.

You can set multiple attributes at the same time with the **`<p:set-attributes>`** step. This step copies all attributes from the root element of the document appearing on its `attributes` port. Example 8.6 copies the attributes `a` and `c` to all the second level elements of whatever is flowing through the pipeline.

Example 8.6 – Adding attributes using the `<p:set-attributes>` step

```
<p:set-attributes match="/*/*">
  <p:with-input port="attributes">
    <dummy a="b" c="d"/>
  </p:with-input>
</p:set-attributes>
```

Deleting stuff: `<p:delete>`

Full step description: the section titled "p:delete" (p. 246).

The **`<p:delete>`** step is simple but effective: it deletes anything in the document flowing through that matches what is specified in its `match` option. If the matched node is an element, its children are deleted also.

Example 8.7 deletes all `<div>` elements with `class="extra"` (and their contents):

Example 8.7 – Deleting elements using the `<p:delete>` step

```
<p:delete match="div[@class eq 'extra']/>
```

Inserting stuff: `<p:insert>`

Full step description: the section titled "p:insert" (p. 259).

The **`<p:insert>`** step inserts documents appearing on its `insertion` port into the documents appearing on its primary `source` port. It's often used to merge the documents flowing through subpipelines into one.

What happens when **`<p:insert>`** executes is dictated by two options:

- The `match` option tells **`<p:insert>`** *where* in the input document to do the insertion.
- The `position` option tells **`<p:insert>`** *how* to perform the insertion. Its value must be one of `first-child`, `last-child`, `before`, or `after`.

The following (not very useful but hopefully illustrative) examples (Example 8.8 and Example 8.9) show the results for two values of position

Example 8.8 – Using **<p:insert>** with position="first-child"

```
<p:insert match="B" position="first-child">
  <p:with-input port-"source">
    <A>
      <B>
        <C/>
      </B>
    </A>
  </p:with-input>
  <p:with-input port="insertion">
    <X/>
  </p:with-input>
</p:insert>
```

This results in:

```
<A>
  <B>
    <X/>
    <C/>
  </B>
</A>
```

Example 8.9 – Using **<p:insert>** with position="before"

The same as Example 8.8 but with position="before" results in:

```
<A>
  <X/>
  <B>
    <C/>
  </B>
</A>
```

Wrapping a sequence: `<p:wrap-sequence>`

Full step description: the section titled "p:wrap-sequence" (p. 291).

A common pattern in XProc pipelines is that some operation, for instance a **`<p:for-each>`** loop, produces multiple documents, but you want to put them back into a single document. That's easy, just add a **`<p:wrap-sequence>`** step (see Example 8.10).

Example 8.10 – Wrapping multiple documents into one with **`<p:wrap-sequence>`**

```
… multiple documents …

<p:wrap-sequence wrapper="new-root-element"/>

… single document …
```

If necessary you can set the namespace and namespace prefix of the wrapping element using options. For advanced usage there's also a `group-adjacent` option that allows more fine-grained control over the wrapping.

Resolving XIncludes: `<p:xinclude>`

Full step description: the section titled "p:xinclude" (p. 293).

XInclude is a standard for including documents (see the section titled "Additional resources" (p. xvii)). For instance, this book is written with every chapter in its own (DocBook) XML file to avoid overly long and hard-to-edit documents. There is an overarching book XML document that brings everything together using XInclude.

XProc makes using XInclude easy by providing a **`<p:xinclude>`** step that resolves all XIncludes in a document. For example, assume a primary document like this stored in `/some/directory`:

```
<primary xmlns:xi="http://www.w3.org/2001/XInclude">
  <xi:include href="secondary.xml"/>
</primary>
```

The `secondary.xml` document looks like this and, here, is stored in the same directory:

```
<secondary/>
```

Running the primary document through a `<p:xinclude>` step (that's all) will result in:

```
<primary xmlns:xi="http://www.w3.org/2001/XInclude">
  <secondary xml:base="file://some/directory/xinclude-secondary.xml"/>
</primary>
```

Storing documents: `<p:store>`

Full step description: the section titled "p:store" (p. 278).

It's often useful to store documents to disk from within your pipeline. For instance because your pipeline generates results and you already know where they need to be stored, instead of passing them to the outside world through output ports, you can just store them where they belong. XProc provides the `<p:store>` step for this.

For example, suppose your pipeline generates an XML document that you need to store on disk, and the storage location has been computed by the pipeline and stored in the `location` attribute on the root element of the document. Example 8.11 shows how you can use this value to store the document in the right place (all non-existent directories in the specified path are tacitly created).

Example 8.11 – Example of storing a document using `<p:store>`

```
<p:store href="{/*/@location}"/>
```

You can pass serialization options, which determine how things will be stored, using `<p:store>`'s `serialization` option, or you can use the document's `serialization` property. See the section titled "Specifying serialization" (p. 95) for details.

What flows out of `<p:store>`'s `result` port is exactly the same as what flows in on its `source` port. In other words, inside your pipeline `<p:store>` acts like a `<p:identity>` step. This is handy for situations, such as debugging, where you want to know what's flowing through the pipeline at a certain point. Just add a `<p:store>` that stores the document flowing through somewhere and inspect it. See also the section titled "Debugging hints" (p. 225).

In XProc 1.0 the `<p:store>` step behaved differently: The `result` port emitted a document containing the absolute URI of the document stored by the step. You can still access this information using the `result-uri` port (see below), but be aware of this change if you're converting 1.0 pipelines into 3.0.

There is a second output port called `result-uri` that will emit an XML document existing of a single `<c:result>` element whose content is the absolute URI of the document stored by the step (for instance `<c:result>file:/my/dir/stored-file.xml</c:result>`).

Changing a document's type: `<p:cast-content-type>`

Full step description: the section titled "p:cast-content-type" (p. 240).

A new kid on the XProc block is **`<p:cast-content-type>`**. It's something of a conversion Swiss Army Knife. You put in a document of type X, specify you need it in type Y and there it is! It can't do everything, but the list of things it *can* do is impressive. For instance, if you have JSON and need XML, Example 8.12 will do the conversion

Example 8.12 – Converting JSON into XML using **`<p:cast-content-type>`**

```
… JSON data flowing

<p:cast-content-type content-type="text/xml"/>

… XML data flowing
```

For the other way around, specify `content-type="application/json"`. Please have a look at its specification for all the wonderful things **`<p:cast-content-type>`** can do for you.

CHAPTER 9

Extension functions

XProc has a set of *extension functions* you can use in XPath expressions. These functions allow you to do things like finding out which XProc processor you're running, determining what iteration your **`<p:for-each>`** loop is in, or working with document properties.

In addition to the functions mentioned here, your XProc processor may provide other, implementation-defined functions. These functions will not be in the XProc namespace. Check your XProc processor's documentation to see if there's anything useful for you.

Environment information related functions

The following functions return information about your XProc processor and the pipeline running:

```
p:system-property($property as xs:string) as xs:string
```

Properties recognized by this function are:

Table 9.1 – Property values for the `p:system-property()`

Property	Description
`p:episode`	Returns a unique string for each invocation of the pipeline processor.
`p:locale`	Returns a string which identifies the language set by the environment (usually the operating system). Use this, for instance, to localize messages.
`p:product-name`	Returns a string containing the name of the XProc processor. This remains constant from one release of the product to the next and across platforms.
`p:product-version`	Returns a string identifying the version of the XProc processor.
`p:vendor`	Returns string identifying the vendor of the XProc processor.

Property	Description
`p:vendor-uri`	Returns a URI which identifies the vendor of the XProc processor, usually the vendor's web site.
`p:version`	Returns the version(s) of XProc implemented by the processor, as a space-separated list. For example, a processor that supports XProc 1.0 would return `'1.0'` and a processor that supports XProc 1.0 and 3.0 would return `'1.0 3.0'`
`p:xpath-version`	Returns the version(s) of XPath implemented by the XProc processor, as a space-separated list. For example, a processor that only supports XPath 3.1 would return `'3.1'` and a processor that supports both XPath 2.0 and 3.1 would return `'2.0 3.1'`.
`p:psvi-supported`	Returns `true` if the implementation supports passing PSVI ("Post Schema Validation Infoset") annotations between steps, `false` otherwise. For more information see the `psvi-required` attribute on `<p:declare-step>` (the section titled "Declaring a step: `<p:declare-step>` " (p. 80)).

`p:step-available($step-name as xs:string) as xs:boolean`

Returns `true` if a particular type of step is understood by the processor.

For instance, `p:step-available('p:identity')` always returns `true`, but the return value of `p:step-available('p:exec')` depends on your processor because **`<p:exec>`** is optional.

`p:version-available($version as xs:string) as xs:boolean`

Returns `true` when the specified XProc version is supported by the processor. Otherwise, it returns `false`.

`p:xpath-version-available($version as xs:string) as xs:boolean`

Returns `true` when the specified XPath version is supported by the XProc processor. Otherwise, it returns `false`.

`p:function-library-importable($library-type as xs:string) as xs:boolean`

This function tells you whether function libraries of a certain type can be imported, understood, and used by the XProc processor. See the section titled "Importing function libraries: `<p:import-functions>`" (p. 108) for more information.

The `$library-type` argument must be the MIME type of the library. Likely values are `application/xslt+xml` or `application/xquery`.

All functions in this section are available for use in `[p:]use-when` decisions (the section titled "The `[p:]use-when` attribute" (p. 75)) and when specifying the (default) value for static options (the section titled "Static options" (p. 105)).

Iteration related functions

`<p:for-each>` and `<p:viewport>` process a sequence of documents. The following functions provide information about where the document currently being processed is in the sequence and how big the sequence is. They are similar to the `position()` and `last()` functions in XPath.

`p:iteration-position() as xs:integer`

Inside a `<p:for-each>` or `<p:viewport>`, this function returns the position of the current document in the sequence of documents being processed. The first document has position 1, the second has position 2, etc.

```
p:iteration-size() as xs:integer
```

Inside a `<p:for-each>` or `<p:viewport>`, this function returns the total number of documents in the sequence that is processed.

Document properties related functions

The following functions support processing the properties of a document flowing through the pipeline (see the section titled "Representations and properties" (p. 37)).

```
p:document-properties($doc as document-node()) as map(xs:QName, item()*)
```

Returns the properties of `$doc` as a map (see the section titled "Map usage" (p. 60)).

```
p:document-property($doc as document-node(), $key as item()) as item()*
```

Returns a single value from the document properties of `$doc`. If the property `$key` does not exist it returns the empty sequence.

For instance, assume you want to do something based on the MIME type of the document flowing through:

```
<p:choose>
  <p:when test="p:document-property(/, 'content-type') eq 'text/xml'">
    …
  </p:when>
  <p:otherwise>
    …
  </p:otherwise>
</p:choose>
```

Other functions

`p:urify($filepath as xs:string, $basedir as xs:string?) as xs:string`

This function turns a file system path into a usable URI on the platform that the processor is running on. It's a convenience function for transforming OS-specific paths into something the processor can use.

A use case might be an XProc pipeline called from an OS batch/command script. This script passes (as an option) a filename, for instance the name of a file to write a result to. However, straight filenames are not always usable by XProc processors. For instance, some processors may want `file:/` appended in front. `p:urify()` makes sure the processor can use the filename.

The specification for `p:urify()` leaves a lot of the exact functionality open and contains many "may" and "implementation dependent" phrases. It can take some experimenting to grasp whether and how the function is useful for you. Here are some highlights:

- The files/directories do not need to actually exist. This function mainly juggles strings.
- When the result is a directory name, `p:urify()` may add a `/` as the last character.
- When `$filepath` contains a relative path, it is resolved against the location provided in `$basedir`. When `$basedir` is empty, the current working directory is used for this.
- Windows and Unix-like file system addressing schemes (including Apple's OS X) must be supported. Support for rarer types, such as VMS, is optional.
- On Windows, slashes and backslashes are considered equivalent.
- The function may try to interpret and remove path components like `.` or `..`
- Whatever comes out may not be a correct URI, but it should be usable by the processor to access a resource on disk.

Table 9.2 shows some examples. In the OS column, W=Windows and U=Unix. In the file and directory names, ... represents the current working directory.

Table 9.2 – Examples of `p:urify()` processing

OS	Input(s)	Possible results

W	`c:\path\to\file`	`file:///c:/path/to/file`
		`file:///C:/path/to/file`
		`file:///c:/path/to/file/` (if it's a directory)

W	`\\hostname\path\to\file`
	`\\hostname/path/to/file`
	`//hostname/path/to/file`
		`file://hostname/path/to/file`

W	`C:/Program Files (x86)`	`file:///C:/Program%20Files%20(x86)` `file:///C:/Program%20Files%20(x86)/`
W	`temp, /`	`file:///C:/temp` `file:///C:/temp/`
W	`[workspace], E:\temp`	`file:///E:/temp/%5Bworkspace%5D` `file:///E:/temp/%5Bworkspace%5D/`
W, U	`@50%.csv`	…`/@50%25.csv`
W, U	`@50%25.csv`	…`/@50%2525.csv`
U	`/etc`	`file:///etc` `file:///etc/`
U	`/etc?foo=bar#fragment`	`file:///etc%3Ffoo=bar%23fragment`

CHAPTER 10

XProc examples and recipes

This chapter contains some examples and recipes using XProc. You can find some of them in a GitHub repository. See the section titled "Using and finding code examples" (p. xvii) for details.

Using <p:identity> to clarify pipeline structure

In the section titled "A word upfront: understandable steps" (p. 115), I showed that XProc code is not always easy to read and understand. How information flows and how ports connect is not always obvious. Since most code spends more time being maintained than being developed, it makes sense to pay attention to clarity and understandability.

The section titled "Doing nothing: **<p:identity>** " (p. 182) introduced the **<p:identity>** step, which does nothing but still serves a useful purpose. The following two examples show how it can clarify code.

Example 10.1 – Supplying a fixed document to the first step's primary input port

```
<p:declare-step xmlns:p="http://www.w3.org/ns/xproc">

  <p:input port="source" primary="true"/>
  <p:output port="result" primary="true"/>

  <!-- Start with starting document: -->
  <some-first-step>
    <p:with-input port="source">
      <starting-document>
        …
      </starting-document>
    </p:with-input>
  </some-first-step>

  <some-second-step>
    …
  </some-second-step>
  …
</p:declare-step>
```

In Example 10.1 the pipeline starts with a fixed document (e.g., a template) included inside the first step using `<p:with-input>`, which supplies the document to the primary input port of the first step.

However, you can also make the creation of this starting document more explicit by giving it its own step using **`<p:identity>`** (see Example 10.2).

Example 10.2 – Starting with a fixed document by creating it using `<p:identity>`

```
<p:declare-step xmlns:p="http://www.w3.org/ns/xproc">

  <p:input port="source" primary="true"/>
  <p:output port="result" primary="true"/>

  <!-- Generate starting document: -->
  <p:identity>
    <p:with-input port="source">
      <starting-document>
        …
      </starting-document>
    </p:with-input>
  </p:identity>

  <some-first-step>
    …
  </some-first-step>

  <some-second-step>
    …
  </some-second-step>

  …

</p:declare-step>
```

Whether you prefer Example 10.1 or Example 10.2 is, of course, personal, but I think Example 10.2 makes the innards of the pipeline more explicit and, therefore, easier to understand by somebody else or yourself in a few months time. That's well worth the couple of extra lines.

You can also use **<p:identity>** in pipelines to make connections clearer. Example 10.3 contains a pipeline that shows one way to take the output of one step and feed it into two other steps.

Example 10.3 – Directly feeding the output of a step into multiple other steps

```
<p:declare-step xmlns:p="http://www.w3.org/ns/xproc">

  ...

  <some-step name="create-important-intermediate-result">
    ...
  </some-step>

  ...

  <some-other-step-1>
    <p:with-input port="source"
                  pipe="result@create-important-intermediate-result"/>
    ...
  </some-other-step-1>

  ...

  <some-other-step-2>
    <p:with-input port="source"
                  pipe="result@create-important-intermediate-result"/>
    ...
  </some-other-step-2>

</p:declare-step>
```

However, you can make the existence of this very important intermediate result even clearer by inserting a (commented) **<p:identity>** step that reads it from the result output port of the previous step and names it for further use (see Example 10.4).

Example 10.4 – Using a `<p:identity>` step to mark the important intermediate result

```
<p:declare-step xmlns:p="http://www.w3.org/ns/xproc">
  …
  <some-step>
    …
  </some-step>

  <!-- We now have created our important intermediate result that … -->
  <p:identity name="important-intermediate-result"/>

  …

  <some-other-step-1>
    <p:with-input port="source" pipe="result@important-intermediate-result"/>
    …
  </some-other-step-1>

  …

  <some-other-step-2>
    <p:with-input port="source" pipe="result@important-intermediate-result"/>
    …
  </some-other-step-2>

</p:declare-step>
```

This has the additional advantage that if you need to change the steps that create your important intermediate result—maybe you need one more step after **`<some-step>`**—you don't have to bother with changing `name` attributes.

Since you're reading from the primary output port of **`<p:identity>`**, one more improvement would be to shorten both `pipe` attributes to `pipe="@important-intermediate-result"`. For me, this makes the connections even clearer: the pattern your eyes are searching for when reading the code is now almost the same in both the `name` and the `pipe` attributes.

Working with document-properties

As explained in the section titled "Representations and properties" (p. 37) and the section titled "Document properties" (p. 63), documents flowing through XProc pipelines carry properties: name-value pairs that you can use in your pipeline to carry additional information or base decisions on. But when? And how?

XProc pre-defines three document properties: `base-uri`, `content-type`, and `serialization`. An obvious application is to use `content-type` when processing multiple documents. A pipeline could, for instance, fetch all files in a directory and do different things with them, depending on their MIME type. This scenario is elaborated in the section titled "Working with other documents" (p. 212).

But what if you want to add your own document properties? For instance, suppose that somewhere in a complicated pipeline you load an important document, and further down the line, you need to know that it is a specific important document. Example 10.5 shows how you can do this.

Example 10.5 – Setting a document property on load

```
<p:declare-step xmlns:p="http://www.w3.org/ns/xproc">

  ...

  <!-- Load the important document: -->
  <p:load href="/some/important/file.xml"
    document-properties="map{ 'status': 'important' }"/>

  ...

  <!-- Base the processing on whether the document is important: -->
  <p:choose>
    <p:when test="p:document-property(., 'status') eq 'important'">
      <!-- Process important documents: -->
      ...
    </p:when>
    <p:otherwise>
      <!-- Process non-important documents: -->
      ...
    </p:otherwise>
  </p:choose>

  ...

</p:declare-step>
```

Example 10.5 shows how to set a document property on load. But what if you want to add a property to a document that is already flowing through the pipeline? For this XProc has the **`<p:set-properties>`** step (see Example 10.6).

Example 10.6 – Setting a property on a document flowing through the pipeline

```
<p:declare-step xmlns:p="http://www.w3.org/ns/xproc">

  …

  <!-- Mark the document flowing here as important: -->
  <p:set-properties properties="map{ 'status': 'important' }" merge="true"/>

  …

</p:declare-step>
```

Notice the `merge="true"` attribute. This tells **`<p:set-properties>`** to leave any existing properties alone and simply add the supplied ones (overwriting existing properties with the same name). If you specify `merge="false"`, all existing properties (including `base-uri`) will be removed, except for `content-type`. `content-type` can't be set, overwritten, or deleted. Even when you specify `merge="false"` it will stay put. Trying to change its value results in an error.

Working with JSON documents

Some XML folks may loath this, but working with JSON is unavoidable these days. It's everywhere and especially in web interfaces. So XProc tried to cater for this and added facilities that make it possible to process JSON documents.

As explained in the section titled "JSON documents" (p. 66), JSON documents flow through the pipeline as one of the data structures you're used to working with in XPath expressions: a JSON object becomes a map, a JSON array becomes an array, etc. JSON data can be inspected and manipulated using XPath expressions. Let's have a look at how this works.[1]

The website Star Wars API,[2] serves Star Wars facts and trivia through a JSON REST API. If you surf to https://swapi.co/api/people/ (use a normal browser), you get a partial list of people in the Star Wars universe in JSON format (see Example 10.7).

---

[1] This section is based on a demo given by Achim Berndzen at XML Prague 2019.

[2] https://swapi.co/

Example 10.7 – JSON Star Wars information (shortened)

```
{
    "count": 87,
    "next": "https://swapi.co/api/people/?page=2",
    "previous": null,
    "results": [
        {
            "name": "Luke Skywalker",
            "height": "172",
            "mass": "77",
            "hair_color": "blond",
            "skin_color": "fair",
            "eye_color": "blue",
            "birth_year": "19BBY",
            "gender": "male",
            "homeworld": "https://swapi.co/api/planets/1/",
            "films": [
                "https://swapi.co/api/films/2/",
            ...
        },
        {
            "name": "C-3PO",
            ...
        },
        ...
    ]
}
```

This list is not complete, it only gives you the first 10 names. It also provides you with the URL to load the next 10 names: `"next": "https://swapi.co/api/people/?page=2"`. This page again has a `"next":` ... entry. This goes on until you see (at page 9) `"next": null`.

OK, let's set ourselves to the task creating a single list of names from these pages. Simply loading the JSON from Example 10.7 into a pipeline is easy (see Example 10.8).

Example 10.8 – Loading the initial JSON (`$SOURCES/examples/working-with-json/starwars-01.xpl`)

```
<p:declare-step xmlns:p="http://www.w3.org/ns/xproc" version="3.0">

  <p:output port="result"/>

  <p:load href="https://swapi.co/api/people"/>

</p:declare-step>
```

If you run this (please do), you'll see the JSON from Example 10.7 (but not as nicely formatted). However, this does not do anything very interesting. Let's start by loading all the additional pages.

One way to do this is to create a subpipeline (the *loader*) that loads a document and inspects it to check whether it references a next document. If so it calls itself recursively to load that one. The result is a sequence of documents (see Example 10.9).

Example 10.9 – Loading the initial JSON
(`$SOURCES/examples/working-with-json/starwars-02.xpl`)

```
<p:declare-step xmlns:p="http://www.w3.org/ns/xproc"
  xmlns:ex="#examples" version="3.0">

  <!-- 1 - Define the output port as a sequence: -->
  <p:output port="result" sequence="true"/>

  <!-- 2 - Define a subpipeline that will call itself recursively to
          load all the documents: -->
  <p:declare-step type="ex:loader">
    <p:output port="result" sequence="true" content-types="json"/>
    <p:option name="url" required="true"/>

    <!-- 3 - Load the requested document: -->
    <p:load href="{$url}"/>
    <!-- 4 - Put the address of the next page in a variable: -->
    <p:variable name="next-url" select=".('next')"/>
    <!-- 5 - If the next page's URL is not (), get it: -->
    <p:if test="$next-url">
      <!-- 6 - Output the loaded document and the next document(s): -->
      <p:output port="result" sequence="true">
        <p:pipe step="copy" port="result"/>
        <p:pipe step="next" port="result"/>
      </p:output>
      <p:identity name="copy"/>
      <ex:loader name="next" url="{$next-url}"/>
    </p:if>
  </p:declare-step>

  <!-- 7 - Call the loader to get all the documents: -->
  <ex:loader url="https://swapi.co/api/people"/>

</p:declare-step>
```

1. Example 10.9 emits a *sequence* of documents (all the JSON documents with people information). Therefore, you have to adjust the output port's type and add a `sequence="true"` attribute to allow this.
2. At the top of the pipeline, define a child pipeline/step that will load the documents. The `type` attribute gives it its name: `type="ex:loader"`. The namespace prefix `ex` is defined at the root element and refers to the (bogus) namespace `#examples`. You can use any namespace except the XProc `p` namespace.
3. Load the document from the URL passed in by the `url` option.
4. Now you need the value of the URL for the next page. But how do you get this? The documents the Star Wars API returns are JSON *objects*. A JSON object flows through an XProc pipeline as an XDM *map*. This map will be the expression *context item* and, therefore, can be addressed by the "dot" (`.`) operator. Knowing that, you can get the value of this map's `next` entry with `.('next')`. Other expressions giving the same result are `map:get(., 'next')` and the terse `.?next`.
5. Then, check whether the `$next-url` variable has a value. A JSON `"next": null` entry will cause the value of `$next-url` to become the empty sequence `()`. This, in turn, stops the subpipeline inside the **`<p:if>`** from executing. This stops the recursion, because the **`<p:if>`** acts like the **`<p:identity>`** step (see the section titled "Single decision: **`<p:if>`** " (p. 159))
6. Each time it is called, the output of the **`<p:if>`** step is the document it received as input followed by the document referred to in `$next-url` (if any). Therefore, you need to give the **`<p:if>`** step an output port that outputs what flowed in followed by the result of recursively loading the next document. Notice that:
   - The output port will emit multiple documents. Therefore, you must set it to `sequence="true"`.
   - The output port has no `primary="true"` attribute. You could add it, but since it's the *only* output port, it's primary by default.
   - The output port has *two* `<p:pipe>` children. One refers to the **`<p:identity>`** step that copies the **`<p:if>`**'s input, and the other refers to the next recursive `ex:loader` step. Having multiple `<p:pipe>` elements on the output port is fine. When you do that, the port will output multiple documents.
7. After defining the `ex:loader` step, the only thing left is to call it in the main pipeline.

If you run Example 10.9, it will emit a sequence of nine JSON documents with information about the Star Wars cast. But the mission was to get the *names* of the characters. To do this, you can add a **<p:identity>** step that performs the extraction expression on every document in turn. Example 10.10 shows how to do this.

Example 10.10 – Loading the initial JSON
($SOURCES/examples/working-with-json/starwars-03.xpl)

```
<p:declare-step xmlns:p="http://www.w3.org/ns/xproc"
  xmlns:ex="#examples" version="3.0">

  <p:output port="result" sequence="true"/>

  <p:declare-step type="ex:loader">
    <p:output port="result" sequence="true" content-types="json"/>
    <p:option name="url" required="true"/>

    <p:load href="{$url}"/>
    <p:variable name="next-url" select=".('next')"/>
    <p:if test="exists($next-url)">
      <p:output port="result" sequence="true">
        <p:pipe step="copy" port="result"/>
        <p:pipe step="next" port="result"/>
      </p:output>
      <p:identity name="copy"/>
      <ex:loader name="next" url="{$next-url}"/>
    </p:if>
  </p:declare-step>

  <ex:loader url="https://swapi.co/api/people"/>

  <p:identity>
    <p:with-input select="for $someone in array:flatten(.('results'))
                          return $someone('name')"/>
  </p:identity>

</p:declare-step>
```

The expression `select="for $someone in array:flatten(.('results')) return $someone('name')"` probably needs some further explanation:

- Every document in the input is a JSON object and, therefore, becomes an XDM map. The people information inside this object/map is in its `results` entry. You can get that information with `.('results')`.
- The value of this `results` entry is an array. Every entry in the array describes a Star Wars character. You need to iterate over all the entries in the array to get all the names. In XPath, you can't easily iterate over an array, but it is easy to iterate over a sequence. Therefore, *flatten* the array into a sequence with `array:flatten(.('results'))` and then iterate over the sequence using an XPath `for` expression.
- Every Star Wars character is described by a JSON object in the array. From this you can extract and return the `name` entry.

Now you can turn the list of names into an XML document and create a nice looking (X)HTML page. I will leave the second step to you.

You can accomplish the first step by adding the following lines after the last **`<p:identity>`** step in Example 10.10 (the full code is in `$SOURCES/examples/working-with-json/starwars-04.xpl`):

```
<p:json-join/>
<p:cast-content-type content-type="application/xml"/>
```

`<p:json-join>` joins all of the JSON documents into a single array. You can then use **`<p:cast-content-type content-type="application/xml">`** to turn the array into an XML document. Finally, You can use a **`<p:xslt>`** step to run an XSLT to generate (X)HTML.

Working with text documents

XProc can also handle text-only documents, such as command files, shell scripts, CSV data, or Markdown. Text can flow through XProc pipelines (the section titled "Text documents" (p. 41)) as a native format. You have several options for processing text:

- The standard step library (Chapter 8) contains steps (all named **<p:text-...>**) for manipulating text. For example, the **<p:text-head>** step returns the first x lines from the beginning of a text document (or all lines *except* the first x). There is also a **<p:text-tail>**. Other things you can do include sorting, joining, and manipulating with regular expressions.

  For instance, Example 10.11 takes a text document and removes all of the lines that start with a pound (#) sign (in script files these are often comments).

  Example 10.11 – Remove lines that start with a # in text files (`$SOURCES/examples/working-with-text/text-01.xpl`)

  ```
  <p:declare-step xmlns:p="http://www.w3.org/ns/xproc" version="3.0">

    <p:input port="source" content-types="text"/>
    <p:output port="result" content-types="text"/>

    <p:text-replace pattern="^.*#.*$" replacement="" flags="m"/>
  </p:declare-step>
  ```

  Notice that the `source` and `result` ports both have the `content-types="text"` attribute, which says the ports will only accept text documents. This attribute is not strictly necessary, but using it explicitly defines what this pipeline can handle and causes the pipeline to raise an error if the input is a non-text document.

  The **<p:text-replace>** step is modelled after the XPath `replace()` function and uses the same options (`flags="m"`, for instance, means "multi-line mode").

- There are some optional steps for working with text documents (see the section titled "Text steps" (p. 320)). For instance, the **<p:markdown-to-html>** does what it name implies; it attempts to convert a text document in Markdown syntax into XHTML.
- For more advanced text processing, you can also use XSLT 3.0. Let's do this and create a pipeline that outputs text as separate `<line>` elements, removing lines that are empty or contain only whitespace (see Examples 10.12 and 10.13).

Example 10.12 – Pipeline that uses XSLT to process text
($SOURCES/examples/working-with-text/text-02.xpl)

```
<p:declare-step xmlns:p="http://www.w3.org/ns/xproc" version="3.0">

  <p:input port="source" content-types="text"/>
  <p:output port="result" content-types="xml"/>

  <p:xslt>
    <p:with-input port="stylesheet" href="text-02.xsl"/>
  </p:xslt>

</p:declare-step>
```

In Example 10.13, the text document is passed to the XSLT stylesheet (Example 10.13) as a single text node.

Example 10.13 – XSLT stylesheet that processes text
($SOURCES/examples/working-with-text/text-02.xsl)

```
<xsl:stylesheet xmlns:xsl="http://www.w3.org/1999/XSL/Transform"
  exclude-result-prefixes="#all"
  version="3.0" expand-text="true">

  <xsl:template match="/">
    <lines>
      <xsl:apply-templates/>
    </lines>
  </xsl:template>

  <xsl:template match="text()">
   <xsl:for-each select="tokenize(., '[&#10;&#13;]+')[normalize-space(.) ne '']">
      <line>{.}</line>
    </xsl:for-each>
  </xsl:template>

</xsl:stylesheet>
```

The first `<xsl:template>` in Example 10.13 matches the document node and creates the root element (`<lines>`). The second `<xsl:template>` matches the (only) text node, which contains the document's text.

It then does the following:

- Tokenizes the input on line boundaries (the regular expression `[

]+` matches a succession of one or more carriage-returns and/or line-feeds)
- Checks whether the line contains anything other than whitespace. The predicate is: `[normalize-space(.) ne '']`.
- Outputs the resulting lines wrapped in a `<line>` element.

Working with other documents

Any document can flow through an XProc pipeline, including binary files. However, there's not much you can do with a binary file. The only steps (currently) that do something with binary documents are **`<p:archive>`**, **`<p:compress>`**, and **`<p:uncompress>`**.

However, one thing you can do with any document is to use the `content-type` property to base actions on. Example 10.14 takes all of the documents in a directory as input and copies them into separate output directories based on content type.

Example 10.14 – Pipeline that sorts files based on their content-type (`$SOURCES/examples/working-with-others/others-01.xpl`)

```
<p:declare-step xmlns:p="http://www.w3.org/ns/xproc"
  xmlns:c="http://www.w3.org/ns/xproc-step" version="3.0">

  <!-- 1 - Define an output port for a simple report document.
    We don't need an input port -->
  <p:output port="result"/>

  <!-- 2 - Define options to pass in the input and output base directory -->
  <p:option name="input-directory" select="'input'"/>
  <p:option name="output-base-directory" select="'output'"/>

  <!-- 3 - Create a list of files in the input directory -->
  <p:directory-list path="{$input-directory}"/>

  <!-- 4 - Loop over all files in the input directory -->
  <p:for-each>
    <p:with-input select="//c:file"/>

    <!-- 5 - Load the file and determine its content-type -->
    <p:variable name="filename" select="/*/@name"/>
    <p:load href="{$input-directory}/{$filename}"/>
    <p:variable name="content-type"
                select="p:document-property(., 'content-type')"/>

    <!-- 6 - Based on the content type, store the document in a
      particular directory -->
    <p:choose>
      <p:when test="$content-type eq 'application/xml'">
        <p:store href="{$output-base-directory}/xml/{$filename}"/>
      </p:when>
      <p:when test="$content-type eq 'image/jpeg'">
        <p:store href="{$output-base-directory}/jpg/{$filename}"/>
      </p:when>
      <p:otherwise>
        <p:store href="{$output-base-directory}/junk/{$filename}"/>
      </p:otherwise>
    </p:choose>

  </p:for-each>

  <!-- 7 - Just return the number of processed documents -->
  <p:count/>

</p:declare-step>
```

1. Define a `result` output port to emit a report on what's done. There's no input data, so there's no input port.
2. Define options for the name of the input directory and the base name of the output directory. Both options specify a default (the `select` attributes). The default names are relative paths, which means they will be resolved based on the location of the pipeline.
3. **`<p:directory-list>`** gets a list of the files in the input directory. The result (with the files provided in the example environment) will be:

```
<c:directory xml:base="…" name="input"
xmlns:c="http://www.w3.org/ns/xproc-step">
  <c:file xml:base="dummy.xml" name="dummy.xml"/>
  <c:file xml:base="kanava.jpg" name="kanava.jpg"/>
  <c:file xml:base="xproc-logo-old.png" name="xproc-logo-old.png"/>
</c:directory>
```

`<p:directory-list>` is an optional step, so your XProc processor might not support it. However, given the broad applicability of this function, it's likely your processor will support it.[3]

4. The **`<p:for-each>`** dissects the output of **`<p:directory-list>`** into separate `<c:file>` entries and loops over them.
5. The file is loaded using **`<p:load>`**. As part of that step, the XProc processor determines the content-type and stores it in the document properties (the section titled "Document properties" (p. 63)). The `content-type` property is then retrieved using an XProc-specific function (the section titled "Document properties related functions" (p. 196)) and stored in the variable `content-type`.
6. Based on the contents of this variable, the **`<p:choose>`** step stores the documents in different output directories.
7. **`<p:choose>`** emits the document it stored, so the result of the **`<p:for-each>`** will be the sequence of documents from the input directory, which is not useful here. To produce a simple report, **`<p:count>`** counts the processed documents and outputs and emits:

```
<c:result>3</c:result>
```

[3] In case you're wondering why it is optional, as are all file/directory related steps, XProc's designers wanted the language to be useful in all environments, including ones that don't have files or directories (like an industrial Programmable Logic Controller).

Working with zip archives

I suppose everyone uses zip files (a.k.a. archives) now and then. The zip format can store multiple files/directories into a single file *and* compress the data. It has many applications: sending a whole directory tree by mail, archiving old projects, etc.

An important application of the zip format is as an overarching storage format for applications. If your application needs multiple files, but you want the user to see only one, you can use the zip format as a container. For instance, most office suites do this: a Microsoft Word `.docx` or Excel `.xlsx` file is actually a zip file with many smaller files inside (most of them in XML format). The ePub ebook format is another example, and there are many more.

XProc is an excellent language for handling zip files. For example, you can extract Microsoft Excel data into a format that's easier to process, turn Word files into DocBook (or the other way around), etc. Given the complexity of the Microsoft Word formats, this is not for the faint of heart, but it certainly can be done.

Let's built a modest application with the following functionality to show how XProc can work with zip files:

- Take a zip archive as input and determine if the file `demo.html` is present in its root. For this demo, I created an HTML page that references an image that is also in the zip (have a look inside `$SOURCES/examples/working-with-zip/input/processable.zip`).
- If `demo.html` is not present, raise an error.
- If `demo.html` file is present, change it slightly and add a reference to another image.
- Produce a new zip archive containing the changes and the new image.

Inspect a zip archive

The first thing to do is inspect the incoming zip archive to check whether `demo.html` is present. For this XProc offers the **`<p:archive-manifest>`** step (see the section titled "p:archive-manifest" (p. 239)). Example 10.15 does this.

Example 10.15 – Pipeline that gets a zip file manifest (`$SOURCES/examples/working-with-zip/zip-01.xpl`)

```
<p:declare-step xmlns:p="http://www.w3.org/ns/xproc" version="3.0">

  <p:input port="source" href="input/processable.zip"/>
  <p:output port="result"/>

  <p:archive-manifest/>

</p:declare-step>
```

A default input file is connected to this pipeline's `source` primary input port, using an `href` attribute on `<p:input>` (see the section titled "Declaring input ports: `<p:input>`" (p. 86)). This is not essential. It's just there for convenience so you can run the pipeline without specifying the input file on the command line.

Example 10.16 shows the results of this pipeline.

Example 10.16 – The manifest for the example archive

```
<c:archive xmlns:c="http://www.w3.org/ns/xproc-step">
  <c:entry name="demo.html"
    href="$SOURCES/examples/working-with-zip/input/processable.zip/demo.html"
    method="deflated" size="282"
    compressed-size="177" time="2019-10-16T09:00:03+02:00"/>
  <c:entry name="img/kanava.jpg"
   href="$SOURCES/examples/working-with-zip/input/processable.zip/img/kanava.jpg"
    method="deflated" size="1101181"
    compressed-size="364737" time="2019-03-14T15:22:48+01:00"/>
</c:archive>
```

The string `$SOURCES` in Example 10.16 is a placeholder here. When you run this example, the result will be the path to where you stored your examples.

The XML returned is in the archive manifest format (see the section titled "p:archive" (p. 231)). This format has more applications that I will get to shortly.

The manifest shows the following:

- The zip file contains two files: `demo.html` and `img/kanava.jpg`.
- The `href` attribute contains the value for the base URI of the file, once it has been extracted from the archive by **`<p:unarchive>`**.
- There's additional data available about things such as the file sizes and dates/times, but I'm going to ignore that information for now.

You can use the manifest to check whether `demo.html` is present and raise an error if it isn't.

Example 10.17 – Pipeline that checks whether demo.html is present in the zip archive (`$SOURCES/examples/working-with-zip/zip-02.xpl`)

```
<p:declare-step xmlns:p="http://www.w3.org/ns/xproc"
  xmlns:c="http://www.w3.org/ns/xproc-step" version="3.0">

  <p:input port="source" href="input/processable.zip"/>
  <p:output port="result"/>

  <!-- Test for the main file being present: -->
  <p:archive-manifest/>
  <p:if test="empty(/c:archive/c:entry[@name eq 'demo.html'])">
    <p:error code="no-demo-html">
      <p:with-input>
        <message>The ZIP file does not contain the correct file.</message>
      </p:with-input>
    </p:error>
  </p:if>

</p:declare-step>
```

When you run this, nothing changes. The output will still be the archive's manifest because the test expression of the **`<p:if>`** returns `false` (`demo.html` is present), which makes it behave as a **`<p:identity>`** step. The result of **`<p:archive-manifest>`** simply falls through and gets emitted on the `result` port.

If you run this with a zip file that does *not* have a file named `demo.html` in its root, you'll get an error message. To see what happens in this case, change the `href` attribute of `<p:input>` to `href="input/not-processable.zip"`.

Extract and change a file from a zip archive

Next let's extract `demo.html` from the zip and change it. Be warned: later on, I am going to abandon the approach described in this section because it does not help with the goal of creating an amended zip file. However, Example 10.18 nicely illustrates some useful things you can do with zip files, so it is worth exploring in its own right.

Example 10.18 – Pipeline that extracts demo.html from the zip archive and changes it (`$SOURCES/examples/working-with-zip/zip-03.xpl`)

```
<p:declare-step xmlns:p="http://www.w3.org/ns/xproc"
  xmlns:c="http://www.w3.org/ns/xproc-step" version="3.0">

  <p:input port="source" href="input/processable.zip"/>
  <p:output port="result"/>

  <!-- Identify the main zip file: -->
  <p:identity name="original-zip-file"/>

  <!-- Test for the main file being present: -->
  <p:archive-manifest/>
  <p:if test="empty(/c:archive/c:entry[@name eq 'demo.html'])">
    <p:error code="no-demo-html">
      <p:with-input>
        <message>The ZIP file does not contain the correct file.</message>
      </p:with-input>
    </p:error>
  </p:if>

  <!-- 1 - Extract the demo.html file: -->
  <p:unarchive include-filter="demo.html">
    <p:with-input pipe="@original-zip-file"/>
  </p:unarchive>

  <!-- 2 - Change it by inserting a reference to another image -->
  <p:insert match="body" position="last-child">
    <p:with-input port="insertion">
      <p>Old logo: <img src="additional-images/old.png" width="100"/></p>
    </p:with-input>
  </p:insert>

</p:declare-step>
```

Several interesting things happen here:

1. The **<p:unarchive>** step extracts documents from zip files.
   - The `include-filter` option tells **<p:unarchive>** to extract only certain files (in this case `demo.html`).
   - The input to **<p:unarchive>**'s `source` port must be an archive. But its implicit connection is to the **<p:if>** step above, which emits the archive's manifest. So the `source` port must be explicitly connected using `<p:with-input>`.

     This is done using a construction described in the section titled "Using **<p:identity>** to clarify pipeline structure" (p. 199). At the top of the pipeline is a **<p:identity>** step that simply provides a name, `original-zip-file`, to the incoming zip file. Then `<p:with-input pipe="@original-zip-file">` connects that to the `source` port.[4]
2. After `demo.html` is extracted, the **<p:insert>** step changes it by inserting a `<p>` element with a reference to the additional image.

The output is the original `demo.html` with a `<p>` element added at the end of the `<body>`:

```
<html>
  <head>
    <title>XProc demo file</title>
  </head>
  <body>
    <p>This file will be processable by our demo XProc pipeline because it
      contains a file called demo.html</p>
    <p>
      <img src="img/kanava.jpg" alt="Kanava" width="100">
    </p>
    <p xmlns:c="http://www.w3.org/ns/xproc-step">Old logo:
      <img src="img/old.png" width="100">
    </p>
  </body>
</html>
```

So what's the namespace declaration (`xmlns:c="http://www.w3.org/ns/xproc-step"`) doing on this brand new `<p>` element? It doesn't do any harm but it's ugly and unnecessary.

---

[4] You might wonder why the `<p:with-input>` does not specify a port name (`port="source"`). You can do that, but it's unnecessary; the default value for the `port` attribute is the step's primary port.

It's there because inline XML inherits most namespace definitions from the surrounding XProc code. And since the pipeline defines `xmlns:c="http://www.w3.org/ns/xproc-step"` on its root element (needed because the archive's manifest is in this namespace), it turns up in the inserted `<p>` element as well.

Fortunately, it's easy to omit this. Just add an `exclude-inline-prefixes="#all"` attribute to the root element and, hocus pocus, it's gone! Please try. You can read about this mechanism in the section titled "Excluding namespace prefixes" (p. 145).

Creating a new zip archive

The last task is to create a new zip archive that incorporates both the changed `demo.html` file and the additional image.

Unfortunately, the setup from Example 10.18 doesn't do the full job, because it only extracts `demo.html`. The new zip archive needs all of the files that were present in the original. So the approach needs to change. Example 10.19 shows how this can be done.

> You might find all the repeated string constants in Example 10.19 annoying, and from a software engineering point of view, using so many constants is not a good practice. The code would improve enormously with the introduction of a few variables that provided logical names for strings like `demo.html`, `img`, and so forth.
>
> However, doing so in an illustrative example would make the expressions more indirect and, therefore, more difficult to understand. For production code, I absolutely recommend that you introduce string variables for all of those repeated values.

Example 10.19 – Pipeline that creates a new zip archive (`$SOURCES/examples/working-with-zip/zip-04.xpl`)

```
<p:declare-step xmlns:p="http://www.w3.org/ns/xproc"
  xmlns:c="http://www.w3.org/ns/xproc-step"
  xmlns:html="http://www.w3.org/1999/xhtml"
  version="3.0" exclude-inline-prefixes="#all">

  <p:input port="source" href="input/processable.zip"/>
  <p:output port="result"/>

  <!-- Identify the main zip file: -->
  <p:identity name="original-zip-file"/>

  <!-- Test for the main file being present: -->
  <p:archive-manifest/>
  <p:if test="empty(/c:archive/c:entry[@name eq 'demo.html'])">
    <p:error code="no-demo-html">
      <p:with-input>
        <message>The ZIP file does not contain the correct file.</message>
      </p:with-input>
    </p:error>
  </p:if>

  <!-- 1 - Change the manifest so it includes the additional image: -->
  <p:insert match="/*" position="last-child">
    <p:with-input port="insertion">
     <c:entry href="{resolve-uri('additional-images/old.png', static-base-uri())}"
        name="img/old.png"/>
    </p:with-input>
  </p:insert>
  <p:identity name="amended-manifest"/>

  <!-- 2 - Extract the zip file: -->
  <p:unarchive>
    <p:with-input pipe="@original-zip-file"/>
  </p:unarchive>

  <!-- 3 - Add a reference to the additional image to the main file: -->
  <p:for-each>
    <p:if test="p:document-property(., 'base-uri') eq 'demo.html'">
      <p:insert match="body" position="last-child"
                xmlns="http://www.w3.org/1999/xhtml">
        <p:with-input port="insertion">
          <p>Old logo: <img src="img/old.png" width="100"/></p>
        </p:with-input>
      </p:insert>
    </p:if>
  </p:for-each>
```

```
  <!-- 4 - Create a new archive and store it: -->
  <p:archive>
    <p:with-input port="manifest" pipe="@amended-manifest"/>
  </p:archive>
  <p:store href="build/zip-result.zip"/>

  <!-- 5 - As a report, output where the new zip is stored: -->
  <p:identity>
    <p:with-input pipe="result-uri"/>
  </p:identity>

</p:declare-step>
```

1. To create a zip archive, you have to supply a manifest to **`<p:archive>`**'s `manifest` port that describes its contents. The section titled "Inspect a zip archive" (p. 215) shows how to extract the manifest for the existing archive and use it as the basis for a new manifest.[5]

   The manifest needs a `<c:entry>` element for the additional file. This element must have (at least) two attributes:

   `name` The `name` attribute holds the name of the (target) entry in the archive. It must be a relative filename. In this case: `img/old.png`.

   `href` The `href` attribute determines the source for the entry:

   - If its value is equal to the base URI of a document (its `base-uri` document property) appearing on **`<p:archive>`**'s `source` port, this document will be stored in the archive.
   - If not, its value is taken as a reference to something on disk (or the web), and the referenced document will be loaded from there. A relative value is interpreted as relative to the base URI of the manifest.

   But in this case, the value needs to be relative to the location of the pipeline. The expression in the `href` attribute does this. It turns a relative filename (`additional-images/old.png`) into an absolute one by resolving it against the pipeline's location, which is returned by `static-base-uri()`.

[5] Although that wouldn't help here, you don't have to supply a manifest to use **`<p:archive>`**. If you don't supply a manifest, **`<p:archive>`** will create a manifest based on the documents it puts into the archive it is creating. The base URI for each document determines its position in the archive. See the section titled "p:archive" (p. 231) for details.

2. The next step is to extract the files in the archive using **<p:unarchive>**. But this time, there is no need to use an include filter, so all files in the archive are extracted and appear on the `result` port. The base URI of each extracted document is the base URI of the archive followed by the path and name of the document inside the archive, for instance: `$SOURCES/examples/working-with-zip/input/processable.zip/img/kanava.jpg`.

3. The only file from the archive you need to modify is `demo.html`:

   - **<p:unarchive>** emits multiple documents, which are processed by **<p:for-each>**.
   - Inside this loop is a **<p:if>** that tests whether the current file needs to be changed (`p:document-property(.,'base-uri') eq 'demo.html'`). If it does, the **<p:insert>** step makes the change.
   - If the current file doesn't need to change, the **<p:if>** will act like a **<p:identity>** step and the (unchanged) document will simply fall through.

   The output of **<p:for-each>** contains all files from the archive with `demo.html` modified.

The base URIs of these files (their `base-uri` document properties) have *not* changed; they're still the base URIs from the archive (the URI of the archive followed by the relative path of the filename in the archive). So using the example input, the **<p:for-each>** loop will output two documents: `demo.html` (slightly modified) with base URI:

`$SOURCES/examples/working-with-zip/input/processable.zip/demo.html`

`kanava.jpg` with base URI:

`$SOURCES/examples/working-with-zip/input/processable.zip/img/kanava.jpg`

These base URIs are also the values of the `<c:entry>` `href` attributes returned by **<p:archive-manifest>**.

4. The **<p:archive>** step (the section titled "p:archive" (p. 231)) takes the documents appearing on its `source` port, processes them using the manifest appearing on its `manifest` port, and produces an archive (zip by default).

   The manifest now contains three entries:

   ```
   <c:entry name="demo.html"
   href="$SOURCES/examples/working-with-zip/input/processable.zip/demo.html"…/>
   ```

   <p:archive> looks for a file on its `source` port with a base URI equal to the value of this entry's `href` attribute and finds `demo.html`, which was changed in step 3. It stores this file in the new archive based on the value of the `name` attribute, also `demo.html`.

   ```
   <c:entry name="img/kanava.jpg"
   href="$SOURCES/examples/working-with-zip/input/processable.zip/img/kanava.jpg"…/>
   ```

   The same happens for this entry (this file was unchanged).

   ```
   <c:entry name="img/old.png"
   href="$SOURCES/examples/working-with-zip/additional-images/old.png"/>
   ```

   Again **<p:archive>** looks for a file on its `source` port with a base URI equal to the value of this entry's `href` attribute, but it's nowhere to be found. It then looks for this file on disk and loads it from there.

   The resulting zip archive is emitted on the `result` port of **<p:archive>**. The subsequent **<p:store>** step saves this to disk.

5. To avoid having a binary document as the pipeline's result, you can use an additional output port of **<p:store>** called `result-uri`, which emits an XML report that shows where the archive was written. The **<p:identity>** step handles this, yielding the following result on the pipeline output (whitespace added for readability):

   ```
   <c:result xmlns:c="http://www.w3.org/ns/xproc-step">
     $SOURCES/examples/working-with-zip/build/zip-result.zip
   </c:result>
   ```

   There are several other ways of dealing with this pipeline's final result:

   - You could completely discard the result. If you don't define an output port for the pipeline (delete `<p:output>` in the prolog), nothing will come out.
   - You could create a more elaborate report with additional information.

   I'll leave this to you as an exercise.

Debugging hints

To conclude this chapter, here are some tips for debugging pipelines.

Follow progress using messages

You can use the `[p:]message` attribute when you invoke a step (Example 10.20).

Example 10.20 – Using a `[p:]message` attribute on step invocations

```
<p:xslt message="Transforming {base-uri(/)}">
  <p:with-input port="stylesheet" href="somexslt.xsl"/>
</p:xslt>

<p:insert message="Inserting other results">
  <p:with-input port="insertion" pipe="some-port@some-step/>
</p:insert>
```

The value of `[p:]message` is an AVT (the section titled "Attribute and Text Value Templates" (p. 68)), so it can contain expressions, like `{base-uri(/)}` in Example 10.20. The result will be a message that looks like this:

```
Transforming file:///some/path/file.xml
```

Whether and where these messages appear is processor dependent. The message will probably appear on the standard (error) console output or in a log file. Consult your XProc processor's documentation for details.

The `[p:]` part in `[p:]message` means that when you use this attribute on your own steps (steps not declared in XProc's default `p:` namespace), you *must* include the `p:` namespace prefix (see Example 10.21).

Example 10.21 – Using a `[p:]message` attribute on a self-defined step

```
<mysteps:do-something p:message="Now doing something">
  ...
</mysteps:do-something>
```

See intermediate results using `<p:store>`

The `<p:store>` step was designed with debugging in mind: It writes the document flowing through it to disk (or the web), but in the pipeline it acts like the `<p:identity>` step. That means you can insert it to store an intermediate result wherever you want, without disturbing the rest of the pipeline. Example 10.22 shows how you might use this feature for debugging.

Example 10.22 – Using `<p:store>` for producing intermediate debug output

```
<p:xslt>
  <p:with-input port="stylesheet" href="somexslt.xsl"/>
</p:xslt>

<p:store href="/my/tmp/files/after-first-transform.xml"/>

<p:xslt>
  <p:with-input port="stylesheet" href="someotherxslt.xsl"/>
</p:xslt>

<p:store href="/my/tmp/files/after-second-transform.xml"/>
```

Inspecting the XML files written to `/my/tmp/files/` can reveal lots of interesting things. For more information about `<p:store>`, see the section titled "Storing documents: `<p:store>` " (p. 190) and the section titled "p:store" (p. 278).

This approach works well, but it has a major drawback. Once the debugging is done and the code goes into production, you'll want to remove the debug-related steps. You could delete or comment them, but when you need to come back to your code for maintenance, you'll probably have to insert or uncomment them again. XProc has a better way to handle debug output, which I describe in the next section.

Turn code on/off with the `[p:]use-when` attribute and static options

As Example 10.22 shows, you may need to switch on debugging code during development and maintenance but switch it off for production. You can do this in XProc with a combination of the `[p:]use-when` attribute (the section titled "The `[p:]use-when` attribute" (p. 75)) and static options (the section titled "Static options" (p. 105)). Example 10.23 enhances Example 10.22 to provide this capability.

Example 10.23 – Turning debug code on/off using `[p:]use-when`

```
<option name="debug" select="true()" static="true"/>

...

<p:xslt>
  <p:with-input port="stylesheet" href="somexslt.xsl"/>
</p:xslt>

<p:store href="/my/tmp/files/after-first-transform.xml" use-when="$debug"/>

<p:xslt>
  <p:with-input port="stylesheet" href="someotherxslt.xsl"/>
</p:xslt>

<p:store href="/my/tmp/files/after-second-transform.xml" use-when="$debug"/>
```

The prolog of the step declares a *static* option called `debug`. For each step you want to turn off for production, add the `[p:]use-when="$debug"` attribute. Now you can turn off the debugging steps by changing the value of the `select` attribute on the `debug` option to `false()`.

When the `[p:]use-when` attribute evaluates to `false`, the code it's on disappears. There's no performance impact on the pipeline.

A better way to do this would be to set the value for this static option in the code to `false` (`select="false()"`). Then set it to `true` when you invoke the processor during development and maintenance. This will prevent you from inadvertently committing code that contains hard-coded debug settings. Setting static options is processor dependent. Consult your processor's documentation for details.

As with `[p:]message`, you need to include the namespace prefix on `[p:]use-when` when you use it in a step that is not declared in XProc's default `p:` namespace (see also the section titled "The `[p:]` notation for attributes" (p. 75)).

APPENDIX A

Standard step library

This appendix provides an overview of the built-in steps that an XProc processor is *required* to implement: the standard step library. In other words: when you're building an XProc pipeline you can be sure that the steps listed here will always be available.

The step descriptions in this appendix were not (re)written for this book; they were generated directly from the specification. This means that the prose might be a bit more terse and formal than you're used to. Also, not all links may have survived the conversion process, so if you miss something, please consult the specification itself (http://spec.xproc.org/). See Appendix D for copyright information about the specification.

At the time this book was written not all step specifications were completely finished. So there may be inconsistencies between what you read here and what you find in practice. Consult the specification (http://spec.xproc.org/) for the latest version.

p:add-attribute

The `p:add-attribute` step adds a single attribute to a set of matching elements. The input document specified on the `source` is processed for matches specified by the selection pattern in the `match` option. For each of these matches, the attribute whose name is specified by the `attribute-name` option is set to the attribute value specified by the `attribute-value` option.

The resulting document is produced on the `result` output port and consists of a exact copy of the input with the exception of the matched elements. Each of the matched elements is copied to the output with the addition of the specified attribute with the specified value.

```
<p:declare-step type="p:add-attribute">
  <p:input port="source" content-types="xml html"/>
  <p:output port="result" content-types="xml html"/>
  <p:option name="match" as="xs:string" select="'/*'"/>
  <p:option name="attribute-name" required="true" as="xs:QName"/>
  <p:option name="attribute-value" required="true" as="xs:string"/>
</p:declare-step>
```

The value of the `match` option *must* be an XSLTSelectionPattern. It is a dynamic error if the selection pattern matches a node which is not an element (C0023).

The value of the `attribute-value` option *must* be a legal attribute value according to XML.

If an attribute with the same name as the expanded name from the `attribute-name` option exists on the matched element, the value specified in the `attribute-value` option is used to set the value of that existing attribute. That is, the value of the existing attribute is changed to the `attribute-value` value.

If multiple attributes need to be set on the same element(s), the `p:set-attributes` step can be used to set them all at once.

This step cannot be used to add namespace declarations. It is a dynamic error if the QName value in the `attribute-name` option uses the prefix "`xmlns`" or any other prefix that resolves to the namespace name `http://www.w3.org/2000/xmlns/` (C0059). Note, however, that while namespace declarations cannot be added explicitly by this step, adding an attribute whose name is in a namespace for which there is no namespace declaration in scope on the matched element may result in a namespace binding being added by namespace fixup.

If an attribute named `xml:base` is added or changed, the base URI of the element *must* also be amended accordingly.

All document properties are preserved.

p:add-xml-base

The `p:add-xml-base` step exposes the base URI via explicit `xml:base` attributes. The input document from the `source` port is replicated to the `result` port with `xml:base` attributes added to or corrected on each element as specified by the options on this step.

```
<p:declare-step type="p:add-xml-base">
  <p:input port="source" content-types="xml html"/>
  <p:output port="result" content-types="xml html"/>
  <p:option name="all" as="xs:boolean" select="false()"/>
  <p:option name="relative" as="xs:boolean" select="true()"/>
</p:declare-step>
```

The value of the `all` option *must* be a boolean.

The value of the `relative` option *must* be a boolean.

It is a dynamic error if the `all` and `relative` options are *both* `true` (C0058).

The `p:add-xml-base` step modifies its input as follows:

- For every element that is a child of the document node: force the element to have an `xml:base` attribute with the document's [base URI] property's value as its value.
- For other elements:
  - If the `all` option has the value `true`, force the element to have an `xml:base` attribute with the element's [base URI] value as its value.
  - If the element's [base URI] is different from the its parent's [base URI], force the element to have an `xml:base` attribute with the following value: if the value of the `relative` option is `true`, a string which, when resolved against the parent's [base URI], will give the element's [base URI], otherwise the element's [base URI].
  - Otherwise, if there is an `xml:base` attribute present, remove it.

All document properties are preserved.

p:archive

The `p:archive` step outputs on its `result` port an archive (usually binary) document, for instance a ZIP file. A specification of the contents of the archive may be specified in a manifest XML document on the `manifest` port. The step produces a report on the `report` port, which contains the manifest, amended with additional information about the archiving.

```
<p:declare-step type="p:archive">
  <p:input port="source" primary="true" content-types="any" sequence="true"/>
  <p:input port="manifest" content-types="xml" sequence="true">
    <p:empty/>
  </p:input>
  <p:input port="archive" content-types="any" sequence="true">
    <p:empty/>
  </p:input>
```

```
  <p:output port="result" primary="true" content-types="any" sequence="false"/>
  <p:output port="report" content-types="application/xml" sequence="false"/>
  <p:option name="format" as="xs:QName" select="'zip'"/>
  <p:option name="relative-to" as="xs:anyURI?"/>
  <p:option name="parameters" as="map(xs:QName, item()*)?"/>
</p:declare-step>
```

The `p:archive` step can perform several different operations on archives. The most common one will likely be creating an archive, but it could also, depending on the archive format, provide services like update, freshen or even merge. The only format implementations *must* support is ZIP. The list of formats supported by the `p:archive` step is implementation-defined.

The `p:archive` step has the following input ports:

`source`

The (primary) `source` port is used to provide documents to be archived (for instance constructed by other steps). How and which of these documents are processed is governed by the document(s) appearing on the other input ports and the combination of options and parameters. See below for details. It is a dynamic error if two or more documents appear on the `p:archive` step's `source` port that have the same base URI or if any document that appears on the `source` port has no base URI (C0084).

`manifest`

The `manifest` port can receive a manifest document that tells the step how to construct the archive. If no manifest document is provided on this port, a default manifest is constructed automatically. See the section titled "The archive manifest" (p. 234). It is a dynamic error if the document on port `manifest` does not conform to the given schema (C0100).

It is a dynamic error if more than one document appears on the port `manifest` (C0112).

The default input for this port is the empty sequence.

`archive`

The `archive` port is used to provide the step with existing archive(s) for operations like update, freshen or merge. Handling of ZIP files supports modifying archives appearing on the `archive` port (the section titled "Handling of ZIP archives" (p. 236)). The list of archive formats that can be modified by `p:archive` is implementation-defined. For instance an implementation that supports archive merging may accept more than one document on the `archive` port.

The default input for this port is the empty sequence.

The `p:archive` step has the following output ports:

`result`

The (primary) `result` port will output the resulting archive.

`report`

The `report` port will output a report about the archiving operation. This will be the same as the manifest (as provided on the `manifest` port or automatically created if there was no manifest provided), optionally amended with additional attributes and/or elements. The semantics of any additional attributes, elements and their values are implementation-defined.

The `p:archive` step has the following options:

`format`

The format of the archive can be specified using the `format` option. Implementations *must* support the ZIP format, specified with the value `zip`. It is implementation-defined what other formats are supported.

`parameters`

The `parameters` option can be used to supply parameters to control the archiving. The semantics of the keys and the allowed values for these keys are implementation-defined. It is a dynamic error if the map `parameters` contains an entry whose key is defined by the implementation and whose value is not valid for that key (C0079).

`relative-to`

The `relative-to` option is used in creating a manifest when no manifest is provided on the `manifest` port. If the option is relative, it is made absolute against the base URI of the element on which it is specified (`p:with-option` or the step in case of a syntactic shortcut value). It is a dynamic error if the base URI is not both absolute and valid according to RFC 3986 (D0064).

The format of the archive is determined as follows:

- If the `format` option is specified, this determines the format of the archive. Implementations *must* support the ZIP format, specified with the value `zip`. It is implementation-defined what other formats are supported. It is a dynamic error if the format of the archive does not match the format as specified in the `format` option (C0081).

- If no `format` option is specified or if its value is the empty sequence, the archive's format will be determined by the step, using the `content-type` document-property of the document on the `archive` port and/or by inspecting its contents. It is implementation-defined how the step determines the archive's format. Implementations *should* recognize archives in ZIP format.

It is a dynamic error if the format of the archive does not match the specified format, cannot be understood, determined and/or processed (C0085).

No document properties are preserved. The archive has no `base-uri`.

The archive manifest

An archive manifest specifies which documents will be considered in processing the archive. Every entry in the archive must have a corresponding entry in the manifest; if no such entry is provided, one will be constructed automatically (see below). If manifest entries are provided for documents that *are not* in the archive, how those are processed depends on the archive type and the parameters passed to the step.

A manifest is represented by a `c:archive` root element:

```
<c:archive>
  <c:entry>*
  <(any)>*
</c:archive>
```

The `c:archive` root element may contain additional implementation-defined attributes.

All entries in the archive must be present as `c:entry` child elements:

```
<c:entry name = xs:string
         href = anyURI
         comment? = xs:string
         method? = xs:string
         level? = xs:string >
  <(any)>*
</c:entry>
```

- The `name` attribute specifies the name of the entry in the archive.
- The `href` attribute must be a valid URI according to RFC 3986. If its value is relative, it is made absolute against the base URI of the manifest. There are two possible cases:
  - If the (absolute) `href` value is exactly the same as the base URI of a document appearing on the `source` port, that document is associated with this entry. If this entry is to be added to the archive, the associated document will be used. (The `serialization` document property can be used to provide serialization properties.)
  - If no document on the `source` port has a base URI that is exactly the same as the (absolute) `href` value, the document at the specified URI is associated with this entry. If this entry is to be added to the archive, the document must be obtained by dereferencing the URI. It is a dynamic error if the resource referenced by the `href` option does not exist, cannot be accessed or is not a file (D0011). These documents are stored in the archive "as is"; they *must not* be parsed and re-serialized.
- The `method` attribute specifies how the entry should be compressed. The default compression method is implementation-defined. Implementations *must* support no compression, specified with the value `none`. It is implementation-defined what other compression methods are supported.
- The `level` attribute specifies the level of compression. The default compression method is implementation-defined. It is implementation-defined what compression levels are supported.

The `p:archive` step *should* strive to retain the order of the `c:entry` elements when constructing the archive. For instance, an e-book in EPUB format has a non-compressed entry that must be first in the archive. It should be possible to construct such an archive using `p:archive`.

The `c:entry` elements may contain additional implementation-defined attributes.

If no manifest entry is provided for a document appearing on the `source` port, the step will create a manifest entry for the document. (If no document arrives on the `manifest` port at all, a complete manifest document will be created.)

In a constructed manifest entry:

- The entry's `href` value is the base URI of the document.
- The entry's `name` value is derived from the base URI of the document and the `relative-to` option.
  - First, the value of the `relative-to` option is made absolute. If the initial substring of the base URI is exactly the same as the resulting absolute value, then the `name` is the portion of the base URI that follows that initial substring.
  - If there is no `relative-to` option or if its value is not the initial substring of the base URI of the document, the name is the *path* portion of the URI (per RFC 3986). If the path portion begins with an initial slash, that slash is removed.

It is a dynamic error if an archive manifest is invalid according to the specification (C0118).

Handling of ZIP archives

The format of the archive can be specified using the `format` option. Implementations *must* support the ZIP format, specified with the value `zip`.

When ZIP archives are processed, every `name` in the manifest must be a relative path without a leading slash.

The `parameters` option can be used to supply parameters to control the archiving. For the `zip` format, the following parameters *must* be supported:

`command`

Specifies what operation to perform. If not specified, its default value is `update`. Implementations must support the values `update`, `create`, `freshen`, and `delete`. The `p:archive` step may support additional, implementation-defined commands for ZIP files. Unless otherwise specified, exactly zero or one ZIP archive can appear on the `archive` port for the commands described below. If no archive appears, a new archive will be created.

`update`

When the `command` parameter is set to `update`, the ZIP archive will be updated:

1. For every entry in the ZIP file:
   - If the manifest contains a `c:entry` with a matching `name`, the entry in the ZIP file is updated with the document identified by the `c:entry` in the manifest.
   - If the manifest does not contain a matching `c:entry`, the ZIP entry name is resolved against the base URI of the ZIP file.
     - If a document exists at that URI and either has no timestamp or has a timestamp more than the timestamp in the ZIP file, the entry in the ZIP file will be updated with the document at the resolved URI.
     - If no document exists at that URI, or the document cannot be accessed, or the document has a timestamp and the timestamp in the ZIP archive is more recent than the timestamp of the document, then the ZIP entry is unchanged.
2. For every `c:entry` in the manifest that does not have a matching entry in the ZIP file, the ZIP file will be updated by adding the document identified by the `c:entry` to the ZIP file.

`create`

When the `command` parameter is set to `create`, the ZIP archive will be created. Creating a ZIP archive behaves exactly like `update` except that any timestamps are ignored; every ZIP entry will be updated or created if there is a `c:entry` or matching document for it.

`freshen`

When the `command` parameter is set to `freshen`, existing files in the ZIP archive may be updated, but no new files will be added. Freshing a ZIP archive behaves exactly like `update` except that only entries that already exist in the ZIP archive are considered.

`delete`

When the `command` parameter is set to `delete`, exactly one document in ZIP format must appear on the `archive` port. For every entry in the ZIP file:

- If the manifest contains a `c:entry` with a matching `name`, the entry in the ZIP file is removed from the ZIP archive.

If the manifest contains `c:entry` elements which do not have a matching entry in the ZIP archive, they are simply ignored.

`level`

Specifies the default compression level for files added to or updated in the archive. If the `level` attribute is specified on a `c:entry`, its value takes precedence for that entry. Values that must be supported for ZIP files are: "`smallest`", "`fastest`", "`default`", "`huffman`", and "`none`".

`method`

Specifies the default compression method for files added to or updated in the archive. If the `method` attribute is specified on a `c:entry`, its value takes precedence for that entry. Values that must be supported for ZIP files are: "`none`" and "`deflated`".

It is a dynamic error if the number of documents on the `archive` does not match the expected number of archive input documents for the given `format` and `command` (C0080).

Implementations of other archive formats *should* use the same parameter names if applicable. The value spaces for these parameters may be format-specific though. The actual parameter names supported by `p:archive` for a particular format are implementation-defined.

p:archive-manifest

The `p:archive-manifest` creates an XML manifest file describing the contents of the archive appearing on its `source` port.

```
<p:declare-step type="p:archive-manifest">
  <p:input port="source" primary="true" content-types="any" sequence="false"/>
  <p:output port="result" primary="true" content-types="application/xml"
sequence="false"/>
  <p:option name="format" as="xs:QName?"/>
  <p:option name="parameters" as="map(xs:QName, item()*)?"/>
  <p:option name="relative-to" as="xs:anyURI?"/>
</p:declare-step>
```

The `p:archive-manifest` step inspects the archive appearing on its `source` port and outputs a manifest describing the contents of the archive on its `result` port.

The format of the archive is determined as follows:

- If the `format` option is specified, this determines the format of the archive. Implementations *must* support the ZIP format, specified with the value `zip`. It is implementation-defined what other formats are supported.
- If no `format` option is specified or if its value is the empty sequence, the archive's format will be determined by the step, using the `content-type` document-property of the document on the `source` port and/or by inspecting its contents. It is implementation-defined how the step determines the archive's format. Implementations *should* recognize archives in ZIP format.

It is a dynamic error if the format of the archive does not match the specified format, cannot be understood, determined and/or processed (C0085).

The `parameters` option can be used to supply parameters to control the archive manifest generation. The semantics of the keys and the allowed values for these keys are implementation-defined. It is a dynamic error if the map `parameters` contains an entry whose key is defined by the implementation and whose value is not valid for that key (C0079).

The `relative-to` option, when present, is used in creating the value of the manifest's `c:entry/@href` attribute. If the option is relative, it is made absolute against the base URI of the element on which it is specified (`p:with-option` or the step in case of a syntactic shortcut value). It is a dynamic error if the base URI is not both absolute and valid according to RFC 3986 (D0064).

The generated manifest has the format as described in the section titled “The archive manifest” (p. 234). Implementations *must* supply an `c:entry` element and its `name` attribute for every entry in the archive. The value of the generated manifest's `c:entry/@href` attribute will be determined in the same way as a base URI of an unarchived document by the section titled “p:unarchive” (p. 285). It is a dynamic error if the `relative-to` option is not present and the document on the `source` port does not have a base URI (C0120). Additional information provided for entries in `p:archive-manifest` is implementation-defined.

No document properties are preserved. The manifest has no `base-uri`.

p:cast-content-type

The `p:cast-content-type` step creates a new document by changing the media type of its input. If the value of the `content-type` option and the current media type of the document on `source` port are the same, this document will appear unchanged on `result` port.

```
<p:declare-step type="p:cast-content-type">
  <p:input port="source" content-types="any"/>
  <p:output port="result" content-types="any"/>
  <p:option name="content-type" required="true" as="xs:string"/>
  <p:option name="parameters" as="map(xs:QName,item()*)?"/>
</p:declare-step>
```

The input document is transformed from one media type to another. It is a dynamic error if the supplied `content-type` is not a valid media type of the form “ *`type/subtype+ext`* ” where “*`+ext`* ” is optional (C0070). It is a dynamic error if the `p:cast-content-type` step cannot perform the requested cast (C0071).

The `parameters` can be used to supply parameters to control casting. The semantics of the keys and the allowed values for these keys are implementation-defined. It is a dynamic error if the map `parameters` contains an entry whose key is defined by the implementation and whose value is not valid for that key (C0079).

All document properties are preserved except the `content-type` property which is updated accordingly and the `serialization` property which is removed by some casting methods.

Casting from an XML media type

- Casting from one XML media type to another simply changes the "`content-type`" document property.
- Casting from an XML media type to an HTML media type changes the "`content-type`" document property and removes any serialization property.
- Casting from an XML media type to a JSON media type converts the XML into JSON. The precise nature of the conversion from XML to JSON is implementation-defined. If the input document is an XML representation of JSON as defined in the XPath 3.1 functions, implementations *must* produce the same result as `fn:parse-json(fn:xml-to-json())` by default. If the input document has a `c:param-set` document element, a map *must* be returned that represents the document's `c:param` elements. The serialization property is removed.
- Casting from an XML media type to a text media type serializes the XML document by calling `fn:serialize($doc, $param)` where `$doc` is the document on the `source` port and `$param` is the serialization property of this document. The resulting string is wrapped by a document node and returned on the `result` port. The serialization property is removed.
- Casting from an XML media type to any other media type *must* support the case where the input document is a `c:data` document. The resulting document will have the specified media type and a representation that is the content of the `c:data` element after decoding the base64 encoded content The serialization property is removed.

  It is a dynamic error if the `c:data` contains content is not a valid base64 string (C0072).

  It is a dynamic error if the `c:data` element does not have a `content-type` attribute (C0073).

  It is a dynamic error if the `content-type` is supplied and is not the same as the `content-type` specified on the `c:data` element (C0074).

  Casting from an XML media type to any other media type when the input document is not a `c:data` document is implementation-defined.

Casting from an HTML media type

- Casting from an HTML media type to an XML media type changes "`content-type`" document property and removes any serialization property.

- Casting from an HTML media type to another HTML media type changes "`content-type`" document property.
- Casting from an HTML media type to a JSON media type is implementation-defined.
- Casting an an HTML media type to a text media type serializes the HTML document by calling `fn:serialize($doc, $param)` where `$doc` is the document on the `source` port and `$param` is the serialization property of this document. The resulting string is wrapped by a document node and returned on the `result` port. The serialization property is removed.
- Casting from an HTML media type to any other media type is implementation-defined.

Casting from a JSON media type

- Casting from a JSON media type to an XML media type converts the JSON into XML. An implementation *must* support the format specified in section "XML Representation of JSON" of the XPath 3.1 functions as default for the resulting XML. It is implementation-defined whether other result formats are supported. The serialization property is removed.
- Casting from a JSON media type to an HTML media type is implementation-defined.
- Casting from a JSON media type to another JSON media type changes "`content-type`" document property.
- Casting from a JSON media type to a text media type serializes the JSON document by calling `fn:serialize($doc, $param)` where `$doc` is the document on the `source` port and `$param` is the serialization property of this document. The resulting string is wrapped by a document node and returned on the `result` port. The serialization property is removed.
- Casting from a JSON media type to any other media type is implementation-defined.

Casting from a text media type

- Casting from a text media type to an XML media type parses the text value of the document on `source` port by calling `fn:parse-xml`. It is a dynamic error if the text value is not a well-formed XML document. The serialization property is removed.

- Casting from a text media type to an HTML media type parses the text value of the document on `source` port into an XPath data model document that contains a tree of elements, attributes, and other nodes. The precise way in which text documents are parsed into the XPath data model is implementation-defined. It is a dynamic error if the text document can not be converted into the XPath data model. The serialization property is removed.

- Casting from a text media type to a JSON media type parses the text value of the document on `source` port by calling `fn:parse-json($doc, $par)` where `$doc` is the text document and `$par` is the `parameter` option. It is a dynamic error if the text document does not conform to the JSON grammar, unless the parameter liberal is true and the processor chooses to accept the deviation (D0057). It is a dynamic error if the parameter duplicates is reject and the text document contains a JSON object with duplicate keys (D0058). It is a dynamic error if the parameter map contains an entry whose key is defined in the specification of `fn:parse-json` and whose value is not valid for that key, or if it contains an entry with the key fallback when the parameter `escape` with `true()` is also present (D0059). The serialization property is removed.

- Casting from a text media type to another text media type changes "`content-type`" document property.

- Casting from a text media type to any other media type is implementation-defined.

Casting from any other media type

- Casting from a non-XML media type to an XML media type produces an XML document with a `c:data` document element. The original media type will be preserved in the `content-type` attribute on the `c:data` element.

```
<c:data content-type = ContentType
        charset? = xs:string
        encoding? = xs:string >
  <!-- … (text) … -->
</c:data>
```

  The content of the `c:data` element is the base64 encoded representation of the non-XML content. The serialization property is removed.

- Casting from any other media type to a HTML media type, a JSON media type or a text document is implementation-defined.

- Casting from any other media type to any other media type is implementation-defined.

p:compare

The `p:compare` step compares two documents for equality.

```
<p:declare-step type="p:compare">
  <p:input port="source" primary="true" content-types="any"/>
  <p:input port="alternate" content-types="any"/>
  <p:output port="result" content-types="application/xml"/>
  <p:output port="differences" content-types="any" sequence="true"/>
  <p:option name="parameters" as="map(xs:QName,item()*)?"/>
  <p:option name="method" as="xs:QName?"/>
  <p:option name="fail-if-not-equal" as="xs:boolean" select="false()"/>
</p:declare-step>
```

This step takes single documents on each of two ports and compares them. If `method` is not specified, or if `deep-equal` is specified, the comparison uses `fn:deep-equal` (as defined in the XPath 3.1 functions). Implementations of `p:compare` *must* support the `deep-equal` method; other supported methods are implementation-defined. It is a dynamic error if the comparison `method` specified in `p:compare` is not supported by the implementation (C0076). It is a dynamic error if the media types of the documents supplied are incompatible with the comparison `method` (C0077).

It is a dynamic error if the documents are not equal according to the specified comparison `method`, and the value of the `fail-if-not-equal` option is `true` (C0019). If the documents are equal, or if the value of the `fail-if-not-equal` option is `false`, a `c:result` document is produced with contents `true` if the documents are equal, otherwise `false`.

If `fail-if-not-equal` is `false`, and the documents differ, an implementation-defined summary of the differences between the two documents may appear on the `differences` port.

No document properties are preserved. The comparison document has no `base-uri`.

p:compress

The `p:compress` step serializes the document appearing on its `source` port and outputs a compressed version of this on its `result` port.

```
<p:declare-step type="p:compress">
  <p:input port="source" primary="true" content-types="any" sequence="false"/>
  <p:output port="result" primary="true" content-types="any" sequence="false"/>
  <p:option name="format" as="xs:QName" select="'gzip'"/>
  <p:option name="serialization" as="map(xs:QName,item()*)?"/>
  <p:option name="parameters" as="map(xs:QName, item()*)?"/>
</p:declare-step>
```

The `p:compress` step first serializes the document appearing on its `source`. It then compresses the outcome of this serialization and outputs the result on its `result` port.

The `p:compress` step has the following options:

`format`

: The format of the compression can be specified using the `format` option. Implementations *must* support the GZIP format, specified with the value `gzip`. It is implementation-defined what other formats are supported. It is a dynamic error if the compression format cannot be understood, determined and/or processed (C0202).

`parameters`

: The `parameters` option can be used to supply parameters to control the compression. The semantics of the keys and the allowed values for these keys are implementation-defined. It is a dynamic error if the map `parameters` contains an entry whose key is defined by the implementation and whose value is not valid for that key (C0079).

`serialization`

: The `serialization` option is provided to control the serialization of content before compression takes place. If the document to be stored has a `serialization` property, the serialization is controlled by the merger of the two maps where the entries in the `serialization` property take precedence. Serialization is described in XProc 3.0.

All document properties are preserved, except for the `content-type` property which is updated accordingly and the `serialization` property which is removed.

p:count

The `p:count` step counts the number of documents in the `source` input sequence and returns a single document on `result` containing that number. The generated document contains a single `c:result` element whose contents is the string representation of the number of documents in the sequence.

```
<p:declare-step type="p:count">
  <p:input port="source" content-types="any" sequence="true"/>
  <p:output port="result" content-types="application/xml"/>
  <p:option name="limit" as="xs:integer" select="0"/>
</p:declare-step>
```

If the `limit` option is specified and is greater than zero, the `p:count` step will count at most that many documents. This provides a convenient mechanism to discover, for example, if a sequence consists of more than 1 document, without requiring every single document to be buffered before processing can continue.

No document properties are preserved. The count document has no `base-uri`.

p:delete

The `p:delete` step deletes items specified by a selection pattern from the `source` input document and produces the resulting document, with the deleted items removed, on the `result` port.

```
<p:declare-step type="p:delete">
  <p:input port="source" content-types="xml html"/>
  <p:output port="result" content-types="text xml html"/>
  <p:option name="match" required="true" as="xs:string"/>
</p:declare-step>
```

The value of the `match` option *must* be an XSLTSelectionPattern. A selection pattern may match multiple items to be deleted.

If an element is selected by the `match` option, the entire subtree rooted at that element is deleted.

It is a dynamic error if the `match` option matches the document node (C0023).

This step cannot be used to remove namespaces. It is a dynamic error if the `match` option matches a namespace node (C0062). Also, note that deleting an attribute named `xml:base` does not change the base URI of the element on which it occurred.

If the resulting document contains exactly one text node, the `content-type` property is changed to `text/plain` and the `serialization` property is removed, while all other document properties are preserved. For other document types, all document properties are preserved.

p:error

The `p:error` step generates a dynamic error using the input provided to the step.

```
<p:declare-step type="p:error">
  <p:input port="source" sequence="true" content-types="text xml"/>
  <p:output port="result" sequence="true" content-types="any"/>
  <p:option name="code" required="true" as="xs:QName"/>
</p:declare-step>
```

This step uses the document provided on its input as the content of the error raised. An instance of the `c:errors` element will be produced on the error output port, as is always the case for dynamic errors. The error generated can be caught by a `p:try` just like any other dynamic error.

For authoring convenience, the `p:error` step is declared with a single, primary output port. With respect to connections, this port behaves like any other output port even though nothing can ever appear on it since the step always fails.

For example, given the following invocation:

```
<p:error xmlns:my="http://www.example.org/error"
         name="bad-document" code="my:unk12">
   <p:input port="source">
     <p:inline>
       <message>The document element is unknown.</message>
     </p:inline>
   </p:input>
</p:error>
```

The error vocabulary element (and document) generated on the error output port would be:

```
<c:errors xmlns:c="http://www.w3.org/ns/xproc-step"
          xmlns:p="http://www.w3.org/ns/xproc"
          xmlns:my="http://www.example.org/error">
```

```
 <c:error name="bad-document" type="p:error"
          code="my:unk12"><message>The document element is unknown.</message>
</c:error>
</c:errors>
```

The `href`, `line` and `column`, or `offset`, might also be present on the `c:error` to identify the location of the `p:error` element in the pipeline.

No document properties are preserved but that's irrelevant as no document is ever produced.

p:filter

The `p:filter` step selects portions of the source document based on a (possibly dynamically constructed) XPath select expression.

```
<p:declare-step type="p:filter">
  <p:input port="source" content-types="xml html"/>
  <p:output port="result" sequence="true" content-types="text xml html"/>
  <p:option name="select" required="true" as="xs:string"/>
</p:declare-step>
```

This step behaves just like an `p:input` with a `select` expression except that the select expression is computed dynamically.

No document properties are preserved. The `base-uri` property of each document will reflect the base URI of the selected node(s).

p:hash

The `p:hash` step generates a hash, or digital "fingerprint", for some value and injects it into the `source` document.

```
<p:declare-step type="p:hash">
  <p:input port="source" primary="true" content-types="xml html"/>
  <p:output port="result" content-types="text xml html"/>
  <p:option name="parameters" as="map(xs:QName,item()*)?"/>
  <p:option name="value" required="true" as="xs:string"/>
  <p:option name="algorithm" required="true" as="xs:QName"/>
  <p:option name="match" as="xs:string" select="'/*/node()'"/>
  <p:option name="version" as="xs:string?"/>
</p:declare-step>
```

The value of the `algorithm` option must be a QName. If it does not have a prefix, then it must be one of the following values: "crc", "md", or "sha".

If a `version` is not specified, the default version is algorithm-defined. For "`crc`" it is 32, for "`md`" it is 5, for "`sha`" it is 1.

A hash is constructed from the string specified in the `value` option using the specified algorithm and version. Implementations *must* support CRC32, MD5, and SHA1 hashes. It is implementation-defined what other algorithms are supported. The resulting hash *should* be returned as a string of hexadecimal characters.

The value of the `match` option must be an XSLTSelectionPattern.

The hash of the specified value is computed using the algorithm and parameters specified. It is a dynamic error if the requested hash algorithm is not one that the processor understands or if the value or parameters are not appropriate for that algorithm (C0036).

The matched nodes are specified with the selection pattern in the `match` option. For each matching node, the string value of the computed hash is used in the output (if more than one node matches, the *same* hash value is used in each match). Nodes that do not match are copied without change.

If the expression given in the `match` option matches an *attribute*, the hash is used as the new value of the attribute in the output. If the attribute is named "`xml:base`", the base URI of the element *must* also be amended accordingly.

If the document node is matched, the entire document is replaced by a text node with the hash. What appears on port `result` is a text document with the text node wrapped in a document node.

If the expression matches any other kind of node, the entire node (and *not* just its contents) is replaced by the hash.

If the resulting document contains exactly one text node, the `content-type` property is changed to `text/plain` and the `serialization` property is removed, while all other document properties are preserved. For other document types, all document properties are preserved.

p:http-request

The `p:http-request` step allows authors to interact with resources over HTTP or related protocols. Implementations *must* support the `http` and `https` protocols. (Implementors are encouraged to support as many protocols as practical. In particular, pipeline authors may attempt to use `p:http-request` to load documents with computed URIs using the `file:` scheme.)

```
<p:declare-step type="p:http-request">
  <p:input port="source" content-types="any" sequence="true"/>
  <p:output port="result" primary="true" content-types="any" sequence="true"/>
  <p:output port="report" content-types="application/json"/>
  <p:option name="href" as="xs:anyURI" required="true"/>
  <p:option name="method" as="xs:string?" select="'GET'"/>
  <p:option name="serialization" as="map(xs:QName,item()*)?"/>
  <p:option name="headers" as="map(xs:string, xs:string)?"/>
  <p:option name="auth" as="map(xs:string, item()+)?"/>
  <p:option name="parameters" as="map(xs:QName, item()*)?"/>
  <p:option name="assert" as="xs:string" select="'.?status-code lt 400'"/>
</p:declare-step>
```

The `p:http-request` step performs the HTTP request specified by the `method` option against the URI specified in the `href` option. In simple cases, for example, a GET request on an unauthenticated URI, nothing else is necessary to form a complete request.

If the method, for example, POST, supports a body, the request body is constructed using the document(s) appearing on the `source` port. For the convenience of pipeline authors, documents may appear on the `source` port even when the request method (such as GET or HEAD) does not define the semantics of a payload. If the semantics are undefined, the documents are ignored when constructing the request unless the `parameters` option specifies "`send-body-anyway`" as `true()`.

The headers for the request come from the `headers` option (see below). If exactly one document appears on the `source` port, its document properties also contribute to the overall request headers.

The response from the HTTP request appears on the `result` and `report` ports. Any documents contained in the response body will appear on the `result` port. Each document in the response will be parsed according to its content-type (but see "`override-content-type`" in the `parameters` option). Details about the outcome of the request will appear as a map on the `report` port. The map will always contain "`status-code`" (an `xs:integer`) and "`headers`" (a `map(xs:string, xs:string)`). The header map may be empty. Header names are converted to lowercase.

The `p:http-request` step has the following options:

`href`

The `href` option specifies the request's IRI. Relative values are resolved against the base URI of the element on which the option is specified (the relevant `p:with-option` or the step element in the case of a syntactic shortcut value).

Fragment identifiers are removed before making the request. Query parameters are passed through unchanged. It is a dynamic error if the URI's scheme is unknown or not supported (C0128). It is the pipeline author's responsibility to escape problematic UTF-8 characters in the `href` value, for example with `escape-html-uri()`.

`method`

The `method` specifies the HTTP request method. The value is implicitly turned into an uppercase string if necessary. It is implementation defined which HTTP methods are supported. An implementation *should* implement at least the methods `GET`, `POST`, `PUT`, `DELETE`, and `HEAD` (for HTTP and HTTPS). It is a dynamic error if the given method is not supported (C0122).

`serialization`

The `serialization` option is used to control the serialization of documents for the request body. If a document has a "`serialization`" document property, the effective value of the serialization options is the union of the two maps, where the entries in the "`serialization`" document property take precedence.

`headers`

The key/value pairs in the `headers` map are used to construct the request headers. Each map key is used as a header name and the value associated with that key in the map is used as the header value.

If a single document appears on the `source` port, then document properties on that document may be added as additional headers. All of the document properties will be used as headers *except* "`base-uri`", "`serialization`" and any property with a name that already appears in the `headers` map. (In other words, if the same header name appears in both places, the value from the map is used and the value from the document properties is ignored.) If multiple documents appear on the `source` port, none of their properties are used in the request headers.

The behavior of the `p:http-request` depends on the headers specified. In particular:

`content-type`

If a `content-type` header is provided, it will be used. For a single document request, this overrides the content type value of the document. If the content type specified begins with "`multipart/`", a multipart request will be sent to the server.

It is a dynamic error if the content-type specified is not a valid content type (C0130).

`transfer-encoding`

If a `transfer-encoding` header is provided, the request *must* be sent with that encoding. It is a dynamic error if the processor cannot support the requested encoding (C0131).

`authorization`

The `authorization` header is used to authenticate a request. If the `auth` *option* is specified, any key or property that would have contributed a header named "`authorization`" (irrespective of case) is ignored. The authorization header is determined exclusively by the `auth` option when it is present.

HTTP headers are case-insensitive but keys in maps are not; be careful when specifying the request headers. It is a dynamic error if the `headers` map contains two keys that are the same when compared in a case-insensitive manner (C0127). (That is, when `fn:uppercase($key1) = fn:uppercase($key2)`.)

`auth`

Many web services are only available to authenticated users, that is, to users who have "logged in". The `auth` option allows the pipeline author to specify information that may be required to generate an "Authorization" header. The standard values support HTTP "Basic" and "Digest" authentication, but other authentication methods are allowed.

The following standard keys are defined:

`username` (`xs:string`)

> The username.

`password` (`xs:string`)

> The password associated with the username.

`auth-method` (`xs:string`)

> The authentication method. Appropriate values for the "`auth-method`" key are "`Basic`" or "`Digest`" but other values are allowed. If the authentication method is "`Basic`" or "`Digest`", authentication is handled as per RFC 2617. The interpretation of values associated with the "`auth-method`" key other than "`Basic`" or "`Digest`" is implementation defined.

`send-authorization` (`xs:boolean`)

> The "`send-authorization`" key can be used to attempt to allow the request to avoid an authentication challenge. If the "`send-authorization`" key is "`true()`", and the authentication method specified by the value associated with the "`auth-method`" key supports generation of an "`Authorization`" header without a challenge, then the header is generated and sent on the first request. If the "`send-authorization`" key is absent or does not have the value "`true`", the first request is sent without an "`Authorization`" header.

Other key value pairs in map "`auth`" are implementation defined. It is a dynamic error if any key in the "`auth`" map is associated with a value that is not an instance of the required type (C0123).

If the initial response to the request is an authentication challenge, the values provided in the `auth` map and any relevant data from the challenge are used to generate an "`Authorization`" header and the request is sent again. If that authorization fails, the request is not retried.

It is a dynamic error if a "`username`" or a "`password`" key is present without specifying a value for the "`auth-method`" key, if the requested `auth-method` isn't supported, or the authentication challenge contains an authentication method that isn't supported (C0003). All implementations *must* support "Basic" and "Digest" authentication per RFC 2617.

parameters

The `parameter` option can be used to provide values for fine tuning the construction of the request and/or handling of the server response. A number of parameters are defined in this specification. It is implementation defined which other key/value pairs in the `parameters` option are supported.

override-content-type (`xs:string`)

Ordinarily, the value of the `content-type` header provided in the server response controls the interpretation of any body in the response. If the "`override-content-type`" parameter is provided, then its value is used to interpret the body. The content-type header that appears on the `report` port is not changed. It is a dynamic error if the response body cannot be interpreted as requested (e.g. `application/json` to override `application/xml` content) (C0030).

http-version (`xs:string`)

The `http-version` parameter indicates which version of HTTP *must* be used for the request. It is a dynamic error if the requested HTTP version is not supported (C0129).

accept-multipart (`xs:boolean`)

If the `accept-multipart` parameter is present and explicitly has the value `false()`, a dynamic error will be raised, if a multipart response is received from the server. This feature is a convenience for pipeline authors as it will raise an error when the multipart request is received, rather than having the presence of a sequence raise an error further along in the pipeline, or simply producing anomalous results. It is a dynamic error if the key "`accept-multipart`" as the value `false()` and a multipart response is detected (C0125).

override-content-encoding (`xs:string`)

If the "`override-content-encoding`" parameter is present, the response will be treated as if the response contained a "`content-encoding`" header with the specified value. The content-encoding header that appears on the `report` port is not changed. It is a dynamic error if the override content encoding cannot be supported (C0132).

permit-expired-ssl-certificate (`xs:boolean`)

If "`permit-expired-ssl-certificate`" is true, then the processor should not reject responses where the server provides an expired SSL certificate.

permit-untrusted-ssl-certificate (`xs:boolean`)

If "`permit-untrusted-ssl-certificate`" is true, then the processor should not reject response where the server provides an SSL certificate which is not trusted, for example, because the certificate authority (CA) is unknown.

follow-redirect (`xs:integer`)

The "`follow-redirect`" parameter allows the pipeline author to specify the step's behaviour in the case of a redirect response. A value of `0` indicates that redirects are not to be followed, `-1` indicates that redirects are to be followed indefinitely, and a specific number indicates the maximum number of redirects to follow. The default behaviour in case of a redirect response is implementation defined.

timeout (`xs:integer`)

If a "`timeout`" is specified, it *must* be a non-negative integer. It controls the time the XProc processor waits for the request to be answered. If a value is given, it is taken as the number of seconds to wait for the response to be delivered. If no response is received after that time, the request is terminated and a status-code `408` is assumed.

fail-on-timeout (`xs:boolean`)

If "`fail-on-timeout`" is true, a dynamic error is raised if a `408` response is received (either as a consequence of setting a value for the "`timeout`" parameter or as status code returned by a server). It is a dynamic error if the value associated with the "`fail-on-timeout`" is associated with `true()` and a HTTP status code `408` is encountered (C0078).

Please note that the "`fail-on-timeout`" parameter is different from the "`timeout`" option on the `p:http-request` step (see specification). If the *step* does not finish in the specified time, `D0053` is raised. If the *request* does not finish in time, and `fail-on-timeout` is true, `C0078` is raised. The actual times after which a timeout is detected may also differ slightly.

status-only (`xs:boolean`)

If the "`status-only`" parameter is true, this indicates that the pipeline author is only interested in the response code. An empty sequence is always returned on the `result` port in this case. The implementation may save resources by ignoring the response body. The map on the `report` will contain the status code and an empty map for "`headers`".

suppress-cookies (`xs:boolean`)

If the "`suppress-cookies`" parameter is true, the implementation *must not* send any cookies with the request.

send-body-anyway (`xs:boolean`)

If the "`send-body-anyway`" parameter is true, and one or more documents appear on the `source` port, a request body is constructed from the documents and sent with the request, even if the semantics of sending a body are not specified for the HTTP method in use.

It is a dynamic error if any key in the "parameters" map is associated with a value that is not an instance of the required type (C0124).

assert (`xs:string`)

The `assert` option can be used by pipeline authors to raise a dynamic error if the response does not fulfill the expectations of the receiver. The option's value (if present) is interpreted as an XPath expression which will be executed using the map that appears on the `report` port as its context item. If the effective boolean value of the expression is `false()`, a dynamic error is raised. It is a dynamic error if the XPath expression in `assert` evaluates to `false` (C0126). Implementations *should* provide an XML representation of the map used as the context item with the error document to enable pipelines to access the error's cause.

No document properties are preserved.

Construction of a multipart request

If more than one document appears on the `source` port, or if the specified "`content-type`" header begins "`multipart/`", a multipart request will be constructed, per RFC 1521. The content type of the request is derived from the "`content-type`" header:

- If the "`content-type`" header specifies a multipart content type, that value will be used as the content type. If the header includes a `boundary` parameter, that value will be used as the boundary.
- If the "`content-type`" header is not specified, "`multipart/mixed`" will be used.
- It is a dynamic error if more than one document appears on the `source` port and a `content-type` header is present and the content type specified is not a multipart content type (C0133).

A multipart request must have a boundary marker, if one isn't specified in the content type, the implementation *must* construct one. It is implementation-defined how a multipart boundary is constructed. Implementations *are not* required to guarantee that the constructed value does not appear accidentally in the multipart data. If it does, the request will be malformed; pipeline authors must provide a boundary if they wish to assure that this cannot happen.

Each document in the sequence is serialized. If the document has a "`serialization`" document property, its values are used to determine how serialization is performed.

All of the document properties *except* "`base-uri`" and "`serialization`" will be used as headers for the MIME part. In particular, this is now the "`id`", "`description`", "`disposition`" and other multipart headers can be provided.

Managing a multipart response

When a multipart response is received, each part is interpreted according to it's content type and a pipeline document is constructed. Any additional headers associated with the part are added to the document properties of the constructed document.

The multipart response is the resulting sequence of documents.

p:identity

The `p:identity` step makes a verbatim copy of its input available on its output.

```
<p:declare-step type="p:identity">
  <p:input port="source" sequence="true" content-types="any"/>
  <p:output port="result" sequence="true" content-types="any"/>
</p:declare-step>
```

If the implementation supports passing PSVI annotations between steps, the `p:identity` step *must* preserve any annotations that appear in the input.

All document properties are preserved.

p:in-scope-names

The `p:in-scope-names` step exposes all of the in-scope variables and options as a set of parameters in a `c:param-set` document.

```
<p:declare-step type="p:in-scope-names">
  <p:output port="result" content-types="application/xml"/>
</p:declare-step>
```

Each in-scope variable and option is converted into a `c:param` element. The resulting `c:param` elements are wrapped in a `c:param-set` and the parameter set document is written to the `result` port. The order in which `c:param` elements occur in the `c:param-set` is implementation-dependent.

For consistency and user convenience, if any of the variables or options have names that are in a namespace, the `namespace` attribute on the `c:param` element *must* be used. Each `name` *must* be an NCName.

The base URI of the output document is the URI of the pipeline document that contains the step.

For consistency with the `p:parameters` step, the `result` port is not primary.

This unlikely pipeline demonstrates the behavior of `p:in-scope-names`:

```
<p:declare-step xmlns:p="http://www.w3.org/ns/xproc"
                name="main" version="1.0">
<p:output port="result">
  <p:pipe step="vars" port="result"/>
</p:output>

<p:option name="username" required="true"/>
<p:option name="password" required="true"/>
<p:variable name="host" select="'http://example.com/'"/>

<p:in-scope-names name="vars"/>

</p:declare-step>
```

Assuming the values supplied for the username and password options are "`user`" and "`pass`", respectively, the output would be:

```
<c:param-set xmlns:c="http://www.w3.org/ns/xproc-step">
  <c:param name="username" namespace="" value="user"/>
  <c:param name="host" namespace="" value="http://example.com/"/>
  <c:param name="password" namespace="" value="pass"/>
</c:param-set>
```

No document properties are preserved.

p:insert

The `p:insert` step inserts the `insertion` port's document into the `source` port's document relative to the matching elements in the `source` port's document.

```
<p:declare-step type="p:insert">
  <p:input port="source" primary="true" content-types="xml html"/>
  <p:input port="insertion" sequence="true" content-types="xml html"/>
  <p:output port="result" content-types="xml html"/>
```

```
  <p:option name="match" as="xs:string" select="'/*'"/>
  <p:option name="position" as="xs:token"
values="('first-child','last-child','before','after')" select="'after'"/>
</p:declare-step>
```

The value of the `match` option *must* be an XSLTSelectionPattern. It is a dynamic error if that pattern matches an attribute or a namespace node (C0023). Multiple matches are allowed, in which case multiple copies of the `insertion` documents will occur. If no elements match, then the document is unchanged.

The value of the `position` option *must* be an NMTOKEN in the following list:

- "`first-child`" - the insertion is made as the first child of the match;
- "`last-child`" - the insertion is made as the last child of the match;
- "`before`" - the insertion is made as the immediate preceding sibling of the match;
- "`after`" - the insertion is made as the immediate following sibling of the match.

It is a dynamic error if the selection pattern matches anything other than an element or a document node and the value of the `position` option is "`first-child`" or "`last-child`" (C0025). It is a dynamic error if the selection pattern matches a document node and the value of the `position` is "`before`" or "`after`" (C0024).

As the inserted elements are part of the output of the step they are not considered in determining matching elements. If an empty sequence appears on the `insertion` port, the result will be the same as the source.

All document properties on the `source` port are preserved. The document properties on the `insertion` port are not preserved or present in the result document.

p:json-join

The `p:json-join` step joins the sequence of documents on port `source` into a single JSON document (an array) appearing on port `result`. If the sequence on port `source` is empty, the empty sequence is returned on port `result`.

```
<p:declare-step type="p:json-join">
  <p:input port="source" sequence="true" content-types="any"/>
  <p:output port="result" content-types="application/json"/>
  <p:option name="flatten-to-depth" as="xs:string?" select="'0'"/>
</p:declare-step>
```

The step inspects the documents on port `source` in turn to create the resulting array:

- If the document under inspection is a JSON document representing an array, the array is copied to the resulting array according to the setting of option `flatten-to-depth`.
- For every other type of JSON document, for XML documents, HTML documents, or text documents, their XDM representation is appended to the resulting array.
- It is implementation defined if `p:json-join` is able to process document types not mentioned yet, i.e. types of binary documents. If a processor supports a given type of documents, an entry is created as described above. It is a dynamic error if a document of an unsupported document type appears on port `source` of `p:json-join` (C0111).

The option `flatten-to-depth` controls whether and to which depth members of an array appearing on port `source` are flattened. It is a dynamic error if `flatten` is neither "`unbounded`", nor a string that may be cast to a non-negative integer (C0119). An integer value of `0`, which is the default, means that no flattening takes place, so the array appearing on port `source` will be contained as an array in the resulting array. An integer value of `1` means that an array on port `source` is flattened, i.e. the members of that array will appear as individual members in the resulting array. Any value greater than `1` means that the flattening is applied recursively to arrays in arrays up to the given depth. A value of "`unbounded`" means that all arrays in arrays will be flattened. As a consequence, the resulting array appearing on port `result` will not have any arrays as members.

No document properties are preserved. The joined document has no `base-uri`.

p:json-merge

The `p:json-merge` step merges the sequence of appearing on port `source` into a single JSON object appearing on port `result`. If the sequence on port `source` is empty, the empty sequence is returned on port `result`.

```
<p:declare-step type="p:json-merge">
  <p:input port="source" sequence="true" content-types="any"/>
  <p:output port="result" content-types="application/json"/>
  <p:option name="duplicates" as="xs:token" values="('reject', 'use-first',
'use-last', 'use-any', 'combine')" select="'use-first'"/>
  <p:option name="key" as="xs:string" select="'concat("_",$p:index)'"/>
</p:declare-step>
```

The step inspects the documents on port `source` in turn to create the resulting map:

- If the document under inspection is a JSON document representing a map, all key-value pairs are copied into the result map unless this map already contains an entry with the given key. In this case the value of option `duplicates` determines the policy for handling duplicate keys as specified for function `map:merge` in the XPath 3.1 functions. It is a dynamic error if duplicate keys are encountered and option `duplicates` has value "`reject`" (C0106).

- For every other type of JSON document, for XML documents, HTML documents, or text documents a new key-value pair is created and put into the resulting map. The key is created by evaluating the XPath expression in option `key` with the inspected document as context item. If the evaluation result is a single atomic value, it is taken as key. If the evaluation result is a node, its string value is taken as key. It is a dynamic error if the evaluation of the XPath expression in option `key` for a given item returns either a sequence, an array, a map, or a function (C0110). Duplicate keys are handled as described above. The XDM representation of the inspected document is taken as value of the key-value pair.

- It is implementation defined if `p:json-merge` is able to process document types not mentioned yet, i.e. types of binary documents. If a processor supports a given type of documents, the key-value pair is created as described above. It is a dynamic error if a document of a not supported document type appears on port `source` of `p:json-merge` (C0107).

An implementation must bind the variable "`p:index`" in the static context of each evaluation of the XPath expression to the position of the document in the sequence of documents on port `source`, starting with "`1`".

No document properties are preserved. The merged document has no `base-uri`.

p:label-elements

The `p:label-elements` step generates a label for each matched element and stores that label in the specified attribute.

```
<p:declare-step type="p:label-elements">
  <p:input port="source" content-types="xml html"/>
  <p:output port="result" content-types="xml html"/>
  <p:option name="attribute" as="xs:QName" select="'xml:id'"/>
  <p:option name="label" as="xs:string" select="'concat("_",$p:index)'"/>
  <p:option name="match" as="xs:string" select="'*'"/>
  <p:option name="replace" as="xs:boolean" select="true()"/>
</p:declare-step>
```

The value of the `label` option is an XPath expression used to generate the value of the attribute label.

The value of the `match` option *must* be an XSLTSelectionPattern. It is a dynamic error if that expression matches anything other than element nodes (C0023).

The value of the `replace` *must* be a boolean value and is used to indicate whether existing attribute values are replaced.

This step operates by generating attribute labels for each element matched. For every matched element, the expression is evaluated with the context node set to the matched element. An attribute is added to the matched element using the attribute name is specified the `attribute` option and the string value of result of evaluating the expression. If the attribute already exists on the matched element, the value is replaced with the string value only if the `replace` option has the value of `true`.

If this step is used to add or change the value of an attribute named "`xml:base`", the base URI of the element *must* also be amended accordingly.

An implementation must bind the variable "`p:index`" in the static context of each evaluation of the XPath expression to the position of the element in the sequence of matched elements. In other words, the first element (in document order) matched gets the value "`1`", the second gets the value "`2`", the third, "`3`", etc.

The result of the p:label-elements step is the input document with the attribute labels associated with matched elements. All other non-matching content remains the same.

All document properties are preserved.

p:load

The `p:load` step has no inputs but produces as its result a document (or documents) specified by an IRI.

```
<p:declare-step type="p:load">
  <p:output port="result" sequence="true" content-types="any"/>
  <p:option name="href" required="true" as="xs:anyURI"/>
  <p:option name="parameters" as="map(xs:QName,item()*)?"/>
  <p:option name="content-type" as="xs:string?"/>
  <p:option name="document-properties" as="map(xs:QName, item()*)?"/>
</p:declare-step>
```

If the option is relative, it is made absolute against the base URI of the element on which it is specified (`p:with-option` or the step in case of a syntactic shortcut value). If the `href` is relative, it is made absolute against the base URI of the element on which it is specified (`p:with-option` or `p:load` in the case of a syntactic shortcut value). It is a dynamic error if the base URI is not both absolute and valid according to RFC 3986 (D0064).

The document or documents identified by the `href` URI are loaded and returned. If the URI protocol supports redirection, then redirects *must* be followed.

It is a dynamic error if the resource referenced by a `p:load` element does not exist or cannot be accessed (D0011).

The behavior of this step depends on the content type of the document or documents loaded. The content type of each document is determined as follows:

1. If a `content-type` property is specified in `document-properties` or `content-type` is present, then each document *must* be interpreted according to that content type. It is a dynamic error if the `content-type` is specified and the document-properties has a "`content-type`" that is not the same (D0062).

2. If the documents are retrieved with a URI protocol that specifies a content type (for example, `http:`), then the document *must* be interpreted according to that content type.

3. In the absence of an explicit type, the content type is implementation-defined.

The `parameters` map contains additional, optional parameters that may influence the way that content is loaded. The interpretation of this map varies according to the content type. Parameter names that are in no namespace are treated as strings using only the local-name where appropriate.

Broadly speaking, there are five categories of data that might be loaded: the section titled "Loading XML data" (p. 265), the section titled "Loading text data" (p. 265), the section titled "Loading JSON data" (p. 265), the section titled "Loading HTML data" (p. 266), and "other" the section titled "Loading binary data" (p. 266) data.

The properties specified in `document-properties` are applied. If the properties do not specify a `base-uri`, the `base-uri` property will reflect the base URI of the loaded document.

Loading XML data

For an XML media type, the content is loaded and parsed as XML.

It is a dynamic error if the loaded content is not a well-formed XML document (D0049).

If the `dtd-validate` parameter is `true`, then DTD validation must be performed when parsing the document. It is a dynamic error if a DTD validation is performed and either the document is not valid or no DTD is found (D0023). It is a dynamic error if the `dtd-validate` parameter is `true` and the processor does not support DTD validation (D0043).

Additional XML parameters are implementation-defined.

Loading text data

For a text media type, the content is loaded as a text document. (A text document is an XPath data model document consisting of a single text node.)

It is a dynamic error if the `content-type` specifies an encoding, which is not supported by the processor (D0060).

Text parameters are implementation-defined.

Loading JSON data

For a JSON media type, the content is loaded and parsed as JSON.

The parameters specified for the `fn:parse-json` function in the XPath 3.1 functions *must* be supported. Additional JSON parameters are implementation-defined.

It is a dynamic error if the loaded content does not conform to the JSON grammar, unless the parameter `liberal` is `true` and the processor chooses to accept the deviation (D0057).

It is a dynamic error if the parameter `duplicates` is `reject` and the value of loaded content contains a JSON object with duplicate keys (D0058).

It is a dynamic error if the parameter map contains an entry whose key is defined in the specification of `fn:parse-json` and whose value is not valid for that key, or if it contains an entry with the key fallback when the parameter `escape` with `true()` is also present (D0059).

Loading HTML data

For an HTML media type, the content is loaded and parsed into an XPath data model document that contains a tree of elements, attributes, and other nodes.

The precise way in which HTML documents are parsed into the XPath data model is implementation-defined.

It is a dynamic error if the loaded document cannot be represented as an HTML document in the XPath data model (D0078).

HTML parameters are implementation-defined.

Loading binary data

An XProc processor may load other, arbitrary data types. How a processor interprets other media types is implementation-defined.

Parameters for other media types are implementation-defined.

p:make-absolute-uris

The `p:make-absolute-uris` step makes an element or attribute's value in the source document an absolute IRI value in the result document.

```
<p:declare-step type="p:make-absolute-uris">
  <p:input port="source" content-types="xml html"/>
  <p:output port="result" content-types="xml html"/>
  <p:option name="match" required="true" as="xs:string"/>
  <p:option name="base-uri" as="xs:anyURI?"/>
</p:declare-step>
```

The value of the `match` option *must* be an XSLTSelectionPattern. It is a dynamic error if the pattern matches anything other than element or attribute nodes (C0023).

The value of the `base-uri` option *must* be an `anyURI`. It is interpreted as an IRI reference. If it is relative, it is made absolute against the base URI of the element on which it is specified (`p:with-option` or `p:make-absolute-uris` in the case of a syntactic shortcut value). It is a dynamic error if the base URI is not both absolute and valid according to RFC 3986 (D0064).

For every element or attribute in the input document which matches the specified pattern, its XPath string-value is resolved against the specified base URI and the resulting absolute IRI is used as the matched node's entire contents in the output.

The base URI used for resolution defaults to the matched attribute's element or the matched element's base URI unless the `base-uri` option is specified. When the `base-uri` option is specified, the option value is used as the base URI regardless of any contextual base URI value in the document. This option value is resolved against the base URI of the `p:option` element used to set the option.

If the IRI reference specified by the `base-uri` option on `p:make-absolute-uris` is absent and the input document has no base URI, the results are implementation-dependent.

All document properties are preserved.

p:namespace-delete

The `p:namespace-delete` step deletes all of the namespaces identified by the specified prefixes from the document appearing on port `source`.

```
<p:declare-step type="p:namespace-delete">
  <p:input port="source" content-types="xml html"/>
  <p:output port="result" content-types="xml html"/>
  <p:option name="prefixes" required="true" as="xs:string"/>
</p:declare-step>
```

The value of option `prefixes` is taken as a space separated list of prefixes. It is a dynamic error if any prefix is not in-scope at the point where the `p:namespace-delete` occurs (C0108).

For any prefix the associated namespace is removed from the elements and attributes in the document appearing on port `source`. The respective elements or attributes in the document appearing on port `result` will be in no namespace.

It is a dynamic error if a namespace is to be removed from an attribute and the element already has an attribute with the resulting name (C0109).

All document properties are preserved.

p:namespace-rename

The `p:namespace-rename` step renames any namespace declaration or use of a namespace in a document to a new IRI value.

```
<p:declare-step type="p:namespace-rename">
  <p:input port="source" content-types="xml html"/>
  <p:output port="result" content-types="xml html"/>
  <p:option name="from" as="xs:anyURI?"/>
  <p:option name="to" as="xs:anyURI?"/>
  <p:option name="apply-to" as="xs:token" select="'all'"
values="('all','elements','attributes')"/>
</p:declare-step>
```

The value of the `from` option *must* be an `anyURI`. It *should* be either empty or absolute, but will not be resolved in any case.

The value of the `to` option *must* be an `anyURI`. It *should* be empty or absolute, but will not be resolved in any case.

The value of the `apply-to` option *must* be one of "`all`", "`elements`", or "`attributes`". If the value is "`elements`", only elements will be renamed, if the value is "`attributes`", only attributes will be renamed, if the value is "`all`", both elements and attributes will be renamed.

It is a dynamic error if the XML namespace (`http://www.w3.org/XML/1998/namespace`) or the XMLNS namespace (`http://www.w3.org/2000/xmlns/`) is the value of either the `from` option or the `to` option (C0014).

If the value of the `from` option is the same as the value of the `to` option, the input is reproduced unchanged on the output. Otherwise, namespace bindings, namespace attributes and element and attribute names are changed as follows:

- Namespace bindings: If the `from` option is present and its value is not the empty string, then every binding of a prefix (or the default namespace) in the input document whose value is the same as the value of the `from` option is

  - replaced in the output with a binding to the value of the `to` option, provided it is present and not the empty string;

  - otherwise (the `to` option is not specified or has an empty string as its value) absent from the output.

  If the `from` option is absent, or its value is the empty string, then no bindings are changed or removed.

- Elements and attributes: If the `from` option is present and its value is not the empty string, for every element and attribute, as appropriate, in the input whose namespace name is the same as the value of the `from` option, in the output its namespace name is

  - replaced with the value of the `to` option, provided it is present and not the empty string;

  - otherwise (the `to` option is not specified or has an empty string as its value) changed to have no value.

  If the `from` option is absent, or its value is the empty string, then for every element and attribute, as appropriate, whose namespace name has no value, in the output its namespace name is set to the value of the `to` option.

  It is a dynamic error if as a consequence of changing or removing the namespace of an attribute the attribute's name is not unique on the respective element (C0092).

- Namespace attributes: If the `from` option is present and its value is not the empty string, for every namespace attribute in the input whose value is the same as the value of the `from` option, in the output

  - the namespace attribute's value is replaced with the value of the `to` option, provided it is present and not the empty string;

- otherwise (the `to` option is not specified or has an empty string as its value) the namespace attribute is absent.

The `apply-to` option is primarily intended to make it possible to avoid renaming attributes when the `from` option specifies no namespace, since many attributes are in no namespace.

Care should be taken when specifying no namespace with the `to` option. Prefixed names in content, for example QNames and XPath expressions, may end up with no appropriate namespace binding.

All document properties are preserved.

p:pack

The `p:pack` step merges two document sequences in a pair-wise fashion.

```
<p:declare-step type="p:pack">
  <p:input port="source" content-types="text xml html" sequence="true"
primary="true"/>
  <p:input port="alternate" sequence="true" content-types="text xml html"/>
  <p:output port="result" sequence="true" content-types="application/xml"/>
  <p:option name="wrapper" required="true" as="xs:QName"/>
</p:declare-step>
```

The step takes each pair of documents, in order, one from the `source` port and one from the `alternate` port, wraps them with a new element node whose QName is the value specified in the `wrapper` option, and writes that element to the `result` port as a document.

If the step reaches the end of one input sequence before the other, then it simply wraps each of the remaining documents in the longer sequence.

In the common case, where the document element of a document in the `result` sequence has two element children, any comments, processing instructions, or white space text nodes that occur between them may have come from either of the input documents; this step does not attempt to distinguish which one.

No document properties are preserved. The result documents do not have a `base-uri` property.

p:parameters

The `p:parameters` step exposes a set of parameters as a `c:param-set` document.

```
<p:declare-step type="p:parameters">
  <p:output port="result" content-types="application/xml"/>
  <p:option name="parameters" as="map(xs:QName,item()*)?"/>
</p:declare-step>
```

Each parameter in the `parameters` map is converted into a `c:param` element. The resulting `c:param` elements are wrapped in a `c:param-set` and the parameter set document is written to the `result` port. The order in which `c:param` elements occur in the `c:param-set` is implementation-dependent.

For consistency and user convenience, *in the output of* `p:parameters`, if any of the parameters have names that are in a namespace, the `namespace` attribute on the `c:param` element *must* be used. Each `name` *must* be an NCName.

The base URI of the output document is the URI of the pipeline document that contains the step.

No document properties are preserved.

The c:param element

A `c:param` is a standard XML representation of a parameter.

```
<c:param name = QName
         namespace? = anyURI
         value? = xs:string
         as? = XPathSequenceType >
  <(any)>*
</c:param>
```

The attributes that can occur on `c:param` are:

`name`

The `name` attribute of the `c:param` must have the lexical form of a QName. (In the output of some steps, such as `p:parameters`, the name will always be an `xs:NCName`, but that is not a general requirement for user-constructed `c:param` elements)

If the `namespace` attribute is not specified, and the `name` contains a colon, then the expanded name of the parameter is constructed using the `name` value and the namespace declarations in-scope on the `c:param` element. It is a dynamic error if the `namespace` attribute is not specified, the `name` contains a colon, and the specified prefix is not in the in-scope namespace bindings (C0087).

If the `namespace` attribute is not specified, and the `name` does not contain a colon, then the expanded name of the parameter is in no namespace.

`namespace`

The namespace URI of the parameter name.

If the `namespace` attribute is specified, then the expanded name of the parameter is constructed from the specified namespace and the `name` value. It is a dynamic error if the `namespace` attribute is specified, the `name` contains a colon, and the specified namespace is not the same as the in-scope namespace binding for the specified prefix (C0083).

`value`

If the parameter value is an atomic type, a lexical representation of its value appears in the `value` attribute. It is a dynamic error if the `value` attribute is specified and the `c:param` element is not empty (C0087).

`as`

The `as` attribute specifies the XPath 3.1 sequence type[1] of the parameter value. It is a dynamic error if the sequence type is not syntactically valid (C0089). The sequence type `item()*` is assumed if no explicit type is provided. It is a dynamic error if the supplied value of a variable or option cannot be converted to the required type (D0036).

Other attributes

Any namespace-qualified attribute names that appear on the `c:param` element are ignored. It is a dynamic error for any unqualified attribute names other than "`name`", "`namespace`", "`as`", or "`value`" to appear on a `c:param` element (C0085).

1 https://www.w3.org/TR/xpath-31/#dt-sequence-type

If the `c:param` element is not empty, then its content, interpreted as a sequence of XML nodes, is the value of the parameter.

The c:param-set element

A `c:param-set` represents a set of parameters on a parameter input.

```
<c:param-set>
  <c:param>*
</c:param-set>
```

The `c:param-set` contains zero or more `c:param` elements. It is a dynamic error if the parameter list contains any elements other than `c:param` (C0084).

Any namespace-qualified attribute names that appear on the `c:param-set` element are ignored. It is a dynamic error for any unqualified attribute names to appear on a `c:param-set` element (C0086).

p:rename

The `p:rename` step renames elements, attributes, or processing-instruction targets in a document.

```
<p:declare-step type="p:rename">
  <p:input port="source" content-types="xml html"/>
  <p:output port="result" content-types="xml html"/>
  <p:option name="match" as="xs:string" select="'/*'"/>
  <p:option name="new-name" required="true" as="xs:QName"/>
</p:declare-step>
```

The value of the `match` option must be an XSLTSelectionPattern. It is a dynamic error if the pattern matches anything other than element, attribute or processing instruction nodes (C0023).

Each element, attribute, or processing-instruction in the input matched by the selection pattern specified in the `match` option is renamed in the output to the name specified by the `new-name` option.

If the `match` option matches an attribute and if the element on which it occurs already has an attribute whose expanded name is the same as the expanded name of the specified `new-name`, then the results is as if the current attribute named "`new-name`" was deleted before renaming the matched attribute.

With respect to attributes named "`xml:base`", the following semantics apply: renaming an *from* "`xml:base`" *to* something else has no effect on the underlying base URI of the element; however, if an attribute is renamed *from* something else *to* "`xml:base`", the base URI of the element *must* also be amended accordingly.

If the pattern matches processing instructions, then it is the processing instruction target that is renamed. It is a dynamic error if the pattern matches a processing instruction and the new name has a non-null namespace (C0013).

All document properties are preserved.

p:replace

The `p:replace` step replaces matching nodes in its primary input with the top-level node(s) of the `replacement` port's document.

```
<p:declare-step type="p:replace">
  <p:input port="source" primary="true" content-types="xml html"/>
  <p:input port="replacement" content-types="text xml html"/>
  <p:output port="result" content-types="text xml html"/>
  <p:option name="match" required="true" as="xs:string"/>
</p:declare-step>
```

The value of the `match` option *must* be an XSLTSelectionPattern. It is a dynamic error if that pattern matches an attribute or a namespace nodes (C0023). Multiple matches are allowed, in which case multiple copies of the `replacement` document will occur.

Every node in the primary input matching the specified pattern is replaced in the output by the top-level node(s) of the `replacement` document. Only non-nested matches are replaced. That is, once a node is replaced, its descendants cannot be matched.

If the document node is matched and port `replacement` contains a text document, the entire document is replaced by the text node. What appears on port `result` is a text document with the text node wrapped in a document node.

If the resulting document contains exactly one text node, the `content-type` property is changed to `text/plain` and the `serialization` property is removed, while all other document properties are preserved. For other document types, all document properties are preserved.

p:set-attributes

The `p:set-attributes` step sets attributes on matching elements.

```
<p:declare-step type="p:set-attributes">
  <p:input port="source" primary="true" content-types="xml html"/>
  <p:output port="result" content-types="xml html"/>
  <p:option name="match" as="xs:string" select="'/*'"/>
  <p:option name="attributes" required="true" as="map(xs:QName,
xs:anyAtomicType)"/>
</p:declare-step>
```

The value of the `match` option *must* be an XSLTSelectionPattern. It is a dynamic error if that pattern matches anything other than element nodes (C0023).

A new attribute is created for each entry in the map appearing on the `attributes` option. The attribute name is taken from the entry's key while the attribute value is taken from the string value of the entry's value.

If an attribute with the same name as one of the attributes to be created already exists, the value specified on the `attributes` option is used. The result port of this step produces a copy of the `source` port's document with the matching elements' attributes modified.

The matching elements are specified by the selection pattern in the `match` option. All matching elements are processed. If no elements match, the step will not change any elements.

If the attributes taken from the `attributes` use namespaces, prefixes, or prefixes bound to different namespaces, the document produced on the `result` output port will require namespace fixup.

If an attribute named `xml:base` is added or changed, the base URI of the element *must* also be amended accordingly.

All document properties are preserved.

p:set-properties

The `p:set-properties` step sets document properties on the source document.

```
<p:declare-step type="p:set-properties">
  <p:input port="source" content-types="any"/>
  <p:output port="result" content-types="any"/>
  <p:option name="properties" required="true" as="map(xs:QName,item()*)"/>
  <p:option name="merge" select="true()" as="xs:boolean"/>
</p:declare-step>
```

The document properties of the document on the `source` port are augmented with the values specified in the `properties` option. The document produced on the `result` port has the same representation but the adjusted property values.

If the `merge` option is true, then the supplied properties are added to the existing properties, overwriting already existing values for a given key. If it is false, the document's properties are replaced by the new set.

It is a dynamic error if a value is assigned to the `serialization` document property that cannot be converted into `map(xs:QName, item()*)` according to the rules in section "QName handling" of XProc 3.0 (D0070).

It is a dynamic error if the `properties` map contains a key equal to the string "`content-type`" (C0069).

If the `properties` map contains a key equal to the string "`base-uri`" the associated value is taken as the new base URI of the resulting document. It is a dynamic error if the base URI is not both absolute and valid according to RFC 3986 (D0064).

If `merge` is true, document properties not overridden by settings in the `properties` map are preserved, otherwise the resulting document has only the `content-type` property and the properties specified in the `properties` map. In particular, if `merge` is false, the `base-uri` property will not be preserved. This means that the resulting document will not have a base URI if the `properties` map does not contain a `base-uri` entry.

p:sink

The `p:sink` step accepts a sequence of documents and discards them. It has no output.

```
<p:declare-step type="p:sink">
  <p:input port="source" content-types="any" sequence="true"/>
</p:declare-step>
```

p:split-sequence

The `p:split-sequence` step accepts a sequence of documents and divides it into two sequences.

```
<p:declare-step type="p:split-sequence">
  <p:input port="source" content-types="xml html" sequence="true"/>
  <p:output port="matched" sequence="true" primary="true" content-types="xml
html"/>
  <p:output port="not-matched" sequence="true" content-types="xml html"/>
  <p:option name="initial-only" as="xs:boolean" select="false()"/>
  <p:option name="test" required="true" as="xs:string"/>
</p:declare-step>
```

The value of the `test` option *must* be an XPathExpression.

The XPath expression in the `test` option is applied to each document in the input sequence. If the effective boolean value of the expression is true, the document is copied to the `matched` port; otherwise it is copied to the `not-matched` port.

If the `initial-only` option is true, then when the first document that does not satisfy the test expression is encountered, it *and all the documents that follow it* are written to the `not-matched` port. In other words, it only writes the initial series of matched documents (which may be empty) to the `matched` port. All other documents are written to the `not-matched` port, irrespective of whether or not they match.

The XPath context for the `test` option changes over time. For each document that appears on the `source` port, the expression is evaluated with that document as the context document. The context position (`position()`) is the position of that document within the sequence and the context size (`last()`) is the total number of documents in the sequence.

In principle, this component cannot stream because it must buffer all of the input sequence in order to find the context size. In practice, if the test expression does not use the `last()` function, the implementation can stream and ignore the context size.

If the implementation supports passing PSVI annotations between steps, the `p:split-sequence` step *must* preserve any annotations that appear in the input.

All document properties are preserved.

p:store

The `p:store` step stores (a possibly serialized version of) its input to a URI. The input is copied to the `result` port. Additionally this step outputs a reference to the location of the stored document on the `result-uri` port.

```
<p:declare-step type="p:store">
  <p:input port="source" content-types="any"/>
  <p:output port="result" content-types="any" primary="true"/>
  <p:output port="result-uri" content-types="application/xml"/>
  <p:option name="href" required="true" as="xs:anyURI"/>
  <p:option name="serialization" as="map(xs:QName,item()*)?"/>
</p:declare-step>
```

The value of the `href` option *must* be an `anyURI`. If it is relative, it is made absolute against the base URI of the element on which it is specified (`p:with-option` or `p:store` in the case of a syntactic shortcut value).

The step attempts to store the document to the specified URI. If the URI scheme "`file:`" is supported, the processor *should* try to create all non existing folders in the URI's path. It is a dynamic error if the URI scheme is not supported or the step cannot store to the specified location (C0050).

The output of this step on the `result-uri` port is a document containing a single `c:result` element whose content is the absolute URI of the document stored by the step.

The `serialization` option is provided to control the serialization of content when it is stored. If the document to be stored has a "serialization" property, the serialization is controlled by the merger of the two maps where the entries in the "serialization" property take precedence. Serialization is described in XProc 3.0.

All document properties are preserved.

p:string-replace

The `p:string-replace` step matches nodes in the document provided on the `source` port and replaces them with the string result of evaluating an XPath expression.

```
<p:declare-step type="p:string-replace">
  <p:input port="source" content-types="xml html"/>
  <p:output port="result" content-types="text xml html"/>
  <p:option name="match" required="true" as="xs:string"/>
  <p:option name="replace" required="true" as="xs:string"/>
</p:declare-step>
```

The value of the `match` option *must* be an XSLTSelectionPattern.

The value of the `replace` option *must* be an XPathExpression.

The matched nodes are specified with the selection pattern in the `match` option. For each matching node, the XPath expression provided by the `replace` option is evaluated with the matching node as the XPath context node. The string value of the result is used in the output. Nodes that do not match are copied without change.

If the expression given in the `match` option matches an *attribute*, the string value of the `replace` expression is used as the new value of the attribute in the output. If the attribute is named "`xml:base`", the base URI of the element *must* also be amended accordingly.

If the document node is matched, the entire document is replaced by the string value of the `replace` expression. What appears on port `result` is a text document with the text node wrapped in a document node.

If the expression matches any other kind of node, the entire node (and *not* just its contents) is replaced by the string value of the `replace` expression.

If the resulting document contains exactly one text node, the `content-type` property is changed to `text/plain` and the `serialization` property is removed, while all other document properties are preserved. For other document types, all document properties are preserved.

p:text-count

The `p:text-count` step counts the number of lines in a text document and returns a single XML document containing that number.

```
<p:declare-step type="p:text-count">
  <p:input port="source" primary="true" sequence="false" content-types="text"/>
  <p:output port="result" primary="true" sequence="false"
content-types="application/xml"/>
</p:declare-step>
```

The `p:text-count` step counts the number of lines in the text document appearing on its `source` port. It returns on its `result` port an XML document containing a single `c:result` element whose contents is the string representing this count.

Lines are identified as described in XML, 2.11 End-of-Line Handling[2]. For the purpose of identifying lines, if the very last character in the text document is a newline (
), that newline is ignored. (It is not a separator between that line and a following line that contains no characters.)

No document properties are preserved. The count document does not have a `base-uri` property.

p:text-head

The `p:text-head` step returns lines from the beginning of a text document.

```
<p:declare-step type="p:text-head">
  <p:input port="source" primary="true" sequence="false" content-types="text"/>
  <p:output port="result" primary="true" sequence="false" content-types="text"/>
  <p:option name="count" required="true" as="xs:integer"/>
</p:declare-step>
```

The `p:text-head` step returns on its `result` port lines from the text document that appears on its `source` port:

- If the `count` option is positive, the `p:text-head` step returns the first `count` lines
- If the `count` option is zero, the `p:text-head` step returns all lines

2 https://www.w3.org/TR/xml/#sec-line-ends

- If the `count` option is negative, the `p:text-head` step returns all lines except the first `count` lines

Lines are identified as described in XML, 2.11 End-of-Line Handling[3]. All lines returned by `p:text-head` are terminated with a single newline (
).

All document properties are preserved.

p:text-join

The `p:text-join` step concatenates text documents.

```
<p:declare-step type="p:text-join">
  <p:input port="source" sequence="true" content-types="text"/>
  <p:output port="result" content-types="text"/>
  <p:option name="separator" as="xs:string?"/>
  <p:option name="prefix" as="xs:string?"/>
  <p:option name="suffix" as="xs:string?"/>
  <p:option name="override-content-type" as="xs:string?"/>
</p:declare-step>
```

The `p:text-join` step concatenates the text documents appearing on its `source` port into a single document on its `result` port. The documents will be concatenated in order of appearance.

- When the `separator` option is specified, its value will be inserted in between adjacent documents.
- When the `prefix` option is specified, the document appearing on the `result` port will always start with its value (also when there are no documents on the `source` port).
- When the `suffix` option is specified, the document appearing on the `result` port will always end with its value (also when there are no documents on the `source` port).

When the `override-content-type` option is specified, the document appearing on the port `result` will have this media type as part of its document properties. It is a dynamic error if the supplied `content-type` is not a valid media type of the form " *type/subtype+ext* " where

[3] https://www.w3.org/TR/xml/#sec-line-ends

"`+ext` " is optional (C0070). It is a dynamic error if the value of option `override-content-type` is not a text media type (C0001).

Concatenating text documents does not require identifying individual lines in each document, consequently no special end-of-line handling is performed.

No document properties are preserved. The joined document has no `base-uri` property.

p:text-replace

The `p:text-replace` step replaces all occurrences of substrings in a text document that match a supplied regular expression with a given replacement string.

```
<p:declare-step type="p:text-replace">
  <p:input port="source" primary="true" sequence="false" content-types="text"/>
  <p:output port="result" primary="true" sequence="false" content-types="text"/>
  <p:option name="pattern" required="true" as="xs:string"/>
  <p:option name="replacement" required="true" as="xs:string"/>
  <p:option name="flags" as="xs:string?"/>
</p:declare-step>
```

The `p:text-replace` step replaces all occurrences of substrings in the text document appearing on its `source` port that match a supplied regular expression with a given replacement string. The result is returned (as another text document) on its `result` port.

This step is a convenience wrapper around the XPath `fn:replace` [4] function to ease text replacements in the document flow of a pipeline.

The `pattern`, `replacement` and `flags` options are specified the same as the parameters with the same names of the `fn:replace` [5] function.

Replacing strings in text documents does not require identifying individual lines in each document, consequently no special end-of-line handling is performed.

All document properties are preserved.

[4] https://www.w3.org/TR/xpath-functions-31/#func-replace
[5] https://www.w3.org/TR/xpath-functions-31/#func-replace

p:text-sort

The `p:text-sort` step sorts lines in a text document.

```
<p:declare-step type="p:text-sort">
  <p:input port="source" primary="true" sequence="false" content-types="text"/>
  <p:output port="result" primary="true" sequence="false" content-types="text"/>
  <p:option name="sort-key" as="xs:string" select="'.'"/>
  <p:option name="order" as="xs:string" select="'ascending'" values="('ascending',
'descending')"/>
  <p:option name="case-order" as="xs:string?" values="('upper-first',
'lower-first')"/>
  <p:option name="lang" as="xs:language?"/>
  <p:option name="collation" as="xs:string"
select="'https://www.w3.org/2005/xpath-functions/collation/codepoint'"/>
  <p:option name="stable" as="xs:boolean" select="true()"/>
</p:declare-step>
```

The `p:text-sort` step sorts the lines in the text document appearing on its `source` port and returns the result as another text document on its `result` port. The sort key is obtained by applying the XPath expression in `sort-key` to each line in turn.

- The `sort-key` is used to obtain a sort key for each of the lines in the document appearing on `source`. The `context item` is the line as an instance of `xs:string`, the `context position` is the number of the line in the document on port `source`, the `context size` is the number of lines in this document. It is a dynamic error if a dynamic XPath error occurred while applying sort-key to a line (C0098). It is a dynamic error if the result of applying `sort-key` to a given line results in a sequence with more than one item (C0099).
- The `order` option defines whether the lines are processed in ascending or descending order. Its value *must* be one of `ascending` or `descending`. The default is `ascending`.
- The `case-order` option defines whether upper-case letters are to be collated before or after lower-case letters. Its value *must* be one of `upper-first` or `lower-first`. The default is language-dependent.
- The `lang` option defines the language whose collating conventions are to be used. The default depends on the processing environment. Its value must be a valid language code (e.g. `en-EN`).
- The `collation` option identifies how strings are to be compared with each other. Its value must be a valid collation URI. The only collation XProc processors *must* support is the Unicode

Codepoint Collation
`http://www.w3.org/2005/xpath-functions/collation/codepoint` [6]. This is also its default. Support for other collations is implementation-defined.

- If the `stable` option is set to `false` this indicates that there is no requirement to retain the original order of items that have equal values for all the sort keys.

Lines are identified as described in XML, 2.11 End-of-Line Handling[7]. For the purpose of identifying lines, if the very last character in the text document is a newline (
), that newline is ignored. (It is not a separator between that line and a following line that contains no characters.) All lines returned by `p:text-sort` are terminated with a single newline (
).

The sort process performed by this step is the same as described in The xsl:sort Element[8]. Options `lang` and `case-order` are only taken into consideration if no value is selected for option `collation`.

All document properties are preserved.

p:text-tail

The `p:text-tail` step returns lines from the end of a text document.

```
<p:declare-step type="p:text-tail">
  <p:input port="source" primary="true" sequence="false" content-types="text"/>
  <p:output port="result" primary="true" sequence="false" content-types="text"/>
  <p:option name="count" required="true" as="xs:integer"/>
</p:declare-step>
```

The `p:text-tail` step returns on its `result` port lines from the text document that appears on its `source` port:

- If the `count` option is positive, the `p:text-tail` step returns the last `count` lines
- If the `count` option is zero, the `p:text-tail` step returns all lines

---

[6] https://www.w3.org/2005/xpath-functions/collation/codepoint/
[7] https://www.w3.org/TR/xml/#sec-line-ends
[8] https://www.w3.org/TR/xslt-30/#xsl-sort

- If the `count` option is negative, the `p:text-tail` step returns all lines except the last `count` lines

Lines are identified as described in XML, 2.11 End-of-Line Handling[9]. All lines returned by `p:text-tail` are terminated with a single newline (
).

All document properties are preserved.

p:unarchive

The `p:unarchive` step outputs on its `result` port specific entries in an archive (for instance from a zip file).

```
<p:declare-step type="p:unarchive">
  <p:input port="source" primary="true" content-types="any" sequence="false"/>
  <p:output port="result" primary="true" content-types="any" sequence="true"/>
  <p:option name="include-filter" as="xs:string*"/>
  <p:option name="exclude-filter" as="xs:string*"/>
  <p:option name="format" as="xs:QName?"/>
  <p:option name="parameters" as="map(xs:QName, item()*)?"/>
  <p:option name="relative-to" as="xs:anyURI?"/>
</p:declare-step>
```

The meaning and interpretation of the `p:unarchive` step's options is as follows:

- The format of the archive is determined as follows:
  - If the `format` option is specified, this determines the format of the archive. Implementations *must* support the ZIP format, specified with the value `zip`. It is implementation-defined what other formats are supported.
  - If no `format` option is specified or if its value is the empty sequence, the archive's format will be determined by the step, using the `content-type` document-property of the document on the `source` port and/or by inspecting its contents. It is implementation-defined how the step determines the archive's format. Implementations *should* recognize archives in ZIP format.

[9] https://www.w3.org/TR/xml/#sec-line-ends

- It is a dynamic error if the format of the archive does not match the specified format, cannot be understood, determined and/or processed (C0085).

- The `parameters` option can be used to supply parameters to control the unarchiving. The semantics of the keys and the allowed values for these keys are implementation-defined. It is a dynamic error if the map `parameters` contains an entry whose key is defined by the implementation and whose value is not valid for that key (C0079).

- If present, the value of the `include-filter` or `exclude-filter` option *must* be a sequence of strings, each one representing a regular expressions as specified in the XPath 3.1 functions, section 7.61 "`Regular Expression Syntax`".

  If neither the `include-filter` option nor the `exclude-filter` option is specified, the `p:unarchive` step outputs on its `result` port all entries in the archive.

  If the `include-filter` option or the `exclude-filter` option is specified, the `p:archive` step outputs on the `result` port the entries from the archive that conform to the following rules:

  - If any `include-filter` pattern matches an archive entry's name, the entry is included in the output.

  - If any `exclude-filter` pattern matches an archive entry's name, the entry is excluded in the output.

  - If both options are provided, the include filter is processed first, then the exclude filter.

  - Names of entries in archives are always relative names. For instance, the name of a file called `xyz.xml` in a `specs` subdirectory in an archive is called in full `specs/xyz.xml` (and not `/specs/xyz.xml`).

  As a result: an item is included if it matches (at least) one of the `include-filter` values and none of the `exclude-filter` values.

- The `relative-to` option, when present, is used in creating the base URI of the unarchived documents. If the option is relative, it is made absolute against the base URI of the element on which it is specified (`p:with-option` or the step in case of a syntactic shortcut value).

The base URI of an unarchived document appearing on the `result` port is:

- If the `relative-to` option is present: Function `p:urify()` is called with the value of this option as second parameter (`$basedir`) and with the relative path of this document as it was in the archive as first parameter

- If the `relative-to` option is *not* present: Function `p:urify()` is called with the value of the base URI of the archive appended with a "/" as second parameter (`$baseDir`) and the relative path of this document as it was in the archive as first parameter

It is a dynamic error if the `relative-to` option is not present and the document on the `source` port does not have a base URI (C0120). It is a dynamic error if the option is not a valid URI according to RFC 3986 (D0064).

For instance, the base URI of an unarchived file called `xyz.xml` that resided in the `specs` subdirectory in an archive with base URI `file:///a/b/c.zip` will become:

- With the `relative-to` option set to `file:///x/y/z`: `file:///x/y/z/specs/xyz.xml`

- Without a `relative-to` option set: `file:///a/b/c.zip/specs/xyz.xml`

No document properties are preserved. The `base-uri` property of each unarchived document is reflective of the base URI of the document.

p:uncompress

The `p:uncompress` step expects on its `source` port a compressed document. It outputs an uncompressed version of this on its `result` port.

```
<p:declare-step type="p:uncompress">
  <p:input port="source" primary="true" content-types="any" sequence="false"/>
  <p:output port="result" primary="true" content-types="any" sequence="false"/>
  <p:option name="format" as="xs:QName?"/>
  <p:option name="parameters" as="map(xs:QName,item()*)?"/>
  <p:option name="content-type" as="xs:string"
select="'application/octet-stream'"/>
</p:declare-step>
```

The compression format of the document appearing on the `source` port is determined as follows:

- If the `format` option is specified, this determines the compression format. Implementations *must* support the GZIP format, specified with the value `gzip`. It is implementation-defined what other formats are supported. It is a dynamic error if the compression format cannot be understood, determined and/or processed (C0202).
- If no `format` option is specified or its value is the empty sequence, the compression format will be determined by the step, using the `content-type` document-property of the document on the `source` port and/or by inspecting its contents. It is implementation-defined how the step determines the compression format. Implementations *should* recognize archives in GZIP format.

The `parameters` option can be used to supply parameters to control the uncompression. The semantics of the keys and the allowed values for these keys are implementation-defined. It is a dynamic error if the map `parameters` contains an entry whose key is defined by the implementation and whose value is not valid for that key (C0079).

Identification of the uncompressed document's content-type is done as follows:

1. If the `content-type` option is specified, the uncompressed document *must* be interpreted according to that content-type. It is a dynamic error if the supplied `content-type` is not a valid media type of the form "*`type/subtype+ext`*" where "*`+ext`*" is optional (C0070). It is a dynamic error if the `p:uncompress` step cannot perform the requested content-type cast (C0201).
2. In the absence of an explicit type, the content will be interpreted as content type `application/octet-stream`.

All document properties are preserved, except for the `content-type` property which is updated accordingly.

p:unwrap

The `p:unwrap` step replaces matched elements with their children.

```
<p:declare-step type="p:unwrap">
  <p:input port="source" content-types="xml html"/>
  <p:output port="result" content-types="application/xml text/plain"/>
```

```
  <p:option name="match" as="xs:string" select="'/*'"/>
</p:declare-step>
```

The value of the `match` option *must* be an XSLTSelectionPattern. It is a dynamic error if that pattern matches anything other than the document node or element nodes (C0023).

Every element in the `source` document that matches the specified `match` pattern is replaced by its children, effectively "unwrapping" the children from their parent. Non-element nodes and unmatched elements are passed through unchanged.

The matching applies to the entire document, not just the "top-most" matches. A pattern of the form `h:div` will replace *all* `h:div` elements, not just the top-most ones.

This step produces a single document; if the document element is unwrapped, the result might not be well-formed XML. If the step produces a document node with a single text child, the result will have content type "`text/plain`".

All document properties are preserved.

p:uuid

The `p:uuid` step generates a UUID and injects it into the `source` document.

```
<p:declare-step type="p:uuid">
  <p:input port="source" primary="true" content-types="xml html"/>
  <p:output port="result" content-types="text xml html"/>
  <p:option name="match" as="xs:string" select="'/*'"/>
  <p:option name="version" as="xs:integer?"/>
</p:declare-step>
```

The value of the `match` option must be an XSLTSelectionPattern. The value of the `version` option must be an integer.

If the `version` is specified, that version of UUID must be computed. It is a dynamic error if the processor does not support the specified `version` of the UUID algorithm (C0060). If the `version` is not specified, the version of UUID computed is implementation-defined.

Implementations *must* support version 4 UUIDs. Support for other versions of UUID, and the mechanism by which the necessary inputs are made available for computing other versions, is implementation-defined.

The matched nodes are specified with the selection pattern in the `match` option. For each matching node, the generated UUID is used in the output (if more than one node matches, the *same* UUID is used in each match). Nodes that do not match are copied without change.

If the expression given in the `match` option matches an *attribute*, the UUID is used as the new value of the attribute in the output. If the attribute is named "`xml:base`", the base URI of the element *must* also be amended accordingly.

If the document node is matched, the entire document is replaced by a text node with the UUID. What appears on port `result` is a text document with the text node wrapped in a document node.

If the expression matches any other kind of node, the entire node (and *not* just its contents) is replaced by the UUID.

If the resulting document contains exactly one text node, the `content-type` property is changed to `text/plain` and the `serialization` property is removed, while all other document properties are preserved. For other document types, all document properties are preserved.

p:wrap

The `p:wrap` step wraps matching nodes in the `source` document with a new parent element.

```
<p:declare-step type="p:wrap">
  <p:input port="source" content-types="xml html"/>
  <p:output port="result" content-types="application/xml"/>
  <p:option name="wrapper" required="true" as="xs:QName"/>
  <p:option name="match" required="true" as="xs:string"/>
  <p:option name="group-adjacent" as="xs:string?"/>
</p:declare-step>
```

The value of the `match` option *must* be an XSLTSelectionPattern. It is a dynamic error if the pattern matches anything other than document, element, text, processing instruction, and comment nodes (C0023).

The value of the `group-adjacent` option *must* be an XPathExpression.

If the node matched is the document node (`match="/"`), the result is a new document where the document element is a new element node whose QName is the value specified in the `wrapper` option. That new element contains copies of all of the children of the original document node.

When the selection pattern does not match the document node, every node that matches the specified `match` pattern is replaced with a new element node whose QName is the value specified in the `wrapper` option. The content of that new element is a copy of the original, matching node. The `p:wrap` step performs a "deep" wrapping, the children of the matching node and their descendants are processed and wrappers are added to all matching nodes.

The `group-adjacent` option can be used to group adjacent matching nodes in a single wrapper element. The specified XPath expression is evaluated for each matching node with that node as the XPath context node. Whenever two or more adjacent matching nodes have the same "group adjacent" value, they are wrapped together in a single wrapper element. Two "group adjacent" values are the same if the standard XPath function `deep-equal()` returns true for them.

Two matching nodes are considered adjacent if and only if they are siblings and either there are no nodes between them or all intervening, non-matching nodes are whitespace text, comment, or processing instruction nodes.

All document properties are preserved.

p:wrap-sequence

The `p:wrap-sequence` step accepts a sequence of documents and produces either a single document or a new sequence of documents.

```
<p:declare-step type="p:wrap-sequence">
  <p:input port="source" content-types="text xml html" sequence="true"/>
  <p:output port="result" sequence="true" content-types="application/xml"/>
  <p:option name="wrapper" required="true" as="xs:QName"/>
  <p:option name="group-adjacent" as="xs:string?"/>
</p:declare-step>
```

The value of the `group-adjacent` option *must* be an XPathExpression.

In its simplest form, `p:wrap-sequence` takes a sequence of documents and produces a single, new document by placing each document in the `source` sequence inside a new document element as sequential siblings. The name of the document element is the value specified in the `wrapper` option.

The `group-adjacent` option can be used to group adjacent documents. The XPath context for the `group-adjacent` option changes over time. For each document that appears on the `source` port, the expression is evaluated with that document as the context document. The context position (`position()`) is the position of that document within the sequence and the context size (`last()`) is the total number of documents in the sequence. Whenever two or more sequentially adjacent documents have the same "group adjacent" value, they are wrapped together in a single wrapper element. Two "group adjacent" values are the same if the standard XPath function `deep-equal()` returns true for them.

No document properties are preserved. The document produced has no `base-uri` property.

p:www-form-urldecode

The `p:www-form-urldecode` step decodes a `x-www-form-urlencoded` string into a JSON representation.

```
<p:declare-step type="p:www-form-urldecode">
  <p:output port="result" content-types="application/json"/>
  <p:option name="value" required="true" as="xs:string"/>
</p:declare-step>
```

A JSON object of the form "`map(xs:string, xs:string+)`" will appear on `result` port. The `value` option is interpreted as a string of parameter values encoded using the `x-www-form-urlencoded` algorithm. Each name/value pair is represented in the JSON object as key/value entry.

It is a dynamic error if the `value` provided is not a properly `x-www-form-urlencoded` value (C0037).

If any parameter name occurs more than once in the encoded string, a sequence will be associated with the respective key. The order in the sequence retains the order of name/value pairs in the encoded string.

The resulting JSON document has no properties apart from `content-type`. In particular, it has no `base-uri`.

p:www-form-urlencode

The `p:www-form-urlencode` step encodes a set of parameter values as a `x-www-form-urlencoded` string.

```
<p:declare-step type="p:www-form-urlencode">
  <p:output port="result" content-types="text/plain"/>
  <p:option name="parameters" required="true"
as="map(xs:string,xs:untypedAtomic+)"/>
</p:declare-step>
```

The map entries of `parameters` option are encoded as a single `x-www-form-urlencoded` string of name/value pairs. This string is returned on the `result` port as a text document.

If more than one value is associated with a given key in `parameters` option, a name/value pair is created for each value.

The resulting text document has no properties apart from `content-type`. In particular, it has no `base-uri`.

p:xinclude

The `p:xinclude` step applies XInclude processing to the `source` document.

```
<p:declare-step type="p:xinclude">
  <p:input port="source" content-types="xml html"/>
  <p:output port="result" content-types="xml html"/>
  <p:option name="fixup-xml-base" as="xs:boolean" select="false()"/>
  <p:option name="fixup-xml-lang" as="xs:boolean" select="false()"/>
</p:declare-step>
```

The value of the `fixup-xml-base` option *must* be a boolean. If it is true, base URI fixup will be performed as per XInclude.

The value of the `fixup-xml-lang` option *must* be a boolean. If it is true, language fixup will be performed as per XInclude.

The included documents are located with the base URI of the input document and are not provided as input to the step.

It is a dynamic error if an XInclude error occurs during processing (C0029).

All document properties are preserved.

p:xquery

The `p:xquery` step applies an XQuery query to the sequence of documents provided on the `source` port.

```
<p:declare-step type="p:xquery">
  <p:input port="source" content-types="any" sequence="true" primary="true"/>
  <p:input port="query" content-types="text xml"/>
  <p:output port="result" sequence="true" content-types="any"/>
  <p:option name="parameters" as="map(xs:QName,item()*)?"/>
  <p:option name="version" as="xs:string?"/>
</p:declare-step>
```

If a sequence of documents is provided on the `source` port, the first document is used as the initial context item. The whole sequence is also the default collection. If no documents are provided on the `source` port, the initial context item is undefined and the default collection is empty.

The `query` port must receive a single document which is either an XML document or a text document. A text document *must* be treated as the query. For an XML document the following rules apply:

- If the document root element is `c:query`, the text descendants of this element are considered the query.

  ```
  <c:query>
    <!-- … (text) … -->
  </c:query>
  ```

- If the document root element is in the XQueryX namespace, the document is treated as an XQueryX-encoded query. Support for XQueryX is implementation-defined.

- Otherwise the string value of the document *must* be treated as the query.

If the step specifies a `version`, then that version of XQuery *must* be used to process the transformation. It is a dynamic error if the specified XQuery version is not available (C0009). If the step does not specify a version, the implementation may use any version it has available and may use any means to determine what version to use, including, but not limited to, examining the version of the query.It is implementation defined which XQuery version(s) is/are supported.

The name/value pairs in option `parameters` are used to set the query's external variables.

It is a dynamic error if a document appearing on port `source` cannot be represented in the XDM version associated with the chosen XQuery version, e (C0101). It is a dynamic error if any key in option `parameters` is associated to a value that cannot be represented in the XDM version associated with the chosen XQuery version, e (C0102).

It is a dynamic error if any error occurs during XQuery's static analysis phase (C0103). It is a dynamic error if any error occurs during XQuery's dynamic evaluation phase (C0104).

The output of this step *may* include PSVI annotations.

The static context of the XQuery processor is augmented in the following way:

Statically known default collection type

`document()*`

Statically known namespaces:

Unchanged from the implementation defaults. No namespace declarations in the XProc pipeline are automatically exposed in the static context.

The dynamic context of the XQuery processor is augmented in the following way:

Context item	The first document that appears on the `source` port.
Context position	`1`
Context size	`1`

Variable values	Any parameters passed in the `parameters` option augment any implementation-defined variable bindings known to the XQuery processor.
Function implementations	The function implementations provided by the XQuery processor.
Current dateTime	The point in time returned as the current dateTime is implementation-defined.
Implicit timezone	The implicit timezone is implementation-defined.
Available documents	The set of available documents (those that may be retrieved with a URI) is implementation-dependent.
Available collections	The set of available collections is implementation-dependent.
Default collection	The sequence of documents provided on the `source` port.

No document properties are preserved. The `base-uri` property of each document will reflect the base URI specified by the query. If the query does not establish a base URI, the document will not have one.

Example

The following pipeline applies XInclude processing and schema validation before using XQuery:

Example A.1 – A Sample Pipeline Document

```
<p:declare-step xmlns:p="http://www.w3.org/ns/xproc"
                version="3.0">
<p:input port="source"/>
<p:output port="result"/>

<p:xinclude/>

<p:validate-with-xml-schema name="validate">
  <p:with-input port="schema" href="http://example.com/path/to/schema.xsd"/>
</p:validate-with-xml-schema>

<p:xquery>
   <p:with-input port="query" href="countp.xq"/>
</p:xquery>

</p:declare-step>
```

Where `countp.xq` might contain:

```
<count>{count(.//p)}</count>
```

p:xslt

The `p:xslt` step invokes an XSLT stylesheet.

```
<p:declare-step type="p:xslt">
  <p:input port="source" content-types="any" sequence="true" primary="true"/>
  <p:input port="stylesheet" content-types="xml"/>
  <p:output port="result" primary="true" sequence="true" content-types="any"/>
  <p:output port="secondary" sequence="true" content-types="any"/>
  <p:option name="parameters" as="map(xs:QName,item()*)?"/>
  <p:option name="global-context-item" as="item()?"/>
  <p:option name="initial-mode" as="xs:QName?"/>
  <p:option name="template-name" as="xs:QName?"/>
  <p:option name="output-base-uri" as="xs:anyURI?"/>
  <p:option name="version" as="xs:string?"/>
</p:declare-step>
```

If `output-base-uri` is relative, it is made absolute against the base URI of the element on which it is specified (`p:with-option` or `p:xslt` in the case of a syntactic shortcut value).

If the step specifies a `version`, then that version of XSLT *must* be used to process the transformation. It is a dynamic error if the specified xslt version is not available (C0038). If the step does not specify a version, the implementation may use any version it has available and may use any means to determine what version to use, including, but not limited to, examining the version of the stylesheet. It is implementation defined which XSLT version(s) is/are supported.

The XSLT stylesheet provided on the `stylesheet` port is invoked. It is a dynamic error if a static error occurs during the static analysis of the XSLT stylesheet (C0093). Any parameters passed in the `parameters` option are used to define top-level stylesheet parameters.

It is a dynamic error if an error occurred during the transformation (C0095). It is a dynamic error if the transformation is terminated by XSLT message termination (C0096). How XSLT message termination errors are reported to the XProc processor is implementation-dependent. Implementations *should* raise an error using the error code from the XSLT step (for example, the `error-code` specified on the `xsl:message` or `err:XTTM9000` if no code is provided).

If XSLT 2.0 or XSLT 3.0 is used, the outputs of this step *may* include PSVI annotations.

The interpretation of the input and output ports as well as for the other options depends on the selected XSLT version.

No document properties are preserved. The `base-uri` property of each document will reflect the base URI specified by the tranformation. If the transformation does not establish a base URI, the document will not have one.

Invoking an XSLT 3.0 stylesheet

The value of `global-context-item` is used as global context item for the stylesheet invocation. If no value is supplied, the empty sequence is supplied to the invocation.

If no value is supplied for `template-name` option an "Apply-template invocation" is performed. The documents that appear on `source` are taken to be the initial match selection. The default collection is undefined. If a value is supplied for the `initial-mode` option, this value is used as the initial-mode for the invocation. It is a dynamic error if the stylesheet does not support a given mode (C0008). If no value is supplied, nothing is supplied to the invocation, so the default behaviour defined for XSLT 3.0 could be applied.

If a value is supplied for option `template-name` a "Call template invocation" is performed. The documents on port `source` are taken as the default collection in this case. Option `initial-mode` is ignored. It is a dynamic error if the stylesheet does not provide a given template (C0056).

Independent of the way the stylesheet is invoked, the principal result(s) will appear on output port `result` while secondary result(s) will appear on output port `secondary`. Whether the raw results are delivered or a result tree is constructed, depends on the (explicit or implicit) setting for attribute `build-tree` of in the output-definition for the respective result. If a result tree is constructed, the result will be a text document if it is a single text node wrapped into a document node. Otherwise it will be either an XML document or an HTML document depending on the attribute `method` on the output-definition for the respective result. If no result tree is constructed, the stylesheet invocation may additionally deliver a sequence of atomic values, maps, or arrays. For each item in this sequence a JSON document will be constructed and appear on the steps output port.

Option `output-base-uri` sets the base output URI per XSLT 3.0 specification. If a final result tree is constructed, this URI is used to resolve a relative URI reference. If no value is supplied for `output-base-uri`, the base URI of the first document in the `source` port's sequence is used. If no document is supplied on port `source` the base URI of the document on port `stylesheet` is used. It is a dynamic error if a document appearing on the `secondary` port has a base URI that is not both absolute and valid according to RFC 3986 (C0121).

If no result tree is constructed for one of secondary results, a sequence of documents sharing the same value for attribute `href` may appear on output port `result`.

Invoking an XSLT 2.0 stylesheet

If a sequence of documents is provided on the `source` port, the first document is used as the initial context node. The whole sequence is also the default collection. If no documents are provided on the `source` port, the initial context node is undefined and the default collection is empty. It is a dynamic error if any document supplied on the source port is not an XML document, an HTML documents, or a Text document if XSLT 2 (C0094).

The value of option `global-context-item` is ignored if a stylesheet is invoked as per XSLT 2.0. The invocation of the transformation is controlled by the `initial-mode` and `template-name` options that set the initial mode and/or named template in the XSLT transformation where processing begins. It is a dynamic error if any key in `parameters` is associated to a value which is not an instance of the XQuery 1 (C0007). It is a dynamic error if the specified initial mode cannot be applied to the specified stylesheet (C0008). It is a dynamic error if the specified template name cannot be applied to the specified stylesheet (C0056).

The primary result document of the transformation, if there is one, appears on the `result` port. At most one document can appear on the `result` port. All other result documents appear on the `secondary` port. The order in which result documents appear on the `secondary` port is implementation dependent.

The `output-base-uri` option sets the context's output base URI per the XSLT 2.0 specification, otherwise the base URI of the `result` document is the base URI of the first document in the `source` port's sequence. If no document is supplied on port `source` the base URI of the document on port `stylesheet` is used. It is a dynamic error if a document appearing on the `secondary` port has a base URI that is not both absolute and valid according to RFC 3986 (C0121).

Invoking an XSLT 1.0 stylesheet

The document provided for `source` is used the transformations source tree. It is a dynamic error if the source port does not contain exactly one XML document or one HTML document if XSLT 1 (C0039). The values supplied for options `global-context-item`, `initial-mode`, and `template-name` are ignored. If XSLT 1.0 is used, an empty sequence of documents *must* appear on the `secondary` port. An XSLT 1.0 step *should* use the value of the `output-base-uri` as the base URI of its output, if the option is specified.

The key/value pairs supplied in `parameters` are used to set top-level parameters in the stylesheet. If the value is an atomic value or a node, its string value is supplied to the stylesheet. It is a dynamic error if an XSLT 1.0 stylesheet is invoked and option `parameters` contains a value that is not an atomic value or a node (C0105).

APPENDIX B

Optional built-in steps overview

This appendix provides an overview of the *optional* built-in steps. Whether or not these steps are supported by your XProc processor is at the mercy of the processor's developer. Check the documentation (or just try it) if you want to find out.

As in Appendix A, the step descriptions were not (re)written for this book; they were generated directly from the specification.

At the time this book was written not all step specifications were completely finished. So there may be inconsistencies between what you read here and what you find in practice. Consult the specification (http://spec.xproc.org/) for the latest version.

Dynamic pipeline execution

Specification: XProc 3.0: dynamic pipeline execution[1]

p:run

The `p:run` step runs a dynamically loaded pipeline.

When this book was completed the description of this step wasn't completely finished. Please consult the online documentation at https://spec.xproc.org/ for the most recent version.

File steps

Specification: XProc 3.0: file steps[2]

p:directory-list

The `p:directory-list` step produces a list of the contents of a specified directory.

[1] https://spec.xproc.org/master/head/run/
[2] https://spec.xproc.org/master/head/file/

```
<p:declare-step type="p:directory-list">
  <p:output port="result" content-type="application/xml"/>
  <p:option name="path" required="true" as="xs:anyURI"/>
  <p:option name="detailed" as="xs:boolean" select="false()"/>
  <p:option name="max-depth" as="xs:string?" select="'1'"/>
  <p:option name="include-filter" as="xs:string*"/>
  <p:option name="exclude-filter" as="xs:string*"/>
</p:declare-step>
```

Conformant processors *must* support directory paths whose scheme is `file`. It is implementation-defined what other schemes are supported by `p:directory-list`, and what the interpretation of 'directory', 'file' and 'contents' is for those schemes. It is a dynamic error if an implementation does not support directory listing for a specified scheme (C0090).

If `path` is relative, it is made absolute against the base URI of the element on which it is specified (`p:with-option` or `p:directory-list` in the case of a syntactic shortcut value). It is a dynamic error if the base URI is not both absolute and valid according to RFC 3986 (D0064). It is a dynamic error if the absolute path does not identify a directory (C0017). It is a dynamic error if the contents of the directory path are not available to the step due to access restrictions in the environment in which the pipeline is run (C0012).

If the `detailed` option is true, the pipeline author is requesting additional information about the matching entries, see the section titled "Directory list details" (p. 305).

The `max-depth` option may contain either the string "`unbounded`" or a string that may be cast to a non-negative integer. An integer value of `0` means that only information about the directory that is given in the `path` option is returned. A `max-depth` of `1`, which is the default, will effect that also information about the top-level directory's immediate children will be included. For larger values of `max-depth`, also the content of directories will be considered recursively up to the maximum depth, and it will be included as children of the corresponding `c:directory` elements.

If present, the value of the `include-filter` or `exclude-filter` option *must* be a sequence of strings, each one representing a regular expressions as specified in the XPath 3.1 functions, section 7.61 "`Regular Expression Syntax`".

The regular expressions will be matched against an item's file system path relative to the top-level path that was given in the `path` option. If the item is a directory, a trailing slash will be appended.

Examples: A file `file.txt` in the directory specified by `path` will remain `file.txt`, a relative path `dir1/file.txt` will remain `dir1/file.txt`, while a relative path `dir1/dir2` will become `dir1/dir2/` if `dir2` is a directory.

Regular expressions that match `a/a/b/file.txt` are, for example, `^/(\w+/){2,3}.+\.txt$`, `a/a/b/`, or `/file\.[^/]+$`.

If any `include-filter` pattern matches the slash-augmented relative path, the entry is included in the output. If a directory's path matches the inclusion regex, the directory's content will not automatically be included, too. They need to match, the regular expression, too. So the filter regex `^dir/` will match the directory content but `^dir/$` won't, and as a consequence the directory's content will not be included in the result.

If a relative path is matched by an include filter, all its ancestor directories starting from the initial directory (but not their content if not included explicitly) will be included, too.

Example B.1 – Sample Directory List Output for a Single File

For a file `a/a/b/file.txt` below the initial directory `/home/jane`, this output will be produced, omitting content that might be present in the intermediate directories:

```
<c:directory xml:base="file:///home/jane/" name="jane">
  <c:directory xml:base="a/" name="a">
    <c:directory xml:base="a/" name="a">
      <c:directory xml:base="b/" name="b">
        <c:file xml:base="file.txt" name="file.txt"/>
      </c:directory>
    </c:directory>
  </c:directory>
</c:directory>
```

If the `exclude-filter` pattern matches the slash-augmented relative path, the entry (and all of its content in case of a directory) is excluded in the output.

If both options are provided, the include filter is processed first, then the exclude filter. As a result, an item is included if it matches (at least) one of the `include-filter` values and none of the `exclude-filter` values.

If no `include-filter` is given, that is, if `include-filter` is an empty sequence, any item will be included in the result (unless it is excluded by `exclude-filter`).

There is no way to specify a list of values using attribute value templates. If the option shortcut syntax is used to provide the `include-filter` or `exclude-filter` option, it will consist of a single regular expression. To specify a list of regular expressions, you must use the `p:with-option` syntax.

The result document produced for the specified directory path has a `c:directory` document element whose base URI, attached as an `xml:base` attribute, is the absolute directory path (expressed as a URI that ends in a slash) and whose `name` attribute (without a trailing slash) is the last segment of the directory path. The same base URI is attached as the resulting document's base-uri property and, accordingly, as its document node's base URI.

```
<c:directory name = xs:string
             uri = anyURI >
  ( <c:file> |
    <c:directory> |
    <c:other> )*
</c:directory>
```

Its contents are determined as follows, based on the entries in the directory identified by the directory path. For each entry in the directory and subject to the rules that are imposed by the `max-depth`, `include-filter`, and `exclude-filter` options, a `c:file`, a `c:directory`, or a `c:other` element is produced, as follows:

- A `c:directory` is produced for each subdirectory not determined to be special. Depending on the values of the three options, it may contain child elements for the directory's content.

- A `c:file` is produced for each file not determined to be special.

  ```
  <c:file name = xs:string
          uri = anyURI
          content-types? = ContentTypes />
  ```

- Any file or directory determined to be special by the `p:directory-list` step may be output using a `c:other` element but the criteria for marking a file as special are implementation-defined.

  ```
  <c:other name = xs:string
           uri = anyURI />
  ```

Each of the elements `c:file`, `c:directory`, and `c:other` has a `name` attribute, whose value is a relative IRI reference, giving the (local) file or directory name.

Each of these element also contains the corresponding resource's URI in an `xml:base` attribute, which may be a relative URI for any but the top-level `c:directory` element. In the case of `c:directory`, it must end in a trailing slash. This way, users will always be able to compute the absolute URI for any of these elements by applying `fn:base-uri()` to it.

Besides the `content-type` property, the resulting document has a `base-uri`. Its value is identical to the top-level element's `xml:base` attribute, that is, to the directory's URI.

Directory list details

If `detailed` is false, then only the `name` and `xml:base` attributes are expected on `c:file`, `c:directory`, or `c:other` elements.

If `detailed` is true, then the pipeline author is expecting additional details about each entry. The following attributes *should* be provided by the implementation:

`content-type`	The `content-type` attribute contains the content type of the respective file. The value "`application/octet-stream`" will be used if the processor is not able to identify another content type.
`readable`	"`true`" if the entry is readable.
`writable`	"`true`" if the entry is writable.
`hidden`	"`true`" if the entry is hidden.
`last-modified`	The last modification time of the entry, expressed as a lexical `xs:dateTime` in UTC.
`size`	The size of the entry in bytes.

The precise meaning of these properties are implementation-defined and may vary according to the URI scheme of the `path`. If the value of an attribute is "`false`" or if it has no meaningful value, the attribute may be omitted.

Any other attributes on `c:file`, `c:directory`, or `c:other` are implementation-defined.

p:file-copy

The `p:file-copy` step copies a file.

```
<p:declare-step type="p:file-copy">
  <p:output port="result" primary="true" content-types="application/xml"/>
  <p:option name="href" required="true" as="xs:anyURI"/>
  <p:option name="target" required="true" as="xs:anyURI"/>
  <p:option name="fail-on-error" as="xs:boolean" select="true()"/>
</p:declare-step>
```

The `p:file-copy` step copies the file or directory named in `href` to the new name specified in `target`. If the target is a directory, the step attempts to move the file into that directory, preserving its base name.

It is a dynamic error if the `href` or `target` option value is not a valid `xs:anyURI` (D0064). If the `href` or `target` is relative, it is made absolute against the base URI of the element on which it is specified (`p:with-option` or `p:file-copy` in the case of a syntactic shortcut value).

If the copy is successful, the step returns a `c:result` element containing the absolute URI of the target.

If an error occurs and `fail-on-error` is `false`, the step returns a `c:error` element which may contain additional, implementation-defined, information about the nature of the error.

If an error occurs and `fail-on-error` is `true`, one of the following errors is raised:

- It is a dynamic error if the resource referenced by the `href` option does not exist, cannot be accessed or is not a file or directory (D0011).
- It is a dynamic error if the URI scheme of the `target` option is not supported or the file or directory cannot be copied to the specified location (C0050).

The resulting document has no properties apart from `content-type`. In particular, it has no `base-uri`.

p:file-create-tempfile

The `p:file-create-tempfile` step creates a temporary file.

```
<p:declare-step type="p:file-create-tempfile">
  <p:output port="result" primary="true" content-types="application/xml"/>
  <p:option name="href" as="xs:anyURI?"/>
  <p:option name="suffix" as="xs:string?"/>
  <p:option name="prefix" as="xs:string?"/>
  <p:option name="delete-on-exit" as="xs:boolean" select="false()"/>
  <p:option name="fail-on-error" as="xs:boolean" select="true()"/>
</p:declare-step>
```

The `p:file-create-tempfile` creates a temporary file. The temporary file is guaranteed not to already exist when the step is called.

If the `href` option is specified it must be the URI of an existing directory. The temporary file is created here. If there is no `href` option specified the location of the temporary file is implementation defined, usually the operating system's default location for temporary files.

It is a dynamic error if the `href` option value is not a valid `xs:anyURI` (D0064). If the `href` is relative, it is made absolute against the base URI of the element on which it is specified (`p:with-option` or `p:file-create-tempfile` in the case of a syntactic shortcut value).

If the `prefix` option is specified, the filename will begin with that prefix. If the `suffix` option is specified, the filename will end with that suffix.

If the `delete-on-exit` option is `true`, an attempt will be made to automatically delete the temporary file when the processor terminates the pipeline. No error will be raised if this is unsuccessful.

If the temporary file creation is successful, the step returns a `c:result` element containing the absolute URI of this file.

If an error occurs and `fail-on-error` is `false`, the step returns a `c:error` element which may contain additional, implementation-defined, information about the nature of the error.

If an error occurs and `fail-on-error` is `true`, one of the following errors is raised:

- It is a dynamic error if the resource referenced by the `href` option does not exist, cannot be accessed or is not a directory (D0011).
- It is a dynamic error if the temporary file could not be created (C0116).

The resulting document has no properties apart from `content-type`. In particular, it has no `base-uri`.

p:file-delete

The `p:file-delete` step deletes a file or a directory.

```
<p:declare-step type="p:file-delete">
  <p:output port="result" primary="true" content-types="application/xml"/>
  <p:option name="href" required="true" as="xs:anyURI"/>
  <p:option name="recursive" as="xs:boolean" select="false()"/>
  <p:option name="fail-on-error" as="xs:boolean" select="true()"/>
</p:declare-step>
```

The `p:file-delete` step attempts to delete the file or directory named in `href`.

It is a dynamic error if the `href` option value is not a valid `xs:anyURI` (D0064). If the `href` option is relative, it is made absolute against the base URI of the element on which it is specified (`p:with-option` or `p:file-delete` in the case of a syntactic shortcut value).

If `href` specifies a directory, it can only be deleted if the `recursive` option is `true` or if the specified directory is empty.

If the delete is successful, the step returns a `c:result` element containing the absolute URI of the deleted file or directory.

If an error occurs and `fail-on-error` is `false`, the step returns a `c:error` element which may contain additional, implementation-defined, information about the nature of the error.

If an error occurs and `fail-on-error` is `true`, one of the following errors is raised:

- It is a dynamic error if the resource referenced by the `href` option does not exist, cannot be accessed or is not a file or directory (D0011).

- It is a dynamic error if an attempt is made to delete a non-empty directory and the `recursive` option was set to `false` (C0113).

The resulting document has no properties apart from `content-type`. In particular, it has no `base-uri`.

p:file-info

The `p:file-info` step returns information about a file, directory or other file system object.

```
<p:declare-step type="p:file-info">
  <p:output port="result" primary="true" content-types="application/xml"/>
  <p:option name="href" required="true" as="xs:anyURI"/>
  <p:option name="fail-on-error" as="xs:boolean" select="true()"/>
</p:declare-step>
```

The `p:file-info` step returns information about the file, directory or other file system object named in the `href` option.

Conformant processors *must* support file infos whose scheme is `file`. It is implementation-defined what other schemes are supported by `p:file-info`, and what the interpretation of 'directory', 'file' and 'contents' is for those schemes. It is a dynamic error if an implementation does not support file info for a specified scheme (C0134).

If `href` is relative, it is made absolute against the base URI of the element on which it is specified (`p:with-option` or `p:file-info` in the case of a syntactic shortcut value). It is a dynamic error if the base URI is not both absolute and valid according to RFC 3986 (D0064). It is a dynamic error if file infos are not available to the step due to access restrictions in the environment in which the pipeline is run (C0135).

If the `href` option is a `file:` URI, the step returns:

- If `href` option references a file: A `c:file` element with standard attributes (see below).
- If `href` option references a directory: A `c:directory` element with standard attributes (see below).

- If `href` option references any other file system object: Implementation defined (for example an `c:other` or `c:device` element). It is advised to use the standard attributes (see below) if applicable.

The following attributes are standard on a returned `c:file` or `c:directory` element. All attributes are optional and must be absent if not applicable. Additional implementation-defined attributes may be present, but they must be in a namespace.

Attribute	Type	Description
`readable`	`xs:boolean`	`true` if the object is readable.
`writable`	`xs:boolean`	`true` if the object file is writable.
`hidden`	`xs:boolean`	`true` if the object is hidden.
`last-modified`	`xs:dateTime`	The last modification time of the object expressed in UTC.
`size`	`xs:integer`	The size of the object in bytes.
`content-type`	`xs:string`	The content type, if the object is a file.

If an error occurs and `fail-on-error` is `false`, the step returns a `c:error` element which may contain additional, implementation-defined, information about the nature of the error.

If an error occurs and `fail-on-error` is `true`, one of the following errors is raised:

- It is a dynamic error if the resource referenced by the `href` option does not exist, cannot be accessed or is not a file, directory or other file system object (D0011).

The resulting document has no properties apart from `content-type`. In particular, it has no `base-uri`.

p:file-mkdir

The `p:file-mkdir` step creates a directory.

```
<p:declare-step type="p:file-mkdir">
  <p:output port="result" primary="true" content-types="application/xml"/>
  <p:option name="href" required="true" as="xs:anyURI"/>
  <p:option name="fail-on-error" as="xs:boolean" select="true()"/>
</p:declare-step>
```

The `p:file-mkdir` create the directory named in the `href` option. If this includes more than one directory component, all of the intermediate components are created. The path separator is implementation-defined.

It is a dynamic error if the `href` option value is not a valid `xs:anyURI` (D0064). If the `href` option is relative, it is made absolute against the base URI of the element on which it is specified (`p:with-option` or `p:file-mkdir` in the case of a syntactic shortcut value).

If the create is successful, the step returns a `c:result` element containing the absolute URI of the directory created.

If an error occurs and `fail-on-error` is `false`, the step returns a `c:error` element which may contain additional, implementation-defined, information about the nature of the error.

If an error occurs and `fail-on-error` is `true`, the following error is raised:

- It is a dynamic error if the directory referenced by the `href` option cannot be created (C0114).

The resulting document has no properties apart from `content-type`. In particular, it has no `base-uri`.

p:file-move

The `p:file-move` step moves a file or directory.

```
<p:declare-step type="p:file-move">
  <p:output port="result" primary="true" content-types="application/xml"/>
  <p:option name="href" required="true" as="xs:anyURI"/>
  <p:option name="target" required="true" as="xs:anyURI"/>
  <p:option name="fail-on-error" as="xs:boolean" select="true()"/>
</p:declare-step>
```

The `p:file-move` step moves the file or directory named in `href` to the new location specified in `target`. If the `target` option specifies an *existing* directory, the step attempts to move the file or directory *into* that directory, preserving its base name.

It is a dynamic error if the href or target option value is not a valid xs:anyURI (D0064). If the href or target is relative, it is made absolute against the base URI of the element on which it is specified (p:with-option or p:file-move in the case of a syntactic shortcut value).

If the href option specifies a device or other special kind of object, the results are implementation-defined.

If the move is successful, the step returns a c:result element containing the absolute URI of the target.

If an error occurs and fail-on-error is false, the step returns a c:error element which may contain additional, implementation-defined, information about the nature of the error.

If an error occurs and fail-on-error is true, one of the following errors is raised:

- It is a dynamic error if the resource referenced by the href option does not exist, cannot be accessed or is not a file or directory (D0011).
- It is a dynamic error if the resource referenced by the target option is an existing file or other file system object (C0115).
- It is a dynamic error if the URI scheme of the target option is not supported or the file or directory cannot be moved to the specified location (C0050).

The resulting document has no properties apart from content-type. In particular, it has no base-uri.

p:file-touch

The p:file-touch step updates the modification timestamp of a file.

```
<p:declare-step type="p:file-touch">
  <p:output port="result" primary="true" content-types="application/xml"/>
  <p:option name="href" required="true" as="xs:anyURI"/>
  <p:option name="timestamp" as="xs:dateTime?"/>
  <p:option name="fail-on-error" as="xs:boolean" select="true()"/>
</p:declare-step>
```

The p:file-touch step updates the modification timestamp of the file specified in the href option. If the file specified by href does not exist, an empty file will be created at the given location.

It is a dynamic error if the `href` option value is not a valid `xs:anyURI` (D0064). If the `href` option is relative, it is made absolute against the base URI of the element on which it is specified (`p:with-option` or `p:file-touch` in the case of a syntactic shortcut value).

If the `timestamp` option is set, the file's timestamp is set to this value. Otherwise the file's timestamp is set to the current system's date and time.

If the operation is successful, the step returns a `c:result` element containing the absolute URI of the file.

If an error occurs and `fail-on-error` is `false`, the step returns a `c:error` element which may contain additional, implementation-defined, information about the nature of the error.

If an error occurs and `fail-on-error` is `true`, the following error is raised:

- It is a dynamic error if the resource referenced by the `href` option does not exist and cannot be created or exists and cannot be accessed (D0011).

The resulting document has no properties apart from `content-type`. In particular, it has no `base-uri`.

Operating system steps

Specification: XProc 3.0: operating system steps[3]

p:os-exec

The `p:os-exec` step runs an external command passing the input that arrives on its `source` port as standard input, reading `result` from standard output, and `errors` from standard error.

```
<p:declare-step type="p:os-exec">
  <p:input port="source" sequence="true" content-types="any"/>
  <p:output port="result" primary="true" content-types="any"/>
  <p:output port="errors" content-types="any"/>
  <p:output port="exit-status" content-types="application/xml"/>
  <p:option name="command" required="true" as="xs:string"/>
  <p:option name="args" select="''" as="xs:string"/>
```

[3] https://spec.xproc.org/master/head/os/

```
  <p:option name="cwd" as="xs:string?"/>
  <p:option name="source-is-xml" select="true()" as="xs:boolean"/>
  <p:option name="result-is-xml" select="true()" as="xs:boolean"/>
  <p:option name="wrap-result-lines" select="false()" as="xs:boolean"/>
  <p:option name="errors-is-xml" select="false()" as="xs:boolean"/>
  <p:option name="wrap-error-lines" select="false()" as="xs:boolean"/>
  <p:option name="path-separator" as="xs:string?"/>
  <p:option name="failure-threshold" as="xs:integer?"/>
  <p:option name="arg-separator" select="' '" as="xs:string"/>
  <p:option name="serialization" as="map(xs:QName,item()*)?"/>
</p:declare-step>
```

The values of the `command`, `args`, `cwd`, `path-separator`, and `arg-separator` options *must* be strings.

The values of the `source-is-xml`, `result-is-xml`, `errors-is-xml`, and `fix-slashes` options *must* be boolean.

The `p:os-exec` step executes the command passed on `command` with the arguments passed on `args`. The processor does not interpolate the values of the `command` or `args` (for example, expanding references to environment variables). It is a dynamic error if the command cannot be run (C0033).

If `cwd` is specified, then the current working directory is changed to the value of that option before execution begins. It is a dynamic error if the current working directory cannot be changed to the value of the `cwd` option (C0034). If `cwd` is not specified, the current working directory is implementation-defined.

If the `path-separator` option is specified, every occurrence of the character identified as the `path-separator` character that occurs in the `command`, `args`, or `cwd` will be replaced by the platform-specific path separator character. It is a dynamic error if the `path-separator` option is specified and is not exactly one character long (C0063).

The value of the `args` option is a string. In order to support passing more than one argument to a command, the `args` string is broken into a sequence of values. The `arg-separator` option specifies the character that is used to separate values; by default it is a single space It is a dynamic error if the `arg-separator` option is specified and is not exactly one character long (C0066).

The following examples of `p:os-exec` are equivalent. The first uses the default `arg-separator`:

```
<p:exec command="someCommand" args="arg1 arg2 arg3"/>
```

The second specifies an alternate separator:

```
<p:exec command="someCommand" args="arg1,arg2,arg3"
 arg-separator=","/>
```

If one of the arguments contains a space (e.g., a filename that contains a space), then you must specify an alternate separator.

The `source` port is declared to accept a sequence so that it can be empty. If no document appears on the `source` port, then the command receives nothing on standard input. If a document does arrive on the `source` port, it will be passed to the command as its standard input. It is a dynamic error if more than one document appears on the `source` port of the `p:os-exec` step (D0006). If `source-is-xml` is true, the value of the `serialization` option is used to convert the input into serialized XML which is passed to the command, otherwise the XPath string-value of the document is passed. Serialization is described in XProc 3.0.

The standard output of the command is read and returned on `result`; the standard error output is read and returned on `errors`. In order to assure that the result will be an XML document, each of the results will be wrapped in a `c:result` element.

If `result-is-xml` is true, the standard output of the program is assumed to be XML and will be parsed as a single document. If it is false, the output is assumed *not* to be XML and will be returned as escaped text.

If `wrap-result-lines` is true, a `c:line` element will be wrapped around each line of output.

```
<c:line>
  <!-- … (text) … -->
</c:line>
```

It is a dynamic error to specify both `result-is-xml` and `wrap-result-lines` (C0035).

The same rules apply to the standard error output of the program, with the `errors-is-xml` and `wrap-error-lines` options, respectively.

If either of the results are XML, they *must* be parsed with namespaces enabled and validation turned off, just like `p:document`.

The `exit-status` port always returns a single `c:result` element which contains the system exit status that the process returned. The specific exit status values returned by a process invoked with `p:os-exec` are implementation-dependent.

If a `failure-threshold` value is supplied, and the exit status is greater than that threshold, then the `p:os-exec` step *must* fail. It is a dynamic error if the exit code from the command is greater than the specified `failure-threshold` value (C0064). This failure, like any step failure, can be captured with a `p:try`.

No document properties are preserved.

p:os-info

The `p:os-info` step returns information about the operating system on which the processor is running.

```
<p:declare-step type="p:os-info">
  <p:output port="result" content-types="application/xml" primary="true"/>
</p:declare-step>
```

The step returns a `c:result` element with attributes describing properties of the system. It *should* include the following properties:

`file-separator`	The file separator; usually `"/"` on Unix, `"\"` on Windows.
`path-separator`	The path separator; usually `":"` on Unix, `";"` on Windows.
`os-architecture`	The operating system architecture, for example `"i386"`.
`os-name`	The name of the operating system, for example `"Mac OS X"`.
`os-version`	The version of the operating system, for example `"10.5.6"`.

`cwd`	The current working directory. On systems which have no concept of a working directory the value of the attribute will be empty.
`user-name`	The login name of the effective user, for example `"ndw"`.
`user-home`	The home directory of the effective user, for example `"/home/ndw"`.

The `c:result` element can contain zero or more `c:environment` elements that identify the environment variables available. These elements have a mandatory `name` and `value` attribute, reflecting name and value of the environment variable. Implementations *should* include all available operating system environment variables.

The exact set of properties returned is implementation-defined.

The resulting document has no properties apart from `content-type`. In particular, it has no `base-uri`.

Mail steps

Specification: XProc 3.0: mail steps[4]

p:send-mail

The `p:send-mail` step sends an email message.

```
<p:declare-step type="p:send-mail">
  <p:input port="source" sequence="true" content-types="xml"/>
  <p:output port="result"/>
</p:declare-step>
```

The first document on the source port is expected to conform to XML format for mail[5] . Any additional documents are treated as attachments.

[4] https://spec.xproc.org/master/head/mail/
[5] https://tools.ietf.org/html/draft-klyne-message-rfc822-xml-03

The `em:content` may contain either text or HTML. To send some other type as the first message body, you must leave the `em:content` element out of the first document and supply the body as a second document.

No document properties are preserved.

Paged media steps

Specification: XProc 3.0: paged media steps[6]

p:css-formatter

The `p:css-formatter` step applies CSS[7] formatting to an XML or HTML document. The output of this step is often, but not necessarily, a PDF document.

```
<p:declare-step type="p:css-formatter">
  <p:input port="source" content-types="xml html"/>
  <p:input port="stylesheet" content-types="text" sequence="true"/>
  <p:output port="result" content-types="any"/>
  <p:option name="parameters" as="map(xs:QName,item()*)?"/>
  <p:option name="content-type" as="xs:string?"/>
</p:declare-step>
```

The document on the `source` port is formatted using one or more CSS stylesheets. The content-type of the output is controlled by the `content-type` option. This option specifies a media type as defined by the IANA Media Types. The option may include media type parameters as well (e.g. "application/someformat; charset=UTF-8"). The use of media type parameters on the `content-type` option is implementation-defined. If the `content-type` option is not specified, the output type is implementation-defined. The default *should* be PDF.

If one or more stylesheets are provided on the `stylesheet` port, they *should* be used. The precise way that the `p:css-formatter` step selects stylesheets is implementation-defined. Because CSS stylesheets may have import statements that rely on relative URI references, it may be more convenient for authors and implementors to allow stylesheets to be specified as a list of URIs (in, for example, one of the `parameters`).

---

6 https://spec.xproc.org/master/head/paged-media/
7 https://www.w3.org/TR/css-2018/

A formatter may take any number of optional rendering parameters via the step's `parameters`; such parameters are defined by the CSS implementation used and are implementation-defined.

The CSS level and the particular CSS features supported by `p:css-formatter` are implementation-defined.

No document properties are preserved.

p:xsl-formatter

The `p:xsl-formatter` step receives an XSL-FO document and renders the content.

```
<p:declare-step type="p:xsl-formatter">
  <p:input port="source" content-types="xml"/>
  <p:output port="result" content-types="any"/>
  <p:option name="parameters" as="map(xs:QName,item()*)?"/>
  <p:option name="content-type" as="xs:string?"/>
</p:declare-step>
```

The content-type of the output is controlled by the `content-type` option. This option specifies a media type as defined by the IANA Media Types. The option may include media type parameters as well (e.g. "application/someformat; charset=UTF-8"). The use of media type parameters on the `content-type` option is implementation-defined.

If the `content-type` option is not specified, the output type is implementation-defined. The default *should* be PDF.

A formatter may take any number of optional rendering parameters via the step's `parameters`; such parameters are defined by the XSL implementation used and are implementation-defined.

The output of this step is a document containing the result of processing. This is often, but not necessarily, a PDF document.

No document properties are preserved.

Text steps

Specification: XProc 3.0: text steps[8]

p:markdown-to-html

The `p:markdown-to-html` step converts a text document in Markdown to XHTML.

```
<p:declare-step type="p:markdown-to-html">
  <p:input port="source" primary="true" content-types="text"/>
  <p:output port="result" primary="true" content-types="html"/>
  <p:option name="parameters" as="map(xs:QName, item()*)?"/>
</p:declare-step>
```

The `p:markdown-to-html` step transforms a text document containing Markdown, for example CommonMark[9] , into HTML. The flavor(s) of Markdown supported and the parameters allowed are implementation-defined..

No document properties are preserved.

Validation steps

Specification: XProc 3.0: validation steps[10]

An important sub-specification was added specifically for the XProc validation steps: Extensible Validation Report Language (XVRL).[11] XVRL defines a common XML vocabulary for validation reports. Its main focus is to express the findings of the most common XML validation languages—Schematron, XML Schema, DTD, and Relax NG—using a unified vocabulary.

All validation steps have an output port called `report` that emits the results of the validation using XVRL.

---

[8] https://spec.xproc.org/master/head/text/
[9] https://spec.commonmark.org/
[10] https://spec.xproc.org/master/head/validation/
[11] https://spec.xproc.org/master/head/xvrl/

Validate with NVDL

The `p:validate-with-nvdl` step applies NVDL validation to the `source` document.

```
<p:declare-step type="p:validate-with-nvdl">
  <p:input port="source" primary="true" content-types="xml html"/>
  <p:input port="nvdl" content-types="xml"/>
  <p:input port="schemas" sequence="true" content-types="text xml"/>
  <p:output port="result" primary="true" content-types="xml html"/>
  <p:output port="report" sequence="true" content-types="xml json"/>
  <p:option name="assert-valid" select="true()" as="xs:boolean"/>
  <p:option name="report-format" select="'xvrl'" as="xs:string"/>
  <p:option name="parameters" as="map(xs:QName,item()*)?"/>
</p:declare-step>
```

The `source` document is validated using the namespace dispatching rules contained in the `nvdl` document.

The dispatching rules may contain URI references that point to the actual schemas to be used. As long as these schemas are accessible, it is not necessary to pass anything on the schemas port. However, if one or more schemas are provided on the `schemas` port, then these schemas should be used in validation.

It is a dynamic error if the `assert-valid` option is `true` and the input document is not valid (C0053).

The output from this step is a copy of the input. The output of this step *may* include PSVI annotations.

All document properties on the `source` port are preserved on the `result` port. No document properties on the `schemas` and `nvdl` ports are preserved. No document properties are preserved on the `report` port.

Validate with RELAX NG

The `p:validate-with-relax-ng` step applies RELAX NG validation to the `source` document.

```
<p:declare-step type="p:validate-with-relax-ng">
  <p:input port="source" primary="true" content-types="xml html"/>
  <p:input port="schema" content-types="text xml"/>
  <p:output port="result" primary="true" content-types="xml html"/>
  <p:output port="report" sequence="true" content-types="xml json"/>
```

```
  <p:option name="dtd-attribute-values" select="false()" as="xs:boolean"/>
  <p:option name="dtd-id-idref-warnings" select="false()" as="xs:boolean"/>
  <p:option name="assert-valid" select="true()" as="xs:boolean"/>
  <p:option name="report-format" select="'xvrl'" as="xs:string"/>
  <p:option name="parameters" as="map(xs:QName,item()*)?"/>
</p:declare-step>
```

The values of the `dtd-attribute-values` and `dtd-id-idref-warnings` options *must* be booleans.

If the `schema` document has an XML media type, then it *must* be interpreted as a RELAX NG Grammar. If the `schema` document has a text media type, then it *must* be interpreted as a RelaxNG Compact Syntax document for validation.

If the `dtd-attribute-values` option is `true`, then the attribute value defaulting conventions of RelaxNG DTD Compatibility are also applied.

If the `dtd-id-idref-warnings` option is `true`, then the validator *should* treat a schema that is incompatible with the ID/IDREF/IDREFs feature of RelaxNG DTD Compatibility as if the document was invalid.

It is a dynamic error if the `assert-valid` option is `true` and the input document is not valid (C0053).

The output from this step is a copy of the input, possibly augmented by application of the RelaxNG DTD Compatibility. The output of this step *may* include PSVI annotations.

Support for RelaxNG DTD Compatibility is implementation defined.

All document properties on the `source` port are preserved on the `result` port. No document properties on the `schema` port are preserved. No document properties are preserved on the `report` port.

Validate with Schematron

The `p:validate-with-schematron` step applies Schematron processing to the `source` document.

```
<p:declare-step type="p:validate-with-schematron">
  <p:input port="source" primary="true" content-types="xml html"/>
  <p:input port="schema" content-types="xml"/>
```

```
  <p:output port="result" primary="true" content-types="xml html"/>
  <p:output port="report" sequence="true" content-types="xml json"/>
  <p:option name="parameters" as="map(xs:QName,item()*)?"/>
  <p:option name="phase" select="'#DEFAULT'" as="xs:string"/>
  <p:option name="assert-valid" select="true()" as="xs:boolean"/>
  <p:option name="report-format" select="'svrl'" as="xs:string"/>
</p:declare-step>
```

It is a dynamic error if the `assert-valid` option is `true` and any Schematron assertions fail or reports succeed (C0054).

A Schematron validation with `assert-valid="true"` will fail if any validation message is produced by `sch:assert` or `sch:report`, even if the severity level of the failed assertion or the successful report is below a certain threshold, for example if there is only an `info` message. (The severity is conventionally conveyed by the `@role` attribute on `sch:assert` or `sch:report`.)

The value of the `phase` option identifies the Schematron validation phase with which validation begins.

The `parameters` option provides name/value pairs which correspond to Schematron external variables, to parameters that influence code generation, or to parameters that influence SVRL to XVRL conversion.

There are multiple Schematron implementations. How the Schematron implementation is selected is implementation-defined. A processor might select an implementation based on the schema's `queryBinding` attribute and/or provide configuration options. In addition, the special parameter map entry `c:implementation` (value: QName) may be used to select a Schematron implementation that the processor supports. The list of supported Schematron implementations and their associated values is implementation-defined. If a requested implementation is not available, the processor may throw an error or select another implementation.

The `parameters` map may contain two special entries, `c:compile` and `c:xvrl`, both are maps. If a code-generating implementation such as Schematron Skeleton is used, the entries of the `c:compile` map, for example `allow-foreign`, will be passed to the code generator. Which parameters the `c:compile` map supports for a given Schematron implementation is implementation-defined.

If the Schematron implementation produces SVRL by default, the SVRL to XVRL conversion can be influenced by the entries of the `c:xvrl` map. The same map, with potentially another set of allowed keys and values, can be used to influence XVRL generation from another reporting language. Which parameters this conversion from native reporting format to XVRL supports is implementation-defined.

All other parameters of the `parameters` option will be passed to the generated code if applicable, or to a hypothetical native Schematron validator that does without code generation.

The `result` output from this step is a copy of the input.

In addition to the mandatory XVRL report, a *Schematron Validation Report Language* (SVRL) report should be provided on the `report` port.

The output of this step *may* include PSVI annotations.

All document properties on the `source` port are preserved on the `result` port. No document properties on the `schema` port are preserved. No document properties are preserved on the `report` port.

Validate with XML Schema

The `p:validate-with-xml-schema` step applies XML Schema validity assessment to the `source` input.

```
<p:declare-step type="p:validate-with-xml-schema">
  <p:input port="source" primary="true" content-types="xml html"/>
  <p:input port="schema" sequence="true" content-types="xml"/>
  <p:output port="result" primary="true" content-types="xml html"/>
  <p:output port="report" sequence="true" content-types="xml json"/>
  <p:option name="use-location-hints" select="false()" as="xs:boolean"/>
  <p:option name="try-namespaces" select="false()" as="xs:boolean"/>
  <p:option name="assert-valid" select="true()" as="xs:boolean"/>
  <p:option name="parameters" as="map(xs:QName,item()*)?"/>
  <p:option name="mode" select="'strict'" as="xs:token" values="('strict','lax')"/>
  <p:option name="version" as="xs:string?"/>
  <p:option name="report-format" select="'xvrl'" as="xs:string"/>
</p:declare-step>
```

The values of the `use-location-hints`, `try-namespaces`, and `assert-valid` options *must* be boolean.

The value of the `mode` option *must* be an NMTOKEN whose value is either "`strict`" or "`lax`".

Validation is performed against the set of schemas represented by the documents on the `schema` port. These schemas must be used in preference to any schema locations provided by schema location hints encountered during schema validation, that is, schema locations supplied for `xs:import` or `xsi:schema-location`, or determined by schema-processor-defined namespace-based strategies, for the namespaces covered by the documents available on the schemas port.

If `xs:include` elements occur within the supplied schema documents, they are treated like any other external documents (see XProc 3.0). It is implementation-defined if the documents supplied on the `schemas` port are considered when resolving `xs:include` elements in the schema documents provided.

The `use-location-hints` and `try-namespaces` options allow the pipeline author to control how the schema processor should attempt to locate schema documents necessary but not provided on the `schema` port. Any schema documents provided on the `schema` port *must* be used in preference to schema documents located by other means.

If the `use-location-hints` option is "`true`", the processor *should* make use of schema location hints to locate schema documents. If the option is "`false`", the processor *should* ignore any such hints.

If the `try-namespaces` option is "`true`", the processor *should* attempt to dereference the namespace URI to locate schema documents. If the option is "`false`", the processor *should not* dereference namespace URIs.

The `mode` option allow the pipeline author to control how schema validation begins. The "`strict`" mode means that the document element must be declared and schema-valid, otherwise it will be treated as invalid. The "`lax`" mode means that the absence of a declaration for the document element does not itself count as an unsuccessful outcome of validation.

If the step specifies a `version`, then that version of XML Schema *must* be used to process the validation. It is a dynamic error if the specified schema version is not available (C0011). If the step does not specify a version, the implementation may use any version it has available and may use any means to determine what version to use, including, but not limited to, examining the version of the schema(s).

It is a dynamic error if the `assert-valid` option is `true` and the input document is not valid (C0053). If the `assert-valid` option is `false`, it is not an error for the document to be invalid. In this case, if the implementation does not support the PSVI, `p:validate-with-xml-schema` is essentially just an "identity" step, but if the implementation *does* support the PSVI, then the resulting document will have additional type information (at least for the subtrees that are valid).

When XML Schema validation assessment is performed, the processor is invoked in the mode specified by the `mode` option. It is a dynamic error if the implementation does not support the specified mode (C0055).

The `result` of the assessment is a document with the Post-Schema-Validation-Infoset (PSVI) (XML Schema) annotations, if the pipeline implementation supports such annotations. If not, the input document is reproduced with any defaulting of attributes and elements performed as specified by the XML Schema recommendation.

All document properties on the `source` port are preserved on the `result` port. No document properties on the `schemas` port are preserved.

APPENDIX C

Namespaces

There are three namespaces associated with and used in XProc:

`http://www.w3.org/ns/xproc`

Prefix convention: **`p:`**

This is the main namespace used for all the XProc elements and some of its attributes.

`http://www.w3.org/ns/xproc-step`

Prefix convention: **`c:`**

This namespace is used for documents that are inputs to and outputs from several standard and optional steps. For instance **`<p:http-request>`** and **`<p:store>`** have defined input or output XML documents in this namespace.

`http://www.w3.org/ns/xproc-error`

Prefix convention: **`err:`**

This namespace is used for XProc errors.

The following namespace comes from XML Schema and is used frequently:

`http://www.w3.org/2001/XMLSchema`

Prefix convention: **`xs:`**

This namespace is used for data types, such as `xs:string` and `xs:boolean`.

APPENDIX D

Copyright credits

Appendix A, Appendix B, and the section titled "The standard step library" (p. 176) in Chapter 8 use material and code examples from the XProc 3.0 Draft Community Group Report available on the date this book went to press (March 13, 2020). A Draft Community Group Report is a proposed standard created by a community of developers interested in the topic. You can find the current version of the report at https://spec.xproc.org.

The text of the XProc 3.0 Draft Community Group Report is subject to the following copyright:

> Copyright © 2018–2020 the Contributors to the XProc 3.0: An XML Pipeline Language specification, published by the XProc Next Community Group[1] under the W3C Community Contributor License Agreement (CLA).[2] A human-readable summary[3] is available.

The source code examples in the XProc 3.0 Draft Community Group Report are subject to the following copyright:

> Copyright © 2020 W3C® (MIT, ERCIM, Keio, Beihang). All Rights Reserved. This work is distributed under the W3C® Software License[4] in the hope that it will be useful, but WITHOUT ANY WARRANTY; without even the implied warranty of MERCHANTABILITY or FITNESS FOR A PARTICULAR PURPOSE.

1 https://www.w3.org/community/xproc-next/
2 https://www.w3.org/community/about/agreements/cla/
3 https://www.w3.org/community/about/agreements/cla-deed/
4 https://www.w3.org/Consortium/Legal/2015/copyright-software-and-document

The code examples in Chapters 1 through 10 (with the exception of Example 6.8, which is from the specification and covered under that license) were created by the author and are covered under the MIT License:

Step Index

This index contains all references to XProc steps in the book. The bold entries point to the detailed step descriptions in Appendix A and Appendix B.

A

C

D

E

F

G

H

I

J

L

M

N

O

P

R

S

T

U

V

W

X

Colophon

About the Author

Erik Siegel is a content engineer and XML specialist who runs Xatapult[5] consultancy in the Netherlands. He specializes in content design and conversions, XML Schemas and transformations, eXist and XProc applications, and XML-related training.

Since 2017, he has been part of the XProc 3.0 editorial team.

About XML Press

XML Press (http://xmlpress.net) was founded in 2008 to publish content that helps technical communicators be more effective. Our publications support managers, social media practitioners, technical communicators, and content strategists and the engineers who support their efforts.

Our publications are available through most retailers, and discounted pricing is available for volume purchases for business, educational, or promotional use. For more information, send email to orders@xmlpress.net or call us at (970) 231-3624.

[5] http://www.xatapult.com

www.ingramcontent.com/pod-product-compliance
Lightning Source LLC
LaVergne TN
LVHW062304060326
832902LV00013B/2041

* 9 7 8 1 9 3 7 4 3 4 7 0 0 *